ADAM
FIRST AND THE LAST

SIMON TURPIN

First printing: July 2023

Master Books® is a division of the New Leaf Publishing Group, LLC.

ISBN: 978-1-68344-345-2
ISBN: 978-1-61458-844-3 (digital)
Library of Congress Control Number: 2023934579

Cover by Diana Bogardus

Please consider requesting that a copy of this volume be purchased by your local library system.

Printed in the United States of America

Please visit our website for other great titles:
www.masterbooks.com

For information regarding promotional opportunities, please contact the publicity department at pr@nlpg.com.

Master Books®
A Division of New Leaf Publishing Group
www.masterbooks.com

Simon Turpin is the executive director and speaker for Answers in Genesis–UK and holds a BA and MA in theology. Simon is married to Jessica, and they home educate their seven children and blog about Christian home education at: LeadingThemOut.com. Simon is also the author of *Scoffers: Responding to Those Who Deliberately Overlook Creation and the Flood.*

Was there ever a real historical first man called Adam? Because of belief in evolution and millions of years, sadly, an increasing number of evangelical theologians are denying a literal first man called Adam. If you deny the "First Adam," not only do you deny the sufficiency of Scripture and undermine its authority, but you ultimately attack the life, teaching, and person of the "Last Adam," our Lord Jesus Christ. The First Adam being supernaturally created from dust by God as recorded in Genesis is important for a coherent, logical, and internally consistent theological understanding of the biblical message of creation, fall, and redemption. This book by Simon Turpin is a powerful apologetics resource to equip Christians to defend the Christian faith in today's world.

— Ken Ham

Introduction

Every generation of Christians must face its own theological challenges and is called "to contend ... for the faith which was once for all delivered to the saints" (Jude 3; NKJV). This generation is no different. Today, however, there is a generation of Christians who do not want to contend for the faith because they tend to think that in an age of intolerance and inclusivism apologetics is being intolerant of others. These Christians argue that we should concentrate solely on telling people about the gospel. There is no doubt that Christians should tell others about the gospel. However, before Jude wrote the above words he had originally intended to write to the believers about their "common salvation" (Jude 3) but was prevented from doing so because of the intrusion of false teachers into the church (Jude 4–19). Jude is not talking about dealing with secondary or tertiary issues, as false teaching strikes at the very heart of the gospel.[1]

False teaching and teachers need to be confronted and cannot be left alone (2 Timothy 2:25; Titus 1:9). It is false teachers who cause division in the church and not those who hold to apostolic doctrine (Jude 19). The danger of those who bring teaching contrary to apostolic doctrine is that it deceives those who are naive (Romans 16:17–18). Christians should not receive teaching that is contrary to apostolic doctrine into their church (2 John 1:10). The intrusion of these false teachers into the church is what caused Jude to write his letter. The purpose of Jude's letter is to urge believers to "contend" for the faith. The term "contend" (*epagōnizomai*) was often used as an athletic image (wrestling) and implies using intense effort on behalf of something. Jude uses this image to exhort his readers to strive intensely to preserve the faith (apostolic teaching, cf. 1 Timothy 4:1, 6:10) that has been handed down to them. This is because it is this faith (doctrine) that believers are to be built up in (Jude 20).

---

1. The false teaching Jude is dealing with is a form of mysticism based on esoteric knowledge (Jude 8–10).

Jude describes this faith as "once for all delivered to the saints." In other words, there is to be nothing added or taken away from it. Just as in Jude's day, believers today need to contend for the faith (apostolic doctrine), as there are those who want to add and take away from it. The idea that we need to simply focus on the gospel (salvation), and not apologetics (contending for the faith), misses the fact that Jude recognized the necessity of apologetics to defend the sound doctrine that the gospel is based upon. Jude's warning to the church may not be popular, but it is very much needed.

The reason our generation needs to contend for the faith is that from childhood we are informed by ideas in our culture that are inherently pagan, and often we are not even aware of this. These ideas are usually accepted uncritically, shaping the way we think (i.e., worldview). One of the most common invasions of secular thought into the Christian mind in our own day is the current pagan understanding of the created realm: evolutionary naturalism. Unfortunately, many Christians uncritically accept the pagan view of the created order into their worldview. Yet the philosophy of evolutionary worldview provides a direct challenge to the biblical worldview. Over the last number of years, the question of whether man was specially created directly from the hand of God or whether he evolved from an ape-like creature has become an increasingly controversial issue within the Church. In today's secular culture it is common to view the biblical history of Adam as a story, myth, or parable.

Although liberal theology has long viewed Adam as a myth, what makes this present debate novel is that this is now also becoming the standard interpretation for many within the evangelical community and, consequently, the problem has become far more intense than when evangelicals first had to deal with it.

New Testament scholar and former Bishop of Durham (UK) N.T. Wright, who believes young-earth creation is false teaching,[2] says in his book *Surprised by Scripture*:

---

2. Wright states, "I wonder whether we are right even to treat the young-earth position as a kind of allowable if regrettable alternative, something we know our cousins down the road get up to but which shouldn't stop us getting together at Christmas … And if, as I suspect, many of us don't think of young-earthism as an allowable alternative, is this simply for the pragmatic reason that it makes it hard for us to be Christians because the wider world looks at those folks and thinks we must be like that too? Or is it — as I suggest it ought to be — because we have glimpsed a positive point that urgently needs to be made and that the young-earth literalism is simply screening out? That's the danger of false teaching: it isn't just that you're making a mess; you are using that mess to cover up something that ought to be brought urgently to light." N.T. Wright, *Surprised by Scripture: Engaging with Contemporary Issues* (London: SPCK, 2014), p. 31.

[J]ust as God chose Israel from the rest of humankind for a special, strange, demanding, vocation, so perhaps what Genesis is telling us is that God chose one pair from the rest of early hominids for a special, strange, demanding, vocation. This pair (call them Adam and Eve if you like) were to be representatives of the whole human race.[3]

Interestingly, Wright goes on to say, "I do not know whether this is exactly what Genesis meant or what Paul meant. But the close and (to a Jewish reader) rather obvious parallel between the vocation of Israel and the vocation of Adam leads me in that direction."[4] If one of the world's leading theologians and former bishop of Durham doesn't know what Genesis or Paul meant, how can anyone else know!? Sadly, viewing Adam as anything other than the first human who was supernaturally created is now becoming a standard interpretation for many within the Christian community. Because many have chosen to reinterpret the Bible with regard to its teaching on the history of Adam, many other biblical teachings are being attacked. For example, the very teachings of Jesus regarding earthly things such as creation and the Flood are being attacked on the basis that, because of His human nature, there was error in some of His teaching. Such evangelical theologians admit that Jesus affirmed the history of such things as Adam, Eve, Noah, and the Flood, but they believe that Jesus was wrong on these matters.

The problem with this is that it raises the question of Jesus' reliability, not only as a prophet, but, more importantly, as our sinless Savior. These theologians go too far when they say that, because of Jesus' human nature and cultural context, He taught and believed erroneous ideas. For example, commenting on Jesus' words in Matthew 19:4–5, theistic evolutionist Dr. Denis Lamoureux states: "Powerful evidence for a strict literal reading of the Genesis creation accounts comes from Jesus himself ... [However,] Jesus accommodated by employing the ancient science of the de novo creation of 'male and female' in Genesis 1:27 to emphasize the inerrant spiritual truth that God is the Creator of human beings."[5] It is interesting that Lamoureux admits that Jesus understood Genesis as literal history, however, he believes the reason why Genesis should not be read "literally" — or, rather, plainly — is because Jesus accommodated His teaching to the beliefs of His first-century audience.[6]

---

3. Ibid., p. 37–38.
4. Ibid., p. 38.
5. Denis O. Lamoureux, *Evolution: Scripture and Nature Say Yes!* (Grand Rapids, MI: Zondervan, 2016), p. 115, 132.
6. Ibid., p. 31.

This is critical because, if we claim Jesus as Lord, what He believed—including on creation, Adam and the Flood — should be extremely important to us. These are vital issues for Christians to think about. We must realize that there are consequences to synthesizing evolution and millions of years with the text of Scripture. Doing so affects not only how the early chapters of Genesis are interpreted, but also the coherency and internal consistency of the biblical message of creation, the Fall, and redemption. Christians need to realize that the idea of evolution and millions of years is not just a side issue, nor is it just about how people understand Genesis 1–11; rather, it has consequences for how we read the rest of Scripture. It is therefore fundamental to the Christian faith. Sadly today, more and more evangelical Christian scholars are having to redefine passages of Scripture because they have adopted the idea of evolution and millions of years into their thinking. These questions may be the biggest doctrinal issues facing our generation, and the church's attitude toward them could be a defining moment in Christianity. This is because they bring into focus whether the clear statements of Scripture are to be accepted, or whether they are to be denied because of "scientific" (i.e., evolutionary naturalism) concerns. The church is facing a crisis because too few of her people and leaders understand the consequences of combining the Bible and evolution. Too many like to go with the cultural flow and be thought of by "the great and the good" as enlightened and intelligent people rather than as "anti-intellectual" or "fundamentalists" (epithet fallacies).

This book will seek to defend the historicity of Adam as a person who existed in space and time, how he was specially created by God, his fall from grace and its impact on his ancestors and creation. It will show that the arguments against this are based, not upon the clear teaching of Scripture, but upon evolutionary presuppositions or influenced by an ancient near Eastern (ANE) view of the world. I will also show why understanding Adam to have been the first man created is important for a coherent, logical, and internally consistent theological understanding of the biblical message of creation, the Fall, and redemption. The latter half of the book will explain the importance of Jesus as the Last Adam in His incarnation, His deity, His death and Resurrection, and His view of Scripture. It will also look at how the Apostles used creation to not only expose the folly of the unbelieving worldview but to share the gospel with unbelievers.

Chapter 1

Adam, Who Art Thou?

It is probably safe to say that the combination of Darwin's theory of evolution in *Origin of Species* and the rise of uniformitarian science in the 1800s has influenced the understanding of Genesis 1–3 more than anything else. Jewish scholar Louis Jacobs acknowledges this with regard to its influence on the understanding of Adam: "There is no doubt that until the nineteenth century Adam and Eve were held to be historical figures, but with the discovery of the great age of the earth … many modern Jews [and Gentiles] have tended … to read the story as a myth."[1] The post-enlightenment emphasis on rationalism (elevating human reason above supernatural revelation) together with the rise of biblical criticism and evolutionary theory laid the foundation for the debate on the subject of the historicity of Adam and whether he was the sole progenitor of the human race. Because of this, critical scholars have long denied the historicity of Adam, as have neo-orthodox theologians. The Swiss theologian Karl Barth, for example, believed that Genesis 1–3 was neither myth nor history but a saga,[2] and denied that Adam was a historical figure. Instead, he preferred to see Adam as being a symbol for everyone.[3]

Today, however, a significant paradigm shift taking has taken place within the evangelical academy in its approach to understanding the identity of Adam. In an article in *Christianity Today* published in 2019, "Ten Theses on Creation and Evolution That (Most) Evangelicals Can Support," the author Todd Wilson (a theistic evolutionist) wrote:

---

1. Louis Jacobs, *The Jewish Religion: A Companion* (Oxford: Oxford University Press, 1995), p. 13–14.
2. Karl Barth, *Church Dogmatics: The Doctrine of Creation*, Vol. 3, Part 1 (Edinburgh: T&T Clark, 1958), p. 90.
3. Karl Barth, *Church Dogmatics: The Doctrine of Reconciliation*, Vol. 4, Part 1 (Edinburgh: T&T Clark, 1956), p. 508–509.

I suspect in 20 years' time, support for Adam and Eve as real persons in a real past will be a minority view even within evangelicalism. Should this come to pass, I remain confident that the Christian faith will survive, even though this will require some reconfiguration of our deepest convictions.[4]

Given everything that has been written on Adam over the past decade, viewing Adam as a real historical individual who was supernaturally created by God is already a minority position within evangelicalism. For a mixture of biblical and scientific reasons, an increasing number of evangelical scholars have come to openly deny the supernatural creation of Adam. This shift has come about largely among evangelicals who are committed to embracing evolution as the way God created the world and formed the first human being — a view referred to broadly as theistic evolution. Theistic evolutionist Dennis Venema provides a helpful definition of the theistic evolutionary position:

This view holds that science is not an enemy to be fought, but rather a means of understanding some of the mechanisms God has used to bring about biodiversity on earth. This view accepts that humans share ancestry with all other forms of life, and that our species arose as a population, not through a single primal pair.[5]

One of the reasons why many theologians either reject Adam as an historical individual or see him as anything other than the originating head of the human race is the supposed evidence from biological evolution. Dr Francis Collins, who was the director of the Human Genome Project and founder of the theistic evolutionary think tank BioLogos, has been greatly influential in this area. In his book *The Language of God* he states: "Population genetics … look at these facts about the human genome and conclude that they point to all members of our species having descended from a common set of founders, approximately 10,000 in number, who lived about 100,000 to 150,000 years ago."[6] Collins is quite clear that mankind descended from a population of around 10,000 and not from two individuals. Collins sees the creation of Adam in Genesis 2 as a "poetic and powerful allegory of God's plan for the entrance of the spiritual nature (the soul) and the Moral Law

4. Todd Wilson, "Ten Theses on Creation and Evolution That (Most) Evangelicals Can Support," *Christianity Today*, January 4, 2019, https://www.christianitytoday.com/ct/2019/january-web-only/ten-theses-creation-evolution-evangelicals.html.

5. Dennis Venema, "Ask an Evolutionary Creationist: A Q&A with Dennis Venema," http://biologos.org/blog/ask-an-evolutionary-creationist-a-qa-with-dennis-venema.

6. Francis Collins, *The Language of God: A Scientist Presents Evidence for Belief* (London: Pocket Books, 2007), p. 126.

into humanity."[7] A number of other proposals for understanding Adam have been suggested by scientists and theologians who embrace evolution or old earth creation model.

Dr Denis Alexander, a leading theistic evolutionist in the UK, believes that Adam was a Neolithic farmer: "God in his grace chose a couple of Neolithic farmers in the Near East ... to whom he chose to reveal himself in a special way, calling them into fellowship with himself — so that they might know him as a personal God."[8] This interpretation of Adam, however, requires that there were Homo sapiens who were not the image bearers of God and therefore could not experience salvation as they were not descendants of Adam (cf. Romans 5:12–19). It also requires an adoptionistic understanding of Adam rather than a special creation of Adam. Furthermore, is this in any way even a possible legitimate exegetical reading of Genesis? It is difficult to imagine that any person without previously being taught this would come to the conclusion that Adam was a Neolithic farmer. The Neolithic period is an evolutionary interpretation of archaeological evidence, not a valid interpretation of Scripture. Alexander's suggested model for understanding Adam and Genesis 1–3 should cause us to be wary, because it is far from the plain reading of Scripture.

Influential evangelical Old Testament scholar, and old-earth creationist, C. John Collins is another of the leading voices in this rethink of Adam's creation. In his book *Did Adam and Eve Really Exist?* he is troublingly unclear on the Genesis account. For example, when it comes to reading the material in Genesis 1–11, Collins believes the "author was talking about what he thought were actual events, using rhetorical and literary techniques to shape the readers' attitudes towards those events."[9] Crucial to his discussion of Genesis 1–11 is how he defines history. Collins describes Genesis 1–11 in its form as "history like"[10] with a "historical core."[11] For Collins, Genesis 1–11 is historical in the sense that the events recorded within it actually happened; however, the description of those events is symbolic since the author uses rhetorical and literary techniques.[12] The high level of (supposed) figurative and pictorial language means that the passage, therefore, should

---

7. Ibid., p. 207.
8. Denis Alexander, *Creation or Evolution: Do We Have to Choose?* (Oxford: Monarch Books, 2008), p. 290. Alexander acknowledges that this is his view on page 303.
9. C. John Collins, *Did Adam and Eve Really Exist? Who They Were and Why It Matters* (Nottingham: Inter-Varsity Press, 2011), p. 16.
10. Ibid., p. 16.
11. Ibid., p. 35.
12. Ibid., p. 34.

not be seen as literal.[13] In fact, Collins constantly warns against a literal reading of Genesis 1–11.[14]

Unfortunately, this is a caricature of the young-earth position as biblical creationists interpret Genesis 1–3 using the historical-grammatical approach, taking the text plainly according to its literary genre (i.e., historical narrative), which of course takes into account such things as metaphors and figures of speech (Genesis 2:23, 4:7, 7:11). Nevertheless, Collins's approach to Genesis allows for the possibility that Adam was merely the head of a tribe rather than the direct ancestor of every human. He states: "If someone should decide that there were, in fact, more human beings than just Adam and Eve at the beginning of mankind, then, in order to maintain good sense, he should envision these humans as a single tribe. Adam would then be the chieftain of this tribe … and Eve would be his wife. This tribe 'fell' under the leadership of Adam and Eve."[15] Collins is uncertain how Adam was formed, other than that God's supernatural intervention was necessary in some way. He states: "The standard young-earth creationist understanding would have Adam and Eve as fresh … creations, with no animal forebears … I think the metaphysics by which the first human beings came about … matter a great deal. This common ground matters more than the differences over where God got the raw material, because either way we are saying that humans are the result of 'special creation.'"[16] The process of Adam's creation, however, is the most crucial part of this debate, as God tells us how He created Adam and where He got the material from (Genesis 2:7). If, however, Adam was not the first man and there were other creatures prior to Adam, what God did with Adam was not that special, and in what sense could he be said to be "the first man" (1 Corinthians 15:45)?

Over the last several years John Walton, an Old Testament scholar who is a specialist in ancient Near Eastern (ANE) studies, has proposed a novel interpretation of Genesis. Walton's primary emphasis in interpreting Genesis is the worldview of the ANE literature.[17] Walton's argument is that, when Genesis 1 is read against its ANE background, it does not speak about the material origins of the world but rather its functional origins. Walton has applied this to the discussion on how Genesis 2–3 understands Adam and

---

13. Ibid., p. 17, 20, and 31.
14. Ibid., p. 33–35, 58, 85, 92 and 124. Unfortunately, Collins does not define what he means by "literal," which leads to his caricaturing of the "literal" position as "literalism" (154).
15. Ibid., p. 121.
16. Ibid., p. 122.
17. John Walton, *The Lost World of Adam and Eve: Genesis 2–3 and the Human Origins Debate* (Downers Grove, IL: InterVarsity Press, 2015), p. 15.

Eve. He argues that in Genesis 2 "the forming accounts of Adam and Eve should be understood archetypally rather than as accounts of how those two individuals were uniquely formed."[18] Nevertheless, Walton does understand Adam and Eve to have been real people who existed in history. Walton bases this on the fact that, in the Old Testament, Adam is part of a genealogy (Genesis 5:1; 1 Chronicles. 1; cf. Luke 3:38) and the New Testament understanding of the entrance of sin and death requires a real event and real people.[19] Yet, Walton insists there are some elements of Adam's profile that are not intended to convey historical elements: his name and his forming account are archetypal.[20] Regarding the Hebrew word *'ādām* in the context of Genesis 2, Walton argues that rather than referring to a proper name (Adam), it means "humankind," which is why he believes Adam is archetypal.[21] The archetypal view allows Walton to argue for other humans having lived before Adam. Walton states:

> Current scientific understanding maintains that there was no first human being because humanity is the result of an evolving population. The evidence of genetics also points to the idea that the genetic diversity that exists in humanity today cannot be traced back to two individuals — a single pair — but that such diversity requires a genetic source population of thousands.... So far in this book, however, the analysis of the relationship of Genesis 1 and 2 has raised the possibility that the Adam and Eve account in Genesis 2 could have come after an en masse creation of humanity in Genesis 1 ... though Adam and Eve should be considered as having been included in that group.[22]

In concluding that Genesis 2–3 is speaking of Adam's functional rather than material creation, Walton is making a very questionable leap from the ANE accounts to the biblical account of creation and offers a false dichotomy between material and functional creation. These ANE texts are totally different in form and function, and contain a distorted worldview (i.e., polytheistic). Walton also allows his interpretation of Genesis to be governed by an evolutionary understanding of history. This is the reason he believes personal evil existed before the Fall of Adam, rather than being the result of his sin (cf. Romans 5:12).[23]

---

18. Ibid., p. 74.
19. Ibid., p. 102–103.
20. Ibid., p. 101.
21. Ibid., p. 61.
22. Ibid., p. 183.
23. Ibid., p. 154.

The idea that Adam did not even exist has become another popular opinion among a number of theologians.[24] Theologian and scientist Dr Denis Lamoureux, who is influential among many evangelicals, argues this way: "My central conclusion … is clear: Adam never existed, and this fact has no impact whatsoever on the foundational beliefs of Christianity.… I simply want evangelicals to be aware that there are born-again Christians who love the Lord Jesus and who do not believe there ever was a first man named '"Adam."'[25] Lamoureux's acceptance of evolution may not have resulted in his giving up his faith in Jesus. However, he has had to reject other vital doctrines of the Christian faith: original sin and the inerrancy of Scripture.[26] In doing so, Lamoureux has given up his foundation for even needing Jesus: if there is no Adam or original sin, why do we need a Savior from our sin?

Lamoureux's primary emphasis on interpreting Genesis is in light of the worldview of the ANE. Lamoureux, therefore, describes Genesis 1 as an "ancient poetic structure"[27] which he believes God used as a vehicle to communicate spiritual truth.[28] Lamoureux believes that Genesis 1 is "ancient science" which leads him to interpret passages that deal with the physical world through what he calls the "message-incident principle." This means that the Bible's spiritual truths are inerrant, but it presents them in the appearance of incidental and errant "ancient science."[29] Lamoureux's belief that Genesis 1 reflects the erroneous "science" of ancient people is an idea based upon a modern assumption and not a biblical one. Understanding Genesis this way is a movement away from a unique worldview that was revealed to the people of Israel (Exodus 20:1–17) and downplays the supernatural revelatory nature of Scripture (2 Timothy 3:16; 2 Peter 1:21).

Because of the supposed conflict between theology and science, another book has appeared, *Adam and the Genome*, which abandons a historical Adam. The book is split into two sections, with biology professor Dennis Venema tackling the scientific issues of the genome while New Testament theologian Scot McKnight deals with Adam from a biblical perspective.

---

24. Peter Enns, *The Evolution of Adam: What the Bible Does and Doesn't Say about Human Origins* (Grand Rapids, MI: Brazos Press. 2012).
25. Denis O. Lamoureux, "Evolutionary Creation View," in Matthew Barret and Ardel B. Caneday (eds.), *Four Views on the Historical Adam* (Grand Rapids, MI: Zondervan, 2013), p. 37–65.
26. Denis Lamoureux, "Beyond Original Sin: Is a Theological Paradigm Shift Inevitable?' *Perspectives on Science and Christian Belief* 67, no. 1 (2015), p. 35–49; Lamoureux, *Evolutionary Creation View*, p. 63.
27. Denis O. Lamoureux, *Evolution: Scripture and Nature Say Yes!* (Grand Rapids, MI: Zondervan, 2016), p. 30.
28. Ibid., p. 86.
29. Ibid., p. 89–90.

McKnight's main thesis throughout his chapters is that there was no historical Adam and that this has no impact on the Bible's redemptive narrative. The primary reason, however, why McKnight believes Genesis should be read as something other than a historical description of events is because he believes it was influenced by the texts of the neighboring ANE peoples (i.e., *Enuma Elish, the Gilgamesh Epic, and Atrahasis*).[30]

McKnight therefore argues that Adam (and Eve) should be viewed as part of the narrative used by Israel in discourse with the other nations in the ANE: a contextual approach to reading Genesis 1–3 immediately establishes that the Adam and Eve of the Bible are a literary Adam and Eve. That is, Adam and Eve are part of a narrative designed to speak into a world that had similar and dissimilar narratives. Making use of this context does not mean Adam and Eve are "fictional," and neither does it mean they are "historical." To be as honest as we can with the text in its context, we need to begin with the undeniable: Adam and Eve are literary — are part of a narrative that is designed to reveal how God wants His people to understand who humans are and what humans are called to do in God's creation.[31] This contextual reading allows McKnight to believe that there is no single interpretation of "Adam and Eve." McKnight points out that from the Second Temple period to the time of the New Testament (530 B.C.– A.D. 90), the "Adam and Eve" of the biblical narrative have been interpreted in a variety of ways. That is why through history "the literary Adam was a wax Adam."[32] Even though many theistic evolutionists look for an actual "Adam" who became head of the human race, chosen from a group of hominids, McKnight rightly points out, "One might suggest that, but it is rather obvious to all readers of Genesis 1–2 that there are no other humans present from whom Adam and Eve could have been chosen."[33] The distinction between Adam as a "literary" figure and Adam as a "historical" figure is foreign to the authors of the New Testament, as they clearly understood Adam as a historical figure who impacted history.

Dr Joshua Swamidass, a professor of laboratory and genomic medicine at Washington University, has given a "novel" model for how mankind may have arisen in his book *The Genealogical Adam and Eve*. Swamidass' view imposes several things on the Bible that simply do not come from an exegesis of the text. For example, Swamidass states, "Looking at Genesis alone, we cannot conclude

30. Venema and Knight, *Adam and the Genome*, p. 111–146.
31. Ibid., p. 118.
32. Ibid., p. 149.
33. Ibid., p. 145.

that all people descend from Adam and Eve."[34] But this overlooks that God's creation of mankind in Genesis 1:26–28 depicts Adam and Eve as the sole original couple. This is why Eve is described as "the mother of all the living" (Genesis 3:20) and the Apostle Paul calls Adam "*the* first man" (1 Corinthians 15:45; cf. Genesis 2:7). Swamidass argues for a real "sinless" Adam and Eve and their Fall from grace, but whose descendants slowly mixed with a pre-existing evolutionary population of humans who were living outside the garden in Eden.[35]

According to Swamidass the "sons of God" are the people outside the garden in Eden and the "daughters of men" are descendants of Adam and Eve.[36] But nowhere does the Bible teach that there were people living outside of the garden in Eden. Although there are different views on the identity of the "sons of God" (Genesis 6:1–4), no one has previously argued that they were those who lived outside the garden. Swamidass also argues that the Fall was not universal but only applied to Adam and Eve and their descendants, but this is contrary to Scripture (cf. Romans 8:20).[37] He also believes that there was a kind of sin in the world before God's command to Adam, and this sin was not held against anyone's account.[38] But again, this is contrary to the biblical view that the wages of sin is death (Romans 6:23). Because Swamidass is committed to deep time and evolution he imposes ideas onto the biblical text that are just not there. The biblical view is that Adam and Eve are the only *genealogical* and *genetic* ancestors of all mankind.

Christian philosopher and apologist Dr. William Lane Craig (WLC) has argued in his book *In Quest of the Historical Adam* that Adam did not exist at the beginning of creation but was selected from the ancestors of *Homo sapiens* known as *Homo heidelbergensis* who lived around 750,000 years ago.[39] In order to place Adam at this point in history, WLC defines the genre of Genesis 1–11 as "mytho-history" and therefore rejects the chronological accuracy of the genealogies in Genesis 5 and 11 (see chapter 5), as he believes chronological calculations are inappropriate for this genre.[40] But why preserve the historical reality of Adam and Noah while rejecting their ages? The identification of Genesis 1–11 as "mytho-history" means the events in those chapters may have happened, but because they are clothed in (supposed)

34. Joshua Swamidass, *The Genealogical Adam and Eve: The Surprising Science of Universal Ancestry* (Downers Grove, IL: InterVarsity Press, 2019), p. 138.
35. Ibid., p. 174.
36. Ibid., p. 136.
37. Ibid., p. 183.
38. Ibid., p. 182-183.
39. William Lane Craig, *In Quest of the Historical Adam: A Biblical and Scientific Exploration* (Grand Rapids, MI: W.B. Eerdmans Publishing Company, 2021), p. 336.
40. Ibid., p. 153–154.

metaphorical and figurative language they should not be taken literally (or plainly).[41] One of the reasons WLC identifies Genesis 1–11 as "mytho-history" is he believes it contains "fantastic" and "inconsistent" elements:

> Despite God's transcendence so dramatically declared in Gen 1, God is portrayed in the story of man's creation in Gen 2 as a humanoid deity worthy of polytheistic myths, as he forms man from the dirt and breathes the breath of life into his nostrils. The same is true of the story of the fall in Gen 3, where God strolls in the cool of the day and searches for the man and woman hiding among the trees; of the story of the flood in Gen 6–9, where God regrets having made man and is pleased with the smell of Noah's burnt offering; and the story of the Tower of Babel in Gen 11, where God comes down to see the city and tower that the people have built. Such anthropomorphic descriptions of God, if interpreted literally, are incompatible with the transcendent God described at the beginning of creation.[42]

WLC's conclusion regarding the transcendent and anthropomorphic descriptions of God is demonstrably false and ignores the context of Genesis 1 and 2 (see chapter 3). WLC dismisses the idea that God walked in the garden as "fantastic" (cf. Genesis 18–19), but if the Creator (John 1:1–3, 14) can walk upon the earth and even upon the sea of Galilee, why not in the garden in Eden? Moreover, the Creator not only breathed physical life into the first man, Adam, but "breathed" new life (symbolizing the Spirit) into the disciples (John 20:22).[43] It should be no surprise that WLC does not accept the supernatural creation of Adam and sees the events of Genesis 1–11 as "mytho history" as over the years he has reinterpreted or rejected biblical doctrine that is ridiculed by the world. WLC already rejects the inerrancy of the Bible (he believes in limited inerrancy), and the doctrine of original sin (see chapter 7). He also holds to an unorthodox view of the nature of Jesus (neo-Apollinarianism) and although he believes it falls short as an analogy, he has likened the doctrine of the Trinity to Cerberus (the three-headed dog of Greek mythology).[44] The corrective lens WLC brings to these doctrines is not derived exegetically from the Bible but is philosophically imposed onto the Bible.

---

41. Ibid., p. 152–157.
42. Ibid., p. 102.
43. Genesis 2:7 (LXX) and John 20:22 both use the Greek word ἐνεφύσησεν *(enephysēsen,* "he breathed on").
44. All these views held by WLC can all be found at his Reasonable Faith website, https://www.reasonablefaith.org/.

The Apostle Paul understood the challenge that philosophy based on human tradition posed to the church in his day. In his Epistle to the Colossians, Paul wrote to them so that no one would "deceive [them] with persuasive words," (Colossians 2:4) and to warn them not to be taken captive by "philosophy … according to human tradition" (Colossians 2:8). WLC has been taken captive by the philosophy of the Big Bang and the evolution of man (both of which are based on the philosophy of naturalism), as well as critical ideologies used by Old Testament theologians.

If you believe the doctrine of creation is divine revelation and is foundational for understanding the world, then you need to realize that today you are in the minority of people who call themselves Christians.

False views of Adam
Metaphor for everyone
Neolithic Farmer
Head of a tribe
Archetype of humanity
Adam did not even exist
Adam's descendants mix with evolutionary population
Homo heidelbergensis
Literary Figure

A major problem with all these varying interpretations of Adam as anything other than the first historical man of the human race is that they are completely out of line with almost all approaches to Adam throughout history. Did first-century Jews think Adam was historical? Yes. Did the New Testament authors think so? Yes. Did Jesus Himself think Adam was historical? Yes. Did the earliest Christians believe this? Yes.[45] Nevertheless, many scholars today claim that it was not until the advent of modern genetics and the discovery of ANE literature that we now know that Adam was not the first person of the human race. If these modern interpretations of Adam are the biblical ones, why did these interpretations not appear until recently?

---

45. For a defense of a historical Adam in early Judaism and throughout church history, see William Van Doodewaard, *The Quest for the Historical Adam: Genesis, Hermeneutics, and Human Origins* (Grand Rapids, MI: Reformation Heritage Books, 2015); and Dr Tom Nettles' chapter, "Adam's Place in the History of the Church's Theology," in Terry Mortenson (ed.), *Searching for Adam: Genesis and the Truth About Man's Origin* (Green Forest, AR: Masters Books, 2016), p. 73–111.

Therefore, to claim that, when you read the Bible in its context, Adam is anything other than the head of the human race is to be in complete disagreement with people in the ancient world and throughout the history of the church, who did not understand Genesis that way.

This has become a serious issue for the church. To understand Genesis this way, Christians have to sacrifice the clear teaching of the Bible to fit with a particular evolutionary view of earth's history. What Christians who accept evolution need to realize is that theistic evolution is not biblical orthodoxy — it does not win the respect of the world (not that the Christian should be looking for the respect of the world — Scripture repeatedly warns Christians against seeking the approval of the world — Luke 6:26; James 4:4; 1 John 4:5) and it is not good science — for it is just as scientifically flawed as naturalistic evolution. Theistic evolutionists (and those Christians who reject biological evolution but accept the millions of years in embracing cosmological and geological evolution) seem to be trying to save Christianity from embarrassment so that the Bible might make sense to those who do not believe. However, the secular academy is hostile to Christianity precisely because secular academia is controlled by evolutionary, millions-of-years thinking.

Belief in supernatural creation stands against a dominant intellectual system that establishes what is called "credibility" in the secular academy. Evangelicals who feel intellectually accountable to the academy then have to come up with another way to understand Genesis. Ultimately, these views of Adam are not based upon credible exegetical conclusions but are the consequence of abandoning the authority of Scripture for the sake of the praise of the academy. The great 20th-century preacher Martyn Lloyd-Jones explained why the issue of Adam is important:

> We must assert that we believe in the being of one first man called Adam, and in one first woman called Eve. We reject any notion of a pre-Adamic man because it is contrary to the teaching of the Scripture.... If we say that we believe the Bible to be the Word of God, we must say that about the whole of the Bible, and when the Bible presents itself to us as history, we must accept it as history.[46]

The reason why we must accept the supernatural creation of the first man Adam is because it is the clear teaching of Scripture.

---

46. Martyn Lloyd-Jones, *What Is an Evangelical?* (Edinburgh: Banner of Truth Trust, 1992), p. 74–75.

❧ The Consequences of Reinterpreting Adam

The atheist philosopher Daniel Dennett, in his book *Darwin's Dangerous Idea*, likened Darwin's idea of natural selection acting on chance variations to a "universal acid" which is so corrosive that nothing can contain it. According to Dennett, Darwinism "eats through virtually every traditional concept — mankind's most cherished beliefs about God, value, meaning, purpose, culture, and morality — everything."[47] How the "universal acid" that is Darwinism erodes Christian doctrine is seen in the beliefs of once-professing Christian and committed Darwinist Karl Giberson, who stated in his book Saving Darwin: How to Be a Christian and Believe in Evolution:

> Acid is an appropriate metaphor for the erosion of my fundamentalism, as I slowly lost my confidence in the Genesis story of creation and the scientific creationism that placed this ancient story within the framework of modern science. Dennett's universal acid dissolved Adam and Eve; it ate through the Garden of Eden; it destroyed the historicity of the events of creation week. It etched holes in those parts of Christianity connected to these stories — the fall, "Christ as second Adam," the origins of sin, and nearly everything else that I counted sacred.[48]

The issue is not whether a person can be a Christian and believe in evolution, but what one has to concede theologically in order to hold on to one's belief in evolution. While it is possible to believe in God and evolution, you cannot be a consistent Christian and believe in evolution. Theistic evolutionists inconsistently reject the supernatural creation of the world yet nevertheless accept the reality of the virgin birth and the miracles and Resurrection of Christ, which are equally at odds with secular interpretations of science. Theistic evolutionists have to tie themselves up in knots in order to ignore the obvious implications of what they believe. The term "blessed inconsistency" should be applied here, as many Christians who believe in evolution do not take it to its logical conclusions. Christians who accept evolution are unwittingly helping to erode belief in the supernatural creation of Adam and other vital doctrines of the Christian faith. This is evidenced in the secular world which often does see the importance of Adam to biblical Christianity, as we see in these words from Peter Bowler:

---

47. Editorial, "Universal Acid," creation.com, https://creation.com/universal-acid, quoting Daniel Dennett, *Darwin's Dangerous Idea: Evolution and the Meanings of Life* (New York: Simon & Schuster, 1995), p. 34–40.
48. Karl W. Giberson, *Saving Darwin: How to Be a Christian and Believe in Evolution* (New York: HarperOne, 2008), p. 10.

If Christians accept that humanity was the product of evolution — even assuming the process could be seen as an expression of the Creator's will — then the whole idea of Original Sin would have to be reinterpreted. Far from falling from an original state of grace in the Garden of Eden, we have risen gradually from our animal origins. And if there was no sin from which we needed salvation, what was the purpose of Christ's agony on the cross? Christ became merely the perfect man who showed us what we could all hope to become when evolution finished its upward course.[49]

For those theistic evolutionists who are trying to make peace with the academic community and attempting to meet the intellectual elites halfway, guess what? The intellectual elites do not want to meet halfway. Bowler, unlike many Christians, recognizes that evolution destroys not only the idea of the creation of Adam but also the concept of original sin and the atonement of Christ. This is a practical consequence of synthesizing evolution with the Bible. Unfortunately, there are many evangelicals who have a high view of Scripture and believe in a historical Adam, yet seem unaware of the consequences of accepting the theory of the process of evolution by which Adam is said to have come into existence. Reformed theologian Michael Horton states: "Whatever one's conclusions concerning the process of human origins, Christian theology stands or falls with a historical Adam and a historical fall."[50] While Horton is correct in what he says concerning a historical Adam, his statement shows a lack of understanding of the origins debate.

As we have seen, many theistic evolutionists today who claim to be evangelical have, because of their beliefs about the process of human origins, rejected or reinterpreted the supernatural creation of Adam and a historical Fall along with him. The debate over whether Adam was supernaturally created is ultimately a debate over whether we trust what the Scriptures clearly teach. If we cannot be certain of the beginning, why would we be certain about what the Scriptures teach elsewhere? The idea of the uncertainty of truth is rampant in our culture, partly due to the influence of postmodernism and its deconstruction of truth, and that is why many believe that the question of Adam's historicity is unimportant. Yet this is not an unimportant matter: it is a theological fact with huge theological implications. As the following chapters seek to demonstrate, if there is no Adam and Eve, the

49. Peter Bowler, *Monkey Trials and Gorilla Sermons* (Cambridge, MA: Harvard University Press, 2007), p. 7.
50. M. Horton, *The Christian Faith: A Systematic Theology for Pilgrims on the Way* (Grand Rapids, MI: Zondervan, 2011), p. 424.

whole of the biblical narrative (creation, Fall, redemption, consummation) falls apart. Adam is essential to the biblical narrative and the gospel. Any attempt to depart from this will only end in an incoherent and inconsistent worldview. Adam is essential to the meta-narrative of the Bible.

Chapter 2

Genesis 1: In the
Space of Six Days

The very first verse of Genesis, possibly the most well known in the Bible, gives us an introduction to the creation of all things: "In the beginning God created the heavens and the earth" (Genesis 1:1; NKJV). It is common today to hear Christian scholars and apologists argue that all Genesis 1 intends to teach us is the fact that God is the creator of all things and not how He created or how long it took Him. If this is the case, then all that is needed to teach that is Genesis 1:1. So why do we have all the excess details in the other 33 verses (Genesis 1:2–2:3)? Because not only does the Bible begin by stating that God is the Creator of everything, the heavens and earth, but in Genesis 1:2–31 we are then told how and when God created the light, darkness, day, night, expanse, waters, dry land, vegetation, plants, fruit trees, sun, moon, stars, sea creatures, birds, livestock, creeping things, beasts of the earth, and, lastly, man in His own image. God did all this for His own glory in the space of six days and then ceased from His work on the seventh day (Genesis 1:1–2:3).

Genesis 1 is a unique, unparalleled, historical account of the creation of all things that took place in time-space history. The literary genre of Genesis 1 is a much-debated issue among scholars, who give a number of suggestions to consider: legend, myth, mytho-history, poetry, theological history, hymn, and exalted prose narrative. There are, however, several compelling reasons to believe that Genesis 1 is an accurate historical narrative portraying real events that took place within six 24-hour days (Exodus 20:11, 31:17).

First, the events of Genesis 1 are a reliable, historical account of the creation of the world and mankind since they were divinely revealed by

God to Moses (Exodus 20:11, 31:17–18). Moses, the author of the Torah (Genesis to Deuteronomy) was the most-qualified candidate to write such a monumental work (including narratives, historical genealogies, law codes, speeches, and poetry), given he was educated in Egypt (Acts 7:22) during a time of great power and international prestige (1526–1486 B.C.).

The Chronology of the Life of Moses		
1526–1486 B.C. Moses in Pharaoh's Court	1486–1446 B.C. Moses in exile in Midian and the final year persuading Pharaoh to let Israel leave Egypt	1446–1406 B.C. Moses with Israel in the Wilderness

Although there is no clear statement in any book of the Torah indicating that Moses wrote every word of all five books, or explicitly that he authored Genesis, this is far from the end of the story (see Exodus 17:14, 34:27; Numbers 33:1–2; Deuteronomy 31:24; cf. Joshua 1:7).

The Torah presumes a knowledge of the narrative in Genesis by quoting and alluding to it, specifically in reference to God's promises to Israel's Patriarchs about the land of Canaan and the great nation they would become (Exodus 2:24, 6:8, 32:13; Leviticus 26:42; Numbers 32:11; Deuteronomy 1:8). Not only that, but prophetic passages in the Torah reference patriarchal promises from the Book of Genesis (Numbers 23:10 cf. Genesis 13:16, 15:5; Numbers 23:21 cf. Genesis 17:8; Numbers 23:24 cf. Genesis 49:9; Numbers 24:9 cf. Genesis 49:9; Numbers 24:9 cf. Genesis 12:3; Numbers 24:17 cf. Genesis 49:10). These references and allusions suggest that the original readers of the Torah had a knowledge of them, or they would be meaningless to them.[1]

In writing the Torah, Moses may have used oral tradition, written sources, or even direct revelation from God (i.e., Genesis 5:1; Exodus 24:15–16, 25:9; Numbers 21:14). The likeliest possible date for the writing of the Torah would be when Moses was at Sinai or in the plains of Moab across from Jericho (Numbers 22:1, 26:63; cf. Deuteronomy 1:5), after the Israelites had come out of Egypt and were about to enter Canaan (1446–1406 B.C.). This would give Moses at least 39 years to write the Torah.[2] Both

1. See Andrews E. Steinmann, *Genesis: Tyndale Old Testament Commentaries* (Downers Grove, IL: InterVarsity Press, 2019), p. 7–8.
2. Even until the time of his death, Moses possessed all his faculties (Deuteronomy 34:7).

internal and external evidence are consistent with Moses being the fundamental author of the Torah (see John 5:45–47).[3]

The scenario of Israel about to enter Canaan helps explain the reason
for God giving Israel Genesis 1–11. Because the people of Israel would have
been influenced by the traditions of the surrounding nations (i.e., first the
Egyptians, then the Canaanites, and later the Babylonians), God wanted to
teach Israel the truth about the past and what He had done in the world.
The purpose of the Torah, then, is to explain who the Israelites were, what
God's plan for them was, and to teach them that He was not only their Creator (Genesis) but also their Redeemer (Exodus), who provides standards of
holiness (Leviticus), protects, and provides for them (Numbers), and keeps
His covenantal promises (Deuteronomy). Genesis 1–11 (Torah), was written to give Israel a worldview to stand against godless peoples of the ANE.

Rather than a redactor piecing together multiple strands of sources (the
Documentary Hypothesis) in the post-exilic period (c. 587 B.C.), the literary
structure of the Torah shows it was intended to be read as a whole book.
For example, the Torah begins with a narrative (Genesis 1–48), which is
followed by a poetic section (Genesis 49) and ends with an epilogue (Genesis 50). This pattern continues throughout the Torah with the exodus and
Sinai-wilderness narratives concluding with poetic sections (Exodus 15;
Numbers 23–24). The final book of the Torah also concludes with a poem
(Deuteronomy 32–33) and is completed with an epilogue (Deuteronomy
34). These poems carry the main theme of the narrative. In all the poems
(except Exodus 15), the main character (i.e., Jacob, Balaam, Moses) indicates
that the fulfillment of these passages will take place in "days to come/the last
days" (Genesis 49:1; Numbers 24:14; Deuteronomy 31:29, cf. 4:30); Moses
uses past events to foreshadow the future. The occurrence of this phrase
indicates that in the composition of the Torah, there was a plan to form the
final work into one book.[4] The perspective of the post-exilic composition
of the Torah cannot explain this literary feature since its interest in Israel's
history would be looking backward and not forward.

Although critical scholars have long claimed that the Torah was not
completed until the post-exilic period, recent evidence from outside of the
Bible demonstrates that Moses could have written the Torah around 1446–

---

3. Mosaic authorship of the Torah does rule out, under the guidance of the Holy Spirit,
later textual updates by subsequent writers (i.e., the name "Chaldeans" in Genesis
11:28). Ur was not known as "of the Chaldeans" until much later than the time of
Moses, so it was most likely updated by a later scribe (cf. Genesis 14:14, 36:31–32).

4. See John Sailhamer, *The Pentateuch as Narrative: A Biblical-Theological Commentary*
(Grand Rapids, MI: Zondervan, 1992), p. 34–37.

1406 B.C. In his 2016 book, *The World's Oldest Alphabet — Hebrew as the Language of the Proto-Consonantal Script*, Dr. Douglas Petrovich argues that it was not the Phoenicians who invented the first alphabet but rather a group of Hebrew sojourners in Egypt (Lahun, Wadi el-Ḥôl) and Sinai (Serâbît el Khadîm, Wadi Nasb) spanning the period from Joseph to Moses (1850–1446 B.C.). If Dr. Petrovich is correct, then the Israelites played a central role in establishing one of the great pillars of civilization: the alphabet. Petrovich identified and translated proto-consonantal Hebrew (PCH) inscriptions of the Egyptian New Kingdom (1560–1069 B.C.) that were written by shepherds, miners, craftspeople, and vintners. This not only confirms that Moses could have written down the Torah in the Hebrew language but that the Israelites were able to read and write (see Deuteronomy 6:9).

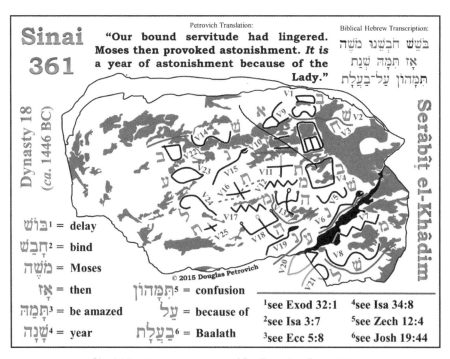

Sinai 361: Image courtesy of Dr. Douglas Petrovich.

In his translations of the inscriptions, Petrovich discovered the name Moses, as well as several other Old Testament figures (Asenath on Sinai 376 c. 1772 B.C. and Ahisamach on Sinai A.D. 375–1480 B.C. — Genesis 41:45; Exodus 31:6) that have never been found outside the Bible. On Sinai 361, part of two fragments of an inscribed stone, the inscription reads, "Our bound servitude had lingered. Moses then provoked astonishment. It is a year of astonishment because of the Lady."[5] Although Sinai 361 is not dated, it is found among other inscriptions in the mines at Serâbît el Khadîm of the Egyptian New Kingdom. The pottery found in those mines was used during the reigns of Thutmose III (the Pharaoh who chased Moses out of Egypt) and Amenhotep II (the Pharaoh of the exodus) — so the pottery dates the inscription (c. 1446 B.C.).

Sinai 361 refers to a year of astonishing events, and one person is named: Moses (Petrovich found that no other grammatical option was even feasible — only *Moses* as a proper noun). All the events described on the inscription refer to the historical period of what we see taking place just before the Israelite exodus from Egypt. The presence of the name Moses on a 15th-century B.C. inscription seriously undermines the idea that the Torah was composed in the post-exilic period. If not, it would have to be proposed (as in the Documentary Hypothesis) that for nearly 1,000 years the name of a leading biblical figure was guessed at correctly by those who are alleged to have redacted the Torah in the post-exilic period. The inscription on Sinai 361 "may stand as the single most important PCH inscription of the entire Bronze Age."[6] If Petrovich's translation of these inscriptions is accurate, then they strongly confirm the reliability of the Old Testament accounts of the Israelite sojourn into Egypt under Jacob, the Israelite exodus from Egypt, and writing of the Torah under Moses.

Second, the literature of Genesis 1 is plainly a historical narrative as it contains a Hebrew verb form the *wayyiqtol* ("and … said", *wāyyōmer*; "and there was," *wāyehi*; "and … saw," *wāyyāre*) which appears 55 times in 34 verses and is a standard marker of historical narrative in the Old Testament.[7] This verb form is characteristic of other historical narratives, such as Genesis 12–50, Exodus, 1 and 2 Samuel, and 1 and 2 Kings. In Genesis 11–12, there is no transition from non-historical to historical, and it is not treated as a separate literary category from Genesis 12–50. Genesis 12 begins with a waw consecutive verb, *wāyyōmer* ("and he said"), indicating that what follows is a continuation of chapter 11 and not a major break in the narrative. There is no major difference in Genesis 1–11 grammatically and in form to

---

5. Douglas Petrovich, *The World's Oldest Alphabet — Hebrew as the Language of the Proto-Consonantal Script* (Jerusalem, Israel: Carta, 2016), p. 158–172.

6. Ibid., 172.

7. Dr. Steven Boyd has undertaken a statistical study on the frequency of the *wayyiqtol* in narrative and poetical accounts and shows, based upon the distribution of verb forms, that Genesis 1 is definitely a narrative and not poetry. Steven W. Boyd, "The Genre of Genesis 1:1–2:3: What Means This Text?" in Terry Mortenson and Thane H. Ury, eds., *Coming to Grips with Genesis: Biblical Authority and the Age of the Earth* (Green Forest, AR: Master Books, 2008), p. 163–192.

the other historical accounts in Genesis because there is no break in the literary style in the first 12 chapters. These are all in the same literary category because they use the same historical marker *tôlĕdōt*: "These are the generations…" (Genesis 2:4, 5:1, 6:9, 10:1, 11:10, 11:27, 25:12, 25:19, 36:1, 36:9, 37:2). Moreover, the biblical chronologies in the Old Testament, such as Genesis 5 and 11 and 1 Chronicles 1:1, present Adam alongside numerous historical individuals, such as Abraham. This clearly demonstrates that the author of Chronicles understood Adam as a historical person who was the head of mankind. The genre of narrative in the Old Testament does not communicate myth but rather real events that took place in history.[8]

Third, while there is debate over artistic features in Genesis 1, there are convincing textual indicators that it is not poetic. Genesis 1 contains no or little figurative language, symbolism, or metaphors. What is more, Genesis 1 lacks the parallelism that is found in poetic accounts of creation (see Psalm 104:1–4). There are those who argue that because Genesis 1 contains symmetry, it is not a normal historical narrative but rather is an artistic arrangement whereby its emphasis is theological not historical. However, this proposes a false dichotomy between history and theology. Why can't the text be addressing both? The Bible's historical claims cannot be separated from its theological claims. The symmetry that has persuaded many scholars of the literary arrangement in Genesis is the supposed parallels between the days:

Environment	Contents
Day 1 — light	Day 4 — luminaries
Day 2 — water and sky	Day 5 — birds and sea creatures
Day 3 — land and plants	Day 6 — land animals and man
Day 7: Sabbath	

However, when examined carefully, the supposed parallels between the days are not there.

- Light on day one is not dependent on the sun, as it was created on day four.

- The waters existed on day one and not only on day two.

- Water was made on day one, but the seas were not made until day three. The sea creatures of day five were to fill the "waters in the seas," which were created on day three, not day two.

---

8. See Abner Chou, "Did God Really Say…? Hermeneutics and History in Genesis 3," *What Really Happened in the Garden: The Reality and Ramifications of the Creation and Fall of Man* (Grand Rapids, MI: Kregel Academic, 2016), p. 36.

- On day four we are told that God made the sun, moon, and stars and placed them in the expanse (Genesis 1:17) created on day two, not on day one.

- Man was created on day six not to rule over the land and vegetation (day three) but over the land animals created on day six and the sea creatures and flying creatures created on day five.

Unfortunately, the literary theory, a more "sophisticated" approach to Genesis 1, seeks to de-historicize the text. Genesis 1 is clearly interested in chronological time ("in the beginning," "one day," "evening and morning," "signs and for seasons").

Fourth, Jesus and the authors of the New Testament treat the early chapters of Genesis as history (rather than myth or allegory). Jesus taught that man was made at the beginning of creation (Mark 10:6; cf. Matthew 19:4–6) and affirmed that Abel, the son of Adam, was the first person to be murdered (Luke 11:51). The reliable historian Luke traces mankind back to the first man Adam (Luke 3:38) and records that the Apostle Paul, in his defense of the gospel in Athens, reminded the Greek philosophers of this fact (Acts 17:26). Jude, the half-brother of Jesus, also views the genealogy in Genesis 5 as accurate history as he identifies Enoch as the seventh from Adam (Jude 14; cf. Genesis 5:1–24). The Apostle Paul establishes Adam as "*the* first man" in relationship of order to mankind (1 Corinthians 15:45). Paul also affirms the order of the creation of Adam and Eve (1 Corinthians 11:8; 1 Timothy 2:13) and argues that the reason why mankind dies is because of the fact we are "in Adam" as he is the one who brought death into the world (1 Corinthians 15:21–22, 26; Romans 5:12). The Apostle Peter clearly understood Genesis as straightforward, historical narrative according to the plain sense of the text as he makes it clear that the world was covered with water on days one and two and was subsequently destroyed by that water through a global Flood (2 Peter 3:5–6). The testimony of the Lord Jesus and the Apostles confirms that Genesis is history and not myth.

Fifth, the historical interpretation comes from the text and not by imposing outside ideas on it, such as evolution or ANE ideas of existence. This was how most scholars understood Genesis 1 before the 18th century, including the Jewish historian Josephus, the early church fathers Theophilus of Antioch, Lactantius, and Basil the Bishop of Caesarea, as well as the Reformers Martin Luther and John Calvin.[9] For example, the 1st century

---

9. See James R. Mook, "The Church Fathers on Genesis, the Flood, and the Age of the Earth," in *Coming to Grips with Genesis: Biblical Authority and the Age of the Earth*, eds. T. Mortenson and T.H. Ury, (Green Forest, AR: Master Books, 2008), p. 23–51.

Jewish historian Josephus understood the creation account in Genesis as historical; of which he said, "In just six days the world, and all that is therein, was made."[10] Likewise the French Reformer John Calvin (1509–1564) affirmed that it took six days to create the world over and against the prevailing view of his day, held by many in the Roman Catholic Church, that the world was made in one moment:

> With the same view Moses relates that the work of creation was accomplished not in one moment, but in six days. By this statement we are drawn away from fiction to the one God who thus divided his works into six days, that we may have no reluctance to devote our whole lives to the contemplation of it.[11]

Calvin also believed that the world had not yet "completed its six thousandth year."[12] However, theistic evolutionists turn to the church fathers Origen (A.D. 185–254) and Augustine (A.D. 354–430) to support their arguments that Genesis can be interpreted figuratively. Even though Origen and Augustine were not influenced by modern science, they did have other influences, including the science (philosophy) of their own respective time. Origen and Augustine were influenced by neo-Platonic philosophy. While both Origen and Augustine did not believe that the days were literally 24 hours, they also did not believe the earth to be ancient. Origen rejected the long ages of the Greeks[13] and Augustine believed "… the evidence of the holy Scriptures, that fewer than 6,000 years have passed since man's first origin."[14] To use Origen and Augustine to justify a figurative reading of Genesis 1, is unwarranted for two reasons. First, they did not believe the days were long periods of time or that the earth was millions of years old. Second, their interpretation of the creation account in Genesis was influenced largely by Greek philosophy, just as many scholars today have been influenced by a worldly philosophy (evolutionary naturalism).

Sixth, because all Scripture is *God-breathed* (2 Timothy 3:16), it is trustworthy and authoritative when it comes to history, and thereby is trustworthy in the scientific inferences from that history (e.g., since the earth was

10. Flavius Josephus, *The Complete Works of Flavius Josephus: The Jewish Historian*, Trans. W. Whiston (Green Forest, AR: New Leaf Press, 2008), p. 1–4.

11. John Calvin, *The Institutes of the Christian Religion* 2nd ed (Peabody, MA: Hendrickson Publications, 2009), p. 91.

12. Ibid., p. 90.

13. See Andrew Sibley, "Origen, origins, and allegory" *Journal of Creation* 32(2) 2018, 110–117.

14. Augustine, *City of God*, Repr. Trans. H. Bettenson (London, England: Penguin Books, 2003), p. 484.

created before the sun, according to Genesis 1, the earth did not evolve by the laws of chemistry and physics from a solar gas cloud around the sun). The supernatural event of creation was not scientifically observable as it was an event that took place in the unobservable past. Therefore, creation is not a scientific fact, rather it is a historical fact that makes science possible, because it was an act of the one true God who is consistent in His nature (which is why we can rely on the uniformity of nature, laws of logic etc.). It is important to remember that the events that take place in creation week involve the supernatural work of the Creator and is unlike the ongoing day-to-day laws of nature that God uses to uphold the present world (cf. Colossians 1:17; Hebrew 1:3). The God of the Bible is not the God of the things we do not understand but of the things we do (and things we do not). Genesis 1 gives us that framework for understanding the origin of all things. It is the fact that God is the Creator of the world that gives us reason to trust our minds that He has given us to study the world around us, as God is responsible for the mind and the creation He has made.

Interpreting Genesis 1 in the historical-grammatical approach understands it as historical narrative, which of course considers such things as metaphors and figures of speech (Genesis 2:23, 4:7, 7:11, 8:21). The plain meaning may be understood as "the meaning intended by the human author, as that sense can be plainly determined by the literary, and historical context."[15] This interpretation of the account of creation in Genesis 1 is crucial in understanding discussions about evolution and the age of the earth and the identity of man as an actual historical person made in the image of God. If Genesis 1 teaches that creation took place in six 24-hour days it would indicate a young earth (see Genesis 5:1–32), thus ruling out the millions of years claimed as fact by secular scientists for the age of the earth and the idea that Adam was an ancestor of a pre-existing evolved hominid creature. If we are going to argue that man was uniquely created by God, with no animal forebears, then we first need to be clear about what Genesis 1 is saying.

 On day one of creation the one true and living God brings space, matter, and time into existence:

> In the beginning, God created the heavens and the earth. The earth was without form and void, and darkness was over the face of the deep. And the Spirit of God was hovering over the face of the waters. And

---

15. Moises Silva, "Has the Church Misread the Bible?" in *Foundations of Contemporary Interpretation: Six Volumes in One*, ed. Moises Silva (Leicester, England: Apollos, 1996), p. 40.

God said, "Let there be light," and there was light. And God saw that the light was good. And God separated the light from the darkness. God called the light Day, and the darkness he called Night. And there was evening and there was morning, the first day (Genesis 1:1–5).

The very first verse of Genesis is one of the most famous verses in the Bible: "In the beginning, God created the heavens and the earth." These words have long been seen by many creationists as God's first creative act. However, that is not the only understanding of Genesis 1:1 among Old Testament scholars and biblical creationists. There is very good reason to view Genesis 1:1 as an introduction or title to the entire creation narrative (cf. Genesis 37:5). Understanding Genesis 1:1 as a title (rather than the first creative act of Day One) means that Day Two is the creation of atmosphere and space (Genesis 1:6–8).[16] There are at least three reasons to understand Genesis 1:1 as an introductory title: 1) the phrase "heaven and earth" is a merism, 2) Genesis 1:1 together with Genesis 2:1–3 functions as an *inclusio* (Genesis 6:9–10 and 9:18–19 introduce and conclude the Flood account), and 3) the grammatical relationship between Genesis 1:1 and 1:2 suggest Genesis 1:1 is an introductory title.[17] Another way of saying this is that Genesis 1:1 tells us, "In the beginning God made everything," and verses 2–31 tell us how He did it.

Moses opens Genesis 1 by telling us that God is interested in time and history (In the beginning).[18] Interestingly, Moses uses the masculine plural noun 'ĕlōhîm to refer to God. Although 'ĕlōhîm can refer to gods (see Exodus 12:12, 20:3), it refers to the one true Creator God when it commonly occurs with singular verbs, as found in Genesis 1:1 (create, bārā').[19] It is God alone who is the Creator of the heavens and the earth and LORD (YHWH) of history (Isaiah 40:28, 42:5, 45:18). The Hebrew verb "create" (bārā) occurs in only four verses in Genesis 1:1–2:3 (Genesis 1:1, 1:21, 1:27x3, 2:3).[20] In the context of Genesis 1:1, the objects of bārā are the

---

16. One of the reasons for not understanding Genesis 1:1 as referring to creation of heaven (i.e., the atmosphere) is that what God does on Day Two with the expanse means that heaven would have been created twice.

17. For a more detailed discussion of Genesis 1:1 as a title, see Dr. Danny Faulkner with Lee Anderson Jr., *The Created Cosmos: What the Bible Reveals About Astronomy* (Green Forest, AR: Master Books, 2016), p. 43–47.

18. The LXX translates the Hebrew word "beginning" (בְּרֵאשִׁית, bĕrē'šît) in Genesis 1:1 as an absolute noun "in the beginning" (ἐν ἀρχῇ, en archē, see John 1:1).

19. Kenneth Mathews, *Genesis 1–11:26: The New American Commentary* Vol. 1A (Nashville TN: B&H Publishing, 1996), p. 127.

20. Although bārā does not inherently refer to creation *ex nihilo*, the context in Genesis 1:1–3 clearly implies this.

heavens and earth and it is used in rest of the chapter in order to designate God's bringing something new into existence (sea creatures and mankind). The verb *bārā'*, with God as its subject, indicates special significance for God as sovereign Creator.[21] Christians often speak of creation as *ex nihilo* (out of nothing, Genesis 1:3, cf. John 1:3, Hebrews 11:3), but technically the creation of all things comes from nothing physical, it does not come from nothing. God, who is spirit (John 4:24), is not nothing! The God who spoke space, time, and the material earth into existence is Himself spaceless, timeless, and immaterial (Psalm 90:2; John 4:24).

In Genesis 1:2 the earth (*'ereṣ*)[22] is not the same as 1:1; as it begins a new subject: "the earth was without form and void, and darkness was over the face of the deep. And the Spirit of God was hovering over the face of the waters" (Genesis 1:2). These words do not follow sequentially from Genesis 1:1 but rather describe the state of the world and the beginning of the creation process which is summarized in 1:1.[23] The earth at this point is pictured as being "without form and void" (*tōhû wābōhû*) or rather "unformed and unfilled." In other words, it is in an unfinished state and is uninhabitable. The reason for this is that throughout days one to six God will form and fill up his creation (Genesis 1:3–31). At this stage in creation the earth was not ready for man to live upon it, but God did not create the earth for it to be empty: "For thus says the LORD, who created the heavens (he is God!), who formed the earth and made it (he established it; he did not create it empty [*tōhû*]), he formed it to be inhabited!" (Isaiah 45:18).

Since God's purpose in forming the earth was for it to be inhabited, it makes sense that creation took place over a short period of time, in six days. Why would God wait billions of years if His whole purpose is to have human life on the earth? It is estimated today, by naturalistic scientists, that the universe is around 13.8 billion years old, which means that man was created after 99.99997 percent of those billions of years had passed. This evolutionary timeline makes no sense considering what the Bible teaches about God's purpose in forming the earth to be inhabited or that God created man at the beginning of creation (Mark 10:6).

What would later become the earth started out covered with water. In Genesis 1:2 the earth is not the earth we live on today, as that did not appear until day three (Genesis 1:9). Rather, it is the raw material God will use to shape into our planet earth. It "is sort of like a lump of clay or a piece of

---

21. Mathews, *Genesis 1–11:26*, p. 129.
22. In Hebrew *'ereṣ* has more than one meaning and can refer to: (1), the whole earth, (2) land, (3) ground, surface of the ground, and (4) people of the land.
23. E.J. Young, *Studies in Genesis One* (P&R Publishing: New Jersey, 1964), p. 30.

stone that an artist acquires but has not yet begun to work on."[24] The presence of darkness over the face of the deep should not lead us to think there was anything imperfect or evil with creation, as it is God who creates the darkness (Isaiah 45:7). It just reflects the fact that no light existed yet upon the earth. The deep (*tehôm*) here is simply a reference to the deep waters of the world's ocean (Genesis 7:11, 8:2; Psalm 106:9). The next mention of water is also in 1:2 when the "Spirit of God was hovering over the face of the waters." The Hebrew word "*rûaḥ*" can be translated either as "spirit," or "wind." The latter term is used to suggest an impersonal force.[25] It is the context that determines the meaning of the word. The verb "hovering" (*měraḥepet*) more properly takes "Spirit" as its subject than "wind." The composite expression "Spirit of God" (*rûaḥ 'ĕlōhîm*) is consistently used in the Torah as a clear reference to the person of the Spirit of God (see Exodus 31:3, 35:31; Numbers 24:2). The Spirit of God is co-participating in creation as he "hovers" (*rāḥap*, Deuteronomy 32:11[26]) over the waters preparing the way for the creative Word of God and the transformation of the earth, readying it for habitation. The Psalmist confirms that it was God's Spirit who transformed the earth: "When you send forth your Spirit, they are created, and you renew the face of the ground" (Psalm 104:30). Notice the Spirit is sent forth by the Father and therefore is distinct from him. The Holy Spirit also had an individual role in creating mankind. In Job 33:4, Elihu acknowledges, "The Spirit of God has made me, and the breath of the Almighty gives me life." The Spirit was actively involved in Elihu's creation, just as He was in the creation of Adam (Genesis 2:7; cf. Genesis 1:26–27).

In Genesis 1:3 God shatters the darkness over the face of the deep: "And God said, 'Let there be light,' and there was light" (Genesis 1:3). God simply speaks ("and God said," *wayyō'mer 'ĕlōhîm*) and His powerful word creates (cf. Genesis 1:6, 9, 11, 14, 20, 24, 26, 29). The divine command "Let there be" is a jussive form of the verb, which is followed by "and it was so," which reveals rapid fulfillment of that command with no process. This is confirmed elsewhere in the Old Testament when creation is described as the result of the dynamic and powerful work of the word of God: "By the word [*logos*, LXX] of the LORD the heavens were made" (Psalm 33:6; cf. 148:1-5; Jeremiah 10:12). God simply spoke, and creation and all other things came into existence (John 1:1–3; Hebrew 11:3).

---

24. Faulkner, *The Created Cosmos*, p. 55.
25. The Jewish Publication Society translates Genesis 1:2: "the earth being unformed and void, with darkness over the surface of the deep and a wind from God sweeping over the water."
26. The verb "hovering" only appears one other time in the Torah in Deuteronomy 32:11, where God is likened to an eagle who "flutters" (*rāḥap*) over his young (Israel) during their wilderness wanderings.

According to the Old Testament, God's Word is living and personal (Genesis 3:8, 15:4–5; cf. 1 Samuel 3:7, 21).[27] This leaves no room for the idea that the universe is eternal, an accident, or a divine emanation, as the eternal God not only spoke creation into being, but He willed it to exist (Revelation 4:11). The fact that God speaks also opens up revelation, as He is someone who communicates with His creatures (Genesis 2:16–17; cf. Hebrews 1:1–2). The God of creation is not silent.

In the New Testament, the Apostle Paul refers to Genesis 1:3 to illustrate the power of the gospel. In 2 Corinthians 4, Paul argues that the mind of the unbeliever has been blinded by the "god of this world" so they may not see the light of the gospel (2 Corinthians 4:4). However, Paul compares the giving of light at creation to the light that shines in the human heart through the gospel to give the light of the knowledge of the glory of God (2 Corinthians 4:6). It is through the light of the gospel that God brings about a "new creation" in believers (2 Corinthians 5:17). Just as when God spoke light into the world at creation, this new life in Christ is instantaneous and not something that comes about over a long period of time.

In Genesis 1:4, God declares the "light" that He spoke into existence to be good and then separates it from the darkness in order to distinguish between day and night. The light God created was natural and physical, but the source of light is not specifically mentioned.[28] Then in Genesis 1:5, God calls the light "day" and the darkness he calls "night." By using the terms "evening" and "morning," Moses qualifies the length of a day as they refer to the end and beginning of a day; as can be seen in the Passover ritual in Deuteronomy 16:4 (cf. Exodus 18:13; Numbers 7:10–84; 1 Samuel 17:16). The initial period is defined in Genesis 1:5 by a cardinal number "one day" (*yôm 'eḥād* — cf. Genesis 27:45; 33:13). Why is this important? Moses is defining what is a day — it is the turning of the earth one time around on its axis to distinguish between the light and the darkness (a period of 24 hours).

 On day two, God begins the process of transforming the formless world that He made on day one.

And God said, "Let there be an expanse in the midst of the waters, and let it separate the waters from the waters." And God made the expanse and separated the waters that were under the expanse from the waters that were above the expanse. And it was

---

27. In Genesis 15, the "word of the LORD" not only speaks to Abram but comes into his tent and takes him outside so that he can number the stars (cf. 1 Samuel 15:10; 2 Samuel 7:4).
28. The light is probably not God since it was God that created the light.

so. And God called the expanse Heaven. And there was evening and there was morning, the second day (Genesis 1:6–8).

The transformation of the formless world begins by God placing an expanse (*rāqîa*) amid the waters (Genesis 1:6). God made the expanse to separate "the waters that were under the expanse from the waters that were above the expanse" (Genesis 1:7). The ancient Egyptians worshiped the sky and sea, but the point Moses is making here is that God is sovereign over these things that He created. This is the first time in Genesis 1 that we are told that God made something. So, not only does God create but He also makes. The Hebrew word *'āśâ* is rightly translated "made" here and in its other uses in this chapter (Genesis 1:7, 11, 12, 16, 25, 26, 31, 2:2). The Hebrew verbs "create" and "make" are used interchangeably for the creation of mankind (Genesis 1:26–27 cf. Genesis 2:4; Isaiah 45:7).[29]

God separates the waters vertically, so that as the expanse that is amid the waters moves outward it takes part of the water with it. At this point, the earth is still covered with water but there is now also water above the expanse (Psalm 148:4). The word for "expanse" or as some translations say "firmament" is *rāqîa*. Its root *rāqa* means to "to hammer," "to spread out," or "to stretch out" (Exodus 39:3), and is descriptive of something that is spread out and transparent (Isaiah 42:5, 44:24). The "expanse" (*rāqîa*) does not refer to a "hard dome" or "vault" that goes across the sky as many theistic evolutionists would believe it teaches. Genesis 1 does not depict the sky as a vault resting on foundations. This view is based on taking an ANE worldview and imposing it on the Bible and interpreting phrases like "pillars of the earth" (Psalm 75:3) in woodenly literal manner. Rather, it is probably best to see the "expanse" (*rāqîa*) as referring to outer space or sky, as not only does God equate the expanse with heaven (Genesis 1:8), but on day four the sun, moon, and stars are placed in the expanse (see Genesis 1:14–17; cf. Psalm 19:1, 4). On day five the "expanse of the heavens" is where the birds fly and the clouds float (Genesis 1:20). But on day two God had made the expanse that is called heaven, and stretched it out (see Isaiah 42:5).[30]

The phrase "God saw that it was good" is absent only on day two of creation week. The reason for this is that Moses probably saw the creation of the expanse as a preliminary stage to the emergence of dry land on day three

29. The fact that in Genesis 1:26–27 there is a parallel between "Let us make" and "So God created" indicates that the verbs "make" and "create" are virtually identical terms in Genesis 1.

30. Since creation was finished by day seven (Genesis 2:2) and the stretching out of the heavens is associated with creation it must refer to a past event (Isaiah 44:24, 45:12; Zechariah 12:1).

(Genesis 1:10) and therefore waited to use the phrase until its appropriate time.[31] The dry land was the place where mankind would live, so only when the dry land appeared on day three, could it be called "good." The earth, for the first two days of creation, is completely covered in water, which is contrary to secular cosmogony that has earth starting out as a hot molten blob. The chronological summary formula for "day" (evening and morning) is followed by a second day (*yôm šēnî*).[32]

 At the beginning of day three, the earth is still unformed and unfilled until God's Word begins to separate things out.

> And God said, "Let the waters under the heavens be gathered together into one place, and let the dry land appear." And it was so. God called the dry land Earth, and the waters that were gathered together he called Seas. And God saw that it was good. And God said, "Let the earth sprout vegetation, plants yielding seed, and fruit trees bearing fruit in which is their seed, each according to its kind, on the earth." And it was so. The earth brought forth vegetation, plants yielding seed according to their own kinds, and trees bearing fruit in which is their seed, each according to its kind. And God saw that it was good. And there was evening and there was morning, the third day (Genesis 1:9–13).

The gathering of the waters together into one place resulted in the formation of dry land; echoing the Apostle Peter's words "the earth was formed out of water and through water" (2 Peter 3:5). The focus of verse 9 is on the waters below which "were gathered together into one place." This seems to suggest that there was a single ocean to begin with. If this is so, then similarly the dry land which God called earth may also have been in one place, suggesting that there was one land mass or supercontinent to begin with. Then God calls "the dry land Earth, and the waters that were gathered together he called Seas. And God saw that it was good" (Genesis 1:10).

With the dry land in place, God says, "Let the earth sprout" and it produced vegetation, plants yielding seed and trees bearing fruit all according to their kind (Genesis 1:11–12). The two different verbs, "sprout" (*dāšā'*) and "brought forth" (*yāṣā'*), used in these verses denote rapid action rather than instantaneous creation. This pattern of rapid mature creation is seen on other

---

31. See Victor Hamilton, *The Book of Genesis Chapters 1–17: The New International Commentary on the Old Testament* (W.B. Eerdmans: Grand Rapids, MI, 1900), p. 124.
32. While the ESV reads "the second day," the Hebrew text does not contain the definite article (nor does the first, third, fourth, or fifth days).

days of creation week (creation of man and the animals from the ground; Genesis 2:7, 19). These things were not created *ex nihilo* (out of nothing) but were made of previously existing material (the earth). The "plants" and "fruit trees" were brought forth out of the ground in a supernatural way that just occurred very quickly. This is part of the supernatural nature of the creation week. It was necessary for the plants and fruit to occur rapidly because they needed to be mature as they were to be food for both man and the animals created on the sixth day (Genesis 1:29–30). God is responsible for the earth's productive powers as he is the one who richly provides food for us and gives it in abundance (cf. Job 36:31). The words "And God saw that it was good" occur twice on day three because two creative acts have taken place: the seas are separated from the dry lands and the earth brought forth vegetation. The chronological summary formula for "day" (evening and morning) is again used, noting a third day (*yôm šĕlîšî*).

 DAY FOUR On day four God now turns the work of His hands towards the heavens, the theater that displays His glory.[33]

> And God said, "Let there be lights in the expanse of the heavens to separate the day from the night. And let them be for signs and for seasons, and for days and years, and let them be lights in the expanse of the heavens to give light upon the earth." And it was so. And God made the two great lights — the greater light to rule the day and the lesser light to rule the night — and the stars. And God set them in the expanse of the heavens to give light on the earth, to rule over the day and over the night, and to separate the light from the darkness. And God saw that it was good. And there was evening and there was morning, the fourth day (Genesis 1:14–19).

God once again commands "Let there be lights," which is nearly identical to Genesis 1:3 when God said, "Let there be light." These lights (*mā'ôr*), the sun, moon, and stars, will take the place of the light ('ôr) source God has provided for the first three days. God places these lights "in the expanse of the heavens," which he had made on day two (Genesis 1:8), which will provide three functions:

1. To separate the day from the night.
2. To be for signs and for seasons and for days and years.
3. To be lights in the expanse of heaven and give light on the earth.

---

33. The reformer John Calvin referred to the heavens (creation) as a theater that displayed God's glorious works.

The sun and the moon are also given a unique purpose:

1. To rule over the day and to rule over the night.

With the sun (greater light) and moon (lesser light) now in the sky, the already existing day and night (Genesis 1:5) now have their appointed dividers. The light of the sun, moon, and stars were also to be for signs and seasons. As signs, they have several purposes in Scripture: to understand the weather (Matthew 16:1–4), to proclaim God's glory (Psalm 19:1), as distressing apocalyptic signs (Isaiah 13:9–13; Joel 2:30–31; Matthew 24:29–31) and even to guide the Magi for the birth of Jesus (Matthew 2:2, 10). The seasons (*mô'ēd*) are probably not just referring to the seasons of the year (i.e., spring, summer, autumn, and winter) but are referring to the appointed liturgical times of the year, so that the Hebrews can keep track of their festivals such as Passover, (spring, Exodus 13:10) and Tabernacles (autumn, Leviticus 23:33–43).[34] Another reason for the sun, moon, and stars being used for days and years is for agricultural purposes.

On day one of creation week, God creates light before the sun, moon, and stars on day 4. But why did God do this? Well, in the Egyptian ANE myths the sun, moon, and stars were worshiped as deities. In Genesis 1, God names the gathering of the waters, seas, the dry land, earth but he does not name the sun (*šemeš*) or the moon (*yārēaḥ*); they are known as the greater light (*hammā'ôr haggādōl*) and the lesser light (*hammā'ôr haqqāṭōn*) (Genesis 1:17).[35] God is communicating to the Israelites (the original audience) that they may have heard that the sun, moon, and stars are gods parading in their victory in the heavens, but they are not to worship or fear them. It is a warning to the people of Israel not to think that the heavenly bodies are deities. Why? Because not only is He warning against idolatry, but He is rejecting and countering myth with history (see Deuteronomy 4:19).

The sun and the moon as the largest objects in the sky that are visible to man are to shine forth and rule or dominate the sky (see Psalm 136:8–9). The stars, like the sun and the moon, are also limited in their importance, as the Hebrew text adds at the end of the verse, almost as an afterthought, "the stars also" (Genesis 1:16).[36] The fact that the stars are not given a role is probably a warning against astrology (Jeremiah 10:2). The question of the creation of the stars on day four raises the question: "How do you get starlight billions of light years away if God created everything in six 24-hour days?" This has been answered several ways.

---

34. On the night of Passover when the Hebrews left Egypt they left on the night of a full moon (Exodus 12:11, 42; 13:3).
35. The Hebrew word for *sun* sounds like the Canaanite god of the sun (*Shapash*).
36. The direct object *'et* אֵת links the stars to the verb "made" at the beginning of verse 16.

Astronomer Dr. Jason Lisle has proposed a helpful answer to the distant starlight issue known as the Anisotropic Synchrony Convention. This is based on an alternative convention that is position-based physics as opposed to velocity-based physics. Albert Einstein left open both options, but did most of his work on velocity-based, and so have most physicists since him. Einstein pointed out that time is not constant in the universe, so our simple equation [Distance = Speed x Time] is not so simple anymore. Dr. Lisle built on this position-based physics and the *one* direction speed of light (which cannot be known), and it solves distant starlight. Based on this convention-based model, light left distant stars and arrived on earth in no time. This fulfills God's statement that these lights were to give light on the earth (Genesis 1:17). Obviously, for an omnipotent God having distant stars shine light on the earth is not a problem.[37]

Astronomer Dr. Danny Faulkner has proposed a different but helpful answer to the distant starlight issue known as the *dasha'* solution:

> But what of the light from astronomical bodies? As we have seen, the plants made on Day Three rapidly came to maturity. The reason for this was that the plants could not fulfill their purpose unless they rapidly matured. In a similar manner, the astronomical bodies could not fulfill their purposes unless they were readily visible. In this sense, the light had to be matured. No one suggests that the rapid development of dry land, plants, birds, land animals, and even man naturally happened. Rather, God rapidly and miraculously brought these things together to maturity. In a similar manner, why could not the light from distant astronomical bodies have undergone the same sort of process? Hence, the *dasha'* solution to the light-travel-time problem proposes that God rapidly and miraculously brought the light of distant astronomical sources to the earth on Day Four.[38]

A problem for some people for not accepting the days of Genesis 1 as 24-hour days is the sun is not made until day four (the obvious reading of the text), and so they believe that the first three days cannot be ordinary days. This, however, is not a problem with the text but is based on the presupposition that the sun is necessary to have a day marked by evening and morning. But to have an evening and morning on the first three days, all

---

37. Dr. Danny R. Faulkner and Bodie Hodge, "What about Distant Starlight Models?" in *The New Answers Book 4*, Ken Ham, General Editor (Green Forest, AR: Master Books, 2013), p. 261–262.
38. See Faulkner, *The Created Cosmos*, p. 219.

that is needed is a light source, which God created on day one (Genesis 1:3), and a rotating earth. Technically, the first three days should not be called "solar days," as the word "solar" means "related to the sun." But they were 24-hour days. God is not dependent upon the sun to produce the phenomenon of light. Genesis is clear that the sun was made (not appeared)[39] on day four. The order of creation also corrects the predominant naturalistic model of cosmology in our day, the big bang. In the big bang cosmology, the stars and sun come before the earth, but in the biblical cosmology the physical earth appears on day three and the sun, moon, and stars are made on day four. On day four of creation week, God shows Himself sovereign over the sun, moon, and stars as they are God's gracious gift to humanity for the order of our time. The chronological summary formula for "day" (evening and morning) is again used, noting a fourth day (*yôm rĕbîʿî*).

 On day five God continues to fill up the world by producing living creatures that will fly above the face of the sky and others that will live in the waters.

> And God said, "Let the waters swarm with swarms of living creatures, and let birds fly above the earth across the expanse of the heavens." So God created the great sea creatures and every living creature that moves, with which the waters swarm, according to their kinds, and every winged bird according to its kind. And God saw that it was good. And God blessed them, saying, "Be fruitful and multiply and fill the waters in the seas, and let birds multiply on the earth." And there was evening and there was morning, the fifth day (Genesis 1:20–23).

These living creatures (*nepeš ḥayyâ*) that God creates on day five are distinct from the vegetation that God made on day three which are not alive. The waters are said to "swarm" with living creatures, which suggests that God created them in great abundance. The flying creatures (*ʿôp*) can include birds, insects, and bats (Leviticus 11:19–20). Interestingly, the word "create" (*bārāʾ*) is used here for the second time (cf. Genesis 1:1) in the narrative, but here it is used for the first living creatures. It occurs next in Genesis 1:27 of the first created human life. Thus, the word "create" is used to mark out the beginning of a new stage in creation, the creation of "living beings": the heavens and earth (Genesis 1:1), living creatures (Genesis 1:21), and mankind (Genesis 1:26). For the first time in the creation account the word

---

39. A word for "appear" (*rāʾâ*) is used in Genesis 1:9 of the dry land but it is not used on Day Four.

"blessing" appears (Genesis 1:22), which is appropriate because "blessing" relates to the giving of life (see Genesis 1:28). God created in the waters the great sea creatures (*tannîn*) such as the whale and the shark, but it is also used elsewhere to speak of large reptiles such as the "dragon" or "serpent" (Exodus 7:9–10; Isaiah 27:1). The Psalmist even calls the great sea creatures to praise their creator (Psalm 148:7). God created these living creatures according to their "kind" (*mîn*, Genesis 1:24–25, 6:20, 7:14).[40] In other words, God established limits for each creature to reproduce within. God then blesses, a central theme in Genesis, the creatures and commands them to be "fruitful and multiply and fill the waters" and "multiply on the earth" The chronological summary formula for "day" (evening and morning) is again used, noting a fifth day (*yôm ḥămîšî*).

DAY SIX   The flow of creation in Genesis 1 leads us to the pinnacle of God's creation on the sixth day when He creates man in His own image:

> And God said, "Let the earth bring forth living creatures according to their kinds — livestock and creeping things and beasts of the earth according to their kinds." And it was so. And God made the beasts of the earth according to their kinds and the livestock

---

40. The biblical "kind" would approximate to the biological classification order of *family*, not *species*.

according to their kinds and the livestock according to their kinds, and everything that creeps on the ground according to its kind. And God saw that it was good.

Then God said, "Let us make man in our image, after our likeness. And let them have dominion over the fish of the sea and over the birds of the heavens and over the livestock and over all the earth and over every creeping thing that creeps on the earth."

So God created man in his own image, in the image of God he created him; male and female he created them.

And God blessed them. And God said to them, "Be fruitful and multiply and fill the earth and subdue it, and have dominion over the fish of the sea and over the birds of the heavens and over every living thing that moves on the earth." And God said, "Behold, I have given you every plant yielding seed that is on the face of all the earth, and every tree with seed in its fruit. You shall have them for food. And to every beast of the earth and to every bird of the heavens and to everything that creeps on the earth, everything that has the breath of life, I have given every green plant for food." And it was so. And God saw everything that he had made, and behold, it was very good. And there was evening and there was morning, the sixth day (Genesis 1:24–31).

Once again, God uses a rapid process to create as He causes the earth to "bring forth" (*yāṣā'*) three categories of living creatures (*nepeš ḥayyâ*) according to their kinds: livestock (*bĕhēmâ*),[41] creeping things (*remeś*),[42] and beasts of the earth (*ḥayyat hā'āreṣ*).[43] This is the sixth time God spoke "it was so" (Genesis 1:7, 9, 11, 15, 24). The same phrase "it was so" or "and so it came to pass" (*wayĕhî-kēn*) is found in 2 Kings 15:12 when a prophecy concerning Jehu is fulfilled exactly the way God said it would be fulfilled. Why say "and it was so" six times? Because the events of creation were accomplished exactly as God had said, what God said He would do, He did.

Just as with the other days (except day two) God declares His creative work to be good. It is only now that the earth is ready for the highpoint of God's creation, man. The prominence of God's creation of man in His own image can be seen in a number of ways: (1) It is God's final act of creation. (2) It is divinely deliberated ("let us make"). (3) The divine expression replaces the impersonal words "let there be" and "let the earth." (4) Man alone is created in

---

41. Domesticated animals such as sheep or cattle.
42. Small animals, including reptiles and amphibians.
43. Non-domesticated animals or wild animals, although at this point, they are vegetarian currently.

God's image and told to rule creation. (5) The verb "create" (*bārā'*) occurs three times in 1:27. (6) This event is given the longest description in Genesis 1. (7) In 1:27 the chiastic structure has an emphasis on image, and (8) mankind is the only direct creation of God.[44]

Mankind is given a unique status among God's creatures. The distinction between mankind and the animals is clear, as His image-bearers they are called to rule over the earth, which the animals are part of (Genesis 1:28; cf. 9:2–3). As creatures made in the image of God, mankind is unique, they are not animals, as they were created as His vice regents to have dominion over the earth and are given certain communicable divine attributes: reason, personality, and morality. Not only that, mankind was originally endowed with knowledge, holiness, and righteousness (Ecclesiastes 7:29; Ephesians 4:24; Colossians 3:10). Because of the Fall, knowledge, righteous, and holiness have been destroyed by sin in man. Knowledge has become ignorance, righteousness has become unrighteousness, and holiness has become perversity (cf. Romans 1:18-32). However, man's rationality, spirituality, and dominion, although distorted, have not been totally lost. In Genesis 9:6, God declares to Noah, after the Flood, that man's life, even though it is fallen, is sacred because he is created in the image of God, which is why there is a death penalty for murdering someone made in God's image. Because of the Fall, the image of God needs to be renewed (Colossians 3:10).

When God creates man in His image He says, "Let us …", but who was He speaking to? The use of the plural "let us … our image … our likeness" has been the source of much scholarly discussion with several suggestions as to what the use of plural pronouns refer to: a plural of majesty,[45] a plural of self-deliberation,[46] or God is addressing His divine council, i.e., the angels.[47]

---

44. See Mathews, *Genesis 1–11:26*, p. 160.

45. This view is generally rejected by scholars today as there is no such thing as a plural of majesty in Hebrew when it comes to verbs and pronouns ("let us make" is a cohortative verb). Old Testament scholar Gerhard Hasel notes: "…there are no certain examples of plurals of majesty with either verbs or pronouns…the verb use in Gn. 1:26 (*āśâh*) is never used with a plural of majesty. There is no linguistic or grammatical basis upon which the 'us' can be considered to be a plural of majesty." Gerhard Hasel, "The Meaning of 'Let us' in Gn. 1:26," *AUSS* 13.1 (1975): p. 63–64.

46. Genesis 3:22 refutes a plural of deliberation as God is not taking counsel with Himself, the speaker is one of that plurality.

47. This view believes that God was speaking to His divine council (i.e., angels cf. 1 Kings 22:19; Job 1:6–12; 2:1, 6; 38:7) who surround His throne seeking their help and counsel in creation. However, there are several reasons why this view is not correct: 1) The language of personal subjects (us, our) cannot be angels, as the whole focus of Genesis 1 is that creation and man are the work of God as the verbs "create" and "make" have God as their subject, no creature is counseling God to do these things. 2) The Bible always ascribes the creation of man to God and not any other creature (see Genesis 1:27,

But none of these make sense of the context or with the teaching of the rest of Scripture. The view that best makes sense of the context of Genesis 1 is that the "let us" statement suggests a plural of persons, so that within the being of God there is a distinction of personalities (God, His Word, and His Spirit) who are involved in an intra-divine deliberation among themselves.[48]

The Hebrew word "let us make" is the first-person plural cohortative verb נַעֲשֶׂה (na 'áśe).[49] What this indicates is that those whom God is speaking to ("let us") are being exhorted to engage in the work of making and creating man (see Genesis 2:7; Job 33:4). The act of creating man is something that the Old Testament ascribes to God alone (Genesis 5:1; Deuteronomy 4:32). He did not consult with any creature (Isaiah 40:14) nor did any creature participate in the creation of man (Nehemiah 9:6). When the verb na 'áśe is used in the Torah it has reference to a plurality of personal subjects who are involved in whatever is being spoken of (see Genesis 11:4; Exodus 19:8; 24:3, 7; Numbers 32:31).[50] It is never used of one person saying, "Let us" (or "we will do") and one person doing it to the exclusion of the group that is being addressed. Genesis 1:27 goes on to state: "So God created man in his own image, in the image of God he created him; male and female he created them." While Genesis 1:26 uses the plural pronouns "us" and "our," Genesis 1:27 uses singular pronouns "his" and "he" to refer to God, who created mankind in "his image" (cf. Genesis 5:1). God reveals Himself as a plural of persons but singular in being (Deuteronomy 6:4; cf. Exodus 3:2, 31:3). Since the doctrine of the Trinity is true, each person must have been present in Genesis 1:26.[51] Why would God (the Father) turn to consult

---

5:1, 2; 6:6; 6:7; 9:6; Deuteronomy 4:32). 3) Man is made in the image and likeness of God, not in the image of any other heavenly being (the world to come belongs to man, God's image bearers, not angels; see Hebrews 2:5–8). 4) The people God is speaking to in Genesis 1:26 share His image (in our image), and nowhere in the Bible are angels said to bear the image of God (Christ died for those who bear His image; see Hebrews 2:9). 5) It is God alone who has the power to create, and He consults with no created being as to how to do this (Isaiah 40:14, 44:24; cf. Job 38–41). 6) The divine council (or angels) are messengers for God, but they are not His counselors (cf. Luke 2:9–14; Revelation 4–5). No one has ever counseled God (Isaiah 40:13 cf. Romans 11:34). 7) The divine counsel is not even explicitly mentioned in Genesis 1, whereas the Spirit of God is.

48. See Hasel, "The Meaning of 'Let us,'" p. 58–66.

49. See Anthony Rodgers "Contra Michael Heiser on Genesis 1:26" June 3rd 2021.https://www.youtube.com/watch?v=_9o59mgmQ3I.

50. Some who hold the "divine council" view argue it is correct because in the Assyrian creation account the gods use the cohortative construct in the creation of man: "Let us slay (two) Lamga gods. With their blood let us create mankind." Genesis 1, however, is not dependent on these superficial similarities from mythological Mesopotamian texts that are totally different in form and function, and contain a distorted worldview (i.e., polytheistic).

51. It is important to remember that the original audience of Genesis 1 was the nation of Israel, who had just been redeemed from Egypt by means of the angel of the LORD and

His divine council when the Son and Spirit have been eternally present with Him?[52] God's speech "let us" in Genesis 1:26 is consistent with belief in plurality within God. Furthermore, even pre-Christian Jewish literature (non-canonical) attributes the act of creating man to the Word of the Lord (cf. Genesis 1:27).[53]

In Genesis 1:27 we have the third occurrence of the verb *bārā'* (3x in 1:27) in reference to the creation of the first human life. However, in Genesis 2:7 we are given a more detailed account of the creation of man when God formed (*yāṣar*), man from the dust of the ground and built (*bānâ*, Genesis 2:22) the woman from the rib which he had taken from the man.[54] Genesis 1:27 is a parallel to Genesis 2:7 where God forms man from the dust of the ground. In his commentary on Genesis, Hebrew expert Franz Delitzsch comments:

> The origin of man, though not brought to pass by a creative fiat, is nevertheless called a creation, ברא, and may be also so called in respect of ii. 7. For the essential characteristic of creation is not the exclusion of existing material, but the achievement, and indeed the miraculous achievement, of something hitherto non-existent....[55]

Even though man, like other living creatures (day five), has the "breath of life" (Genesis 2:7) they are separate from the other created living creatures in that they are made in the image of God.

After God blesses man, He then reveals His purpose for creating them as He tells them to be "fruitful and multiply and fill the earth" and to "subdue" (*kābash*) and have "dominion" (*rādāh*) (or rule) over every living thing that

---

the Holy Spirit (see Exodus 3:2, 23:20–23, 31:3, 35:31).The people of Israel knew God as their Savior through the threefold activity of the Lord (YHWH) as seen in Isaiah 63 — the Father in verse 8 (cf. 63:16), the Son in verse 9 ("angel of his presence," i.e., "the angel of the Lord"), and the Holy Spirit in verses 10 and 14. The context of Isaiah 63:8–14 looks back to the exodus when God saved Israel by means of the "angel of his presence" ("he redeemed them") and the Holy Spirit/the Spirit of the Lord (who was "in the midst of them" and "gave them rest"). Isaiah 63:8–14 shows a distinction between the Father, the angel of his presence (the Son), and the Holy Spirit.

52. The Son and Spirit as divine persons are also involved in creative work (Psalm 33:6; Job 33:4; cf. John 1:1–3, 6:63).

53. Commenting on Genesis 1:27, the Jerusalem Targum states: "And the Word of the Lord created man in His likeness, in the likeness of the presence of the Lord He created him, the male and his yoke-fellow He created them." A Targum is an Aramaic translation and explanation of the Old Testament.

54. The creation of man involved more than just the formation of his body as God breathed into him the breath of life and he became a living creature (Genesis 2:7).

55. Franz Delitzsch, *A New Commentary on Genesis*, Trans. Sophia Taylor, Vol. 1 (Edinburgh: T&T Clark, 1888), p. 101.

moves on the earth (Genesis 1:28). Some theistic evolutionists believe these words (*kābash* and *rādāh*) imply that the first humans were to make a warlike conquest on the earth because it needed to be subdued, implying the earth wasn't "very good" (cf. Genesis 1:31). They even suggest that this means animals could be killed for food and clothing (cf. Genesis 1:29). However, this is reading a meaning into the text that is not there. It is true that these verbs elsewhere in the Old Testament express a violent display of force (Nehemiah 5:5; Ezekiel 34:4), but that is not the meaning here. God created mankind to be His viceroys (royal figures, cf. Psalm 8:4–6) who would represent Him by "ruling" (*rādâ*) peacefully and wisely over His creation. Adam was expected to a have a responsible care over that which he rules. He was to rule with compassion and not violent force over creation. The Torah forbade a master to rule over his servants with harshness (Leviticus 25:43).

Adam was blessed and commanded by God to rule over the entire creation, and to worship Him in the Garden in Eden by working and keeping it (Genesis 2:15). In this role, Adam's "kingly and priestly activity in the garden was to be a beginning fulfillment of the commission in 1:28 and was not limited to the garden's original earthly boundaries but was to be extended over the whole world."[56] Adam's task, then, was to spread the goodness of the Garden in Eden over the entire earth. Like Adam, king Solomon brought about a benevolent rule that resulted in peace and safety with each man under his own fig tree (1 Kings 4:24–26). Solomon even spoke of beasts, birds, reptiles, and fish (1 Kings 4:33). These are the same categories of animals that mankind was to rule over in Genesis 1 (Genesis 1:26–28). The call to have dominion over creation requires strength and energy which God provides for them (and the animals) in the form of plants and fruit (Genesis 1:29–30). Adam's dominion (rule) needs to be understood in terms of the creation being declared "very good" (Genesis 1:31). It was not a harsh or oppressive rule that we see in a fallen world (cf. Leviticus 26:17).

Prior to God creating mankind in His image, He had already stated six times that His creation was "good" (Genesis 1:4, 10, 12, 18, 21, 25). But when God had finished creating, He declared His creation to be "very good" (*tôb me'od*, Genesis 1:31). When *tôb* (good) is accompanied by *me'od* (very), it is a moral evaluation implying much more than a beautiful creation. The phrase "very good" indicates that "God created the world perfect"[57] with

56. G.K. Beale, *The Temple and the Church's Mission: A Biblical Theology of the Dwelling Place of God*, New Studies in Biblical Theology 17 (Downers Grove, IL: InterVarsity, 2004), p. 68.

57. Critical Old Testament scholar Gerhard von Rad says of the phrase "very good": "… expressed and written in a world full of innumerable troubles, preserves an inalienable concern of faith: no evil was laid upon the world by God's hand; neither was his

no evil in it. The goodness of God's creation reflects His moral character, as goodness belongs to Him alone and is reflected in His works (1 Chronicles 16:34; Psalm 34:8, 100:5, 106:1; cf. Luke 18:19). The main contextual pointer surrounding "very good" in Genesis 1:29–30 indicates that man and the animals had a vegetarian diet before the Fall, which of course rules out carnivorous activity or the killing of animals for food or clothes (cf. Genesis 3:21). Old Testament scholar Victor Hamilton, who is not a young-earth creationist, acknowledges this interpretation:

> At no point is anything (human beings, animals, birds) allowed to take the life of another living being and consume it for food. The dominion assigned to the human couple over the animal world does not include the prerogative to butcher. Instead, humankind survives on a vegetarian diet.[58]

It is a fallacy to read the present state of the world, which includes death, disease, war, famine, subjugation of people, and predators, back into the biblical account of creation in Genesis 1. This assumes that the things we observe in our present fallen world are the way they have always been (i.e., influenced by an evolutionary worldview).

Even after the Fall, Adam and Eve were to eat the herb of the field (Genesis 3:17–19), and it is not until after the Flood that God states, "Every moving thing that lives shall be food for you. And as I gave you the green plants, I give you everything." (Genesis 9:3). However, some argue that since man ate plants there was some death before the Fall. This overlooks the fact that plants are never the subject of "life"[59] which is the description of humans, land animals, and sea creatures (Genesis 1:20–21, 24, 30; 2:7; 6:19–20; 9:10–17). The Bible uses terms such as "wither" or "fade" to describe their cessation (Psalm 37:2, 102:11; Isaiah 64:6).[60]

Furthermore, it is the breath of life that separates humans and animals (Genesis 2:7, 6:17) from plants because when it is gone, they cease to exist (2 Samuel 1:9; 1 Kings 17:21–22). Blood is the sign of life in both humans

---

omnipotence limited by any kind of opposing power whatever. When faith speaks of creation, and in doing so directs its eye toward God, then it can only say that God created the world perfect." Gerhard von Rad, *Genesis: Old Testament Library* (London: SCM Press LTD, 1961), p. 61.

58. Hamilton, *Genesis 1–17*, p. 140.

59. G. Gerleman, "Life," in *The Theological Lexicon of the Old Testament, vol. 1* (ed. E. Jenni and C. Westermann. Trans. M. E. Biddle; Peabody, Massachusetts: Hendrickson Publishers, 1997) 414.

60. The only mention of death referring to a plant is in Job 14:8 where the stump of a tree is said to die. This is a common objection to the argument that plants don't die. A closer look at the context of Job 14:8 shows that the tree is not dead but only appears so (Job 14:7–9).

and animals (Genesis 4:10, 9:4–6), and its shedding causes the loss of life (Leviticus 17:11, 14). Plants do not die in the same sense animals and humans do because they are not living in the same sense that humans and animals are. Genesis 9:3 clearly describes that a change in diet is permitted at this time (i.e., after the Flood). In the beginning, God gave mankind "the green plants," an obvious reference to the vegetarian diet prescribed for Adam, Eve, and the animals in Genesis 1:29–30. But it is only after the Flood that God states that everything that moves shall be food for them. In other words, prior to that time, man was not permitted to eat animals, but following the flood, God instituted a change and man could then eat meat. In the context of Genesis 1, there is no danger implied, because God's creation is morally "very good."[61]

As God's image-bearers, mankind is supposed to model His perfect rule. God gave mankind the responsibility of representing Him in His creation, which means we should act as He would. For example, even in a fallen world, God calls us to show kindness to animals (Exodus 23:12; Proverbs 12:10; Jonah 4:11), but if animals were suffering and being mistreated in God's "very good" world, then this would not reflect well on His character and render His creation "not very good." However, God is not wasteful or indifferent with His creation, nor does He act in a cruel or harmful way towards it; therefore, we should not. The misuse of God's creation is a result of our sin and not being obedient to His command. In this context then, the fact that God declares His creation to be "very good" rules out the possibility of death and suffering before the Fall of man in Genesis 3. The Bible links the reality of death and suffering and natural disasters to the sin of the first man which thereby brought corruption into God's "very good" creation (Genesis 2:17, 3:17–19; Romans 5:12, 8:19–22; 1 Corinthians 15:21–22).

There are some who argue that there must have been death before the Fall because mammals such as whales, who do not live on green vegetation but on live sea food, must have caused death while eating.[62] In doing this they rule out the possibility of the existence of other foods for these animals before the Fall. It is also suggested that no animal death before human sin makes the existence of predator's problematic.[63] These problems for no animal death before the Fall are understandable, but they can be answered within a biblical framework. The Bible never uses the Hebrew term *nepeš*

---

61. Some argue that Psalm 104 refers to death in Genesis 1, but this is talking about the world post-fall.
62. John Lennox, *Seven Days that Divide the World: The Beginning According to Genesis and Science* (Grand Rapids, MI: Zondervan, 2011), p. 78.
63. Ibid., p. 79.

ḥayyâ (living soul/creature) when referring to invertebrates, but it does when referring to fish and humans (Genesis 1:20, 2:7). Also, insects do not have the same sort of "blood" that vertebrates do, yet "the life of the flesh is in the blood" (Leviticus 17:11). It is reasonable then to assume that the pre-Fall diet of animals could have included invertebrates. Even so, if we consider the fact that God foreknew the Fall (1 Peter 1:18–20; Ephesians 3:11; Revelation 13:8), then it is also logical that God "programmed creatures with the information for attack and defense features, which they would need in a cursed world. This information was "switched on" at the Fall."[64]

The chronological summary formula for a "day" (evening and morning) is again used, but for the first time the definite article appears (*yôm haššiššî*, "a day, the sixth") to indicate the completion of the work of creation upon that day.[65] God's creation is now complete, and He is ready to cease from His work. God's creative work in creation took six days, just as He told Moses on Mount Sinai: "For in six days the LORD made heaven and earth, the sea, and all that is in them…" (Exodus 20:11).

 DAY SEVEN It is important to keep in mind that God finished creating on the sixth day, as day seven is about the completion of the heavens and earth:

> Thus the heavens and the earth were finished, and all the host of them. And on the seventh day God finished his work that he had done, and he rested on the seventh day from all his work that he had done. So God blessed the seventh day and made it holy, because on it God rested from all his work that he had done in creation (Genesis 2:1–3).

God is not still working on the seventh day as He had finished working the prior day. The seventh day was not a day of creation but a day of rest (Genesis 2:3). God had finished (*kālâ*) all His work, referring to everything in heaven and earth and their host (*ṣābā'*) being completed (the sun, moon, and stars = heavenly host, Deuteronomy 4:19). The words of Genesis 2:1 introduce the completion of God's creation. The verbs "finished," "rested," and "blessed" indicate the uniqueness of this day. God's rest has nothing to do with Him being tired (Isaiah 40:28), as the Hebrew verb for "rested" is

---

64. Jonathan Sarfati, *Refuting Compromise: A Biblical and Scientific Refutation of "Progressive Creationism" (Billions of Years), as Popularized by Astronomer Hugh Ross* (Green Forest, AR: Master Books, 2004), p. 212.

65. See C.F. Keil and F. Delitzsch, *Biblical Commentary on the Old Testament, Vol. 1: The Pentateuch,* Trans. J. Martin (Grand Rapids, MI: Eerdmans Publishing, 1980), p. 50.

šābat and has to do with "the cessation of creative activity."[66] God's "rest" should be seen in the fact that He is satisfied with His work. The later rest period that God gave to the people of Israel was founded upon this creation ordinance (see Exodus 20:8–11). God blesses creation (Genesis 1:22, 28) on day seven and made it holy (*qādaš*) as it is to be devoted to Him (Isaiah 58:13; cf. Mark 2:23–28).

It has been suggested by some that day seven is not a 24-hour day because it lacks the refrain "evening and morning."[67] However, this misunderstands the use of this phrase throughout the creation week. Notice that in each of the first six days there is a structure, which is not mentioned on the seventh day, to shape each of the days:

1. "God said ..."
2. "Let there be ..."
3. "There was ..."
4. "God saw that it was good."
5. "There was evening and morning ..."

Because day seven is not a day of creation but a day of rest, it is not necessary to use the "evening and morning" formula used in day one through day six since it has a "rhetorical function that marks the transition from a concluding day to the following day."[68] Yet it is not only evening and morning that is absent from day seven, but the other parts of the formula are also absent. The formula is used to describe God's work of creation. The formula is not used on the seventh day because God had already finished creating (Genesis 2:1–3). Furthermore, no terminator phrase is needed for the seventh day, like the others, since the terminator to this day is the *tôlēdôt* ("these are the generations of ..." Genesis 2:4) as the next section of the narrative is about to begin.

The text of Genesis 1, together with Exodus 20:8–11 and Exodus 31:17, gives a clear indication that the days are 24 hours long. Exodus 20:8–11 has a number of connections with the creation week: a six-plus-one pattern, the "heavens and the earth," "rested the seventh day," "blessed," and "made it holy." All of this suggests that one of God's purposes in creating the heavens and the earth within six 24-hour days, followed by a literal day of rest, was to set up a pattern for His people to follow. Exodus 20:11 also teaches that

---

66. Mathews, *Genesis 1–11:26*, p. 178.
67. See C. John Collins, *Genesis 1–4: A Linguistic, Literary, and Theological Commentary* (Philipsburg, NJ: P&R Publishing, 2006), p. 125.
68. See Robert V. McCabe, "A Critique of the Framework Interpretation of the Creation Week," in *Coming to Grips with Genesis: Biblical Authority and the Age of the Earth*, eds. T. Mortenson and T.H. Ury, (Green Forest, AR: Master Books, 2008), p. 242.

God made everything in six days using an adverbial accusative of time ("in six days"), which indicates the duration of God's creative activity.[69] The pattern of the creation week is also mentioned in Exodus 31:16–18, as Israel's observance of the Sabbath was a sign of the Mosaic covenant:

> Therefore the people of Israel shall keep the Sabbath, observing the Sabbath throughout their generations, as a covenant forever. It is a sign forever between me and the people of Israel that in six days the LORD made heaven and earth, and on the seventh day he rested and was refreshed.
>
> And he gave to Moses, when he had finished speaking with him on Mount Sinai, the two tablets of the testimony, tablets of stone, written with the finger of God.

Not only did God speak the words of the commandments to Israel, but He also wrote them upon tablets of stone (Exodus 32:16). This is significant since it is the only part of Scripture that is said to be written directly by the hand of God (Deuteronomy 9:10). Even though the words "finger of God" is figurative language, this should not take away from the fact that something extremely unique took place when God gave these commandments to Moses. Both Exodus 20:8–11 and 31:16–18 make it clear that the events of Genesis 1:1–2:3 occurred in six 24-hour days and affirm that the creation week was a literal, historical week. The seven days of creation week are reflected in the seven days in the Flood narrative (Genesis 7:4, 10; 8:10–12) and the seven days of Moses on Mount Sinai (Exodus 24:16).[70]

Some argue that because day seven is not a 24-hour day it is therefore unending, implying that we are still in God's Sabbath rest. John 5:17 and Hebrews 4:3–11 are usually cited to support this claim. If the seventh day is unending, then this surely raises a serious theological problem: how could God curse the creation (Genesis 3) while at the same time bless and sanctify the seventh day? The idea of being blessed and cursed at the same time would have been foreign to an Israelite audience, for they understood that if they obeyed God's commands, they would be blessed, and if they disobeyed them, they would be cursed (Deuteronomy 28). The use of John 5:17 and Hebrews 4 to show that the Sabbath day continues to the present day proves no such thing. John 5:17 says, "But Jesus answered them, 'My Father has been working until now, and I have been working.'" In context, Jesus is

69. Bruce K. Waltke and M. O'Connor, *An Introduction to Biblical Hebrew Syntax* (Winona Lake, IN: Eisenbrauns, 1990), p. 171.
70. See Warren H. Johns, "A New Flood Chronology Based on Seven-Day Creation Cycles," *Answers Research Journal* 15 (2022): p. 74–75.

referring to God's providential and redemptive work, not His creative work. The verse says nothing about the seventh day continuing. Hebrews 4:3 is referring to the spiritual rest that all believers enter through faith in Christ. Hebrews 4 quotes Genesis 2:2 and Psalm 95:7–11, and these are used by the author as an argument to warn of the danger of unbelief. Again, the text does not say that the seventh day continues but rather that God's rest (from His creation work) continues.

The fact that the seventh day (*yôm haššĕbîʿî*), like the other days, is numbered is further evidence that it is a day of 24 hours (Genesis 2:2–3). The number seven (x3 in 2:2–3) is also a symbol of the excellence of creation. God's blessing of creation is not of a physical aspect (animals, man) but of a specific time (the seventh day). Day seven was a unique day because it was when God ceased from His work as a pattern for His people to follow (Exodus 20:10–11).

Chapter 3
Genesis 2: Defending the Supernatural Creation of Adam

In order to deny the historicity of Adam or identify him as something other than the first human created by God, theistic evolutionists have had to make three hermeneutical moves to blunt the meaning of Genesis 2:7 while still claiming that they have a "high view" of Genesis 1–3. The first move is to identify the literary genre of Genesis 1–11 in such a way that it is interpreted mainly symbolically. The reason given for this is that Genesis 1–11 is meant to teach theology and not history. The second move is to interpret Genesis 1–11 in the light of other creation myths from the ancient Near East (ANE). It is said that these ANE creation myths help us to read the Genesis account and that the similarities which exist between the accounts lead us to the conclusion that Genesis is not historical but is to be understood as myth or even mytho-history. The third move is to hold that Genesis 1 and 2 are contradictory accounts. The reason for this is the supposed contradictions between Genesis 1 and Genesis 2:

- Genesis 1 portrays God as transcendent and sovereign over creation speaking it into existence and is called ʾĕlōhîm, whereas, in Genesis 2 God is called YHWH ʾĕlōhîm, who is immanent and actively involved in creation.

- Genesis 2 says there were no plants when God created mankind, yet plants come on day three and mankind on day six in Genesis 1.

- Genesis 1 says that God created the animals first and then mankind on day six. In Genesis 2, Adam is formed before the animals.

- If the days in Genesis 1 are 24-hour days, then how could the events of Genesis 2 all take place in a 24-hour day (i.e., naming all the animals)?

Consequently, theistic evolutionists argue that these chapters cannot be understood as factual history and it is, therefore, best to read them in a symbolical way. Making these three hermeneutical moves frees up theistic evolutionists to say that Genesis 2:7 does not mean what it says: that God formed the first man Adam supernaturally from the dust of the ground.

❧ Context of Genesis 2

Before looking at the text of Genesis 2, it is first necessary to establish the context of the narrative. Theistic evolutionists often view Genesis 2 as either a secondary and contradictory account of creation to that in chapter 1[1] or a sequel chapter to it.[2] There are, however, a number of reasons for understanding chapter 2 as a historical account of the sixth day of creation.[3] As in chapter 1, an essential grammatical characteristic of Old Testament Hebrew narrative, the *waw consecutive*, occurs 21 times in 22 verses (Genesis 2:4–25), indicating that it is a historical narrative.[4] The *tôlĕdōt* headings in the earlier chapters of Genesis ("This is the history/genealogy of …" — Genesis 2:4; 5:1; 6:9; 10:1; 11:10, 27) also identify these verses as part of the same literary category as Genesis 12–50 (Genesis. 25:12, 19; 36:1, 9; 37:2). In the New Testament, Genesis 2 is clearly understood to be an account of historical events (Matthew 19:4–5; 1 Timothy. 2:13–14). Genesis 1 and 2 are not contradictory accounts of creation but have different purposes. Genesis 1 focuses on the order of creation (one day, day two, day three, day four, day five, the sixth day, the seventh day), whereas Genesis 2 focuses on the pinnacle of creation, mankind, who was created in the image of God on the sixth day.

---

1. Dennis Lamoureux, *Evolutionary Creation: A Christian Approach to Evolution* (Cambridge: Lutterworth Press, 2008), p. 198–199; Tremper Longman III, "What Genesis 1–2 Teaches (and What It Doesn't)," in J. Daryl Charles (ed.), *Reading Genesis 1–2: An Evangelical Conversation* (Peabody, MA: Hendrickson, 2013), p. 108; and Denis Alexander, *Creation or Evolution: Do We Have to Choose?* p. 194–196.
2. John Walton, *The Lost World of Adam and Eve*, p. 63–69.
3. C.J. Collins rightly does not see Genesis 2 as a contradictory account of creation to Genesis 1 but "as an elaboration of the events of the sixth day of Genesis 1." Collins, *Did Adam and Eve Really Exist?* p. 53.
4. Robert McCabe, "A Critique of the Framework Interpretation of the Creation Week", in Terry Mortenson and Thane H. Ury (eds.), *Coming to Grips with Genesis: Biblical Authority and the Age of the Earth* (Green Forest, AR: Master Books, 2008), p. 217.

❧ Genesis 2:4: The History of the Heaven and Earth

> These are the generations of the heavens and the earth when they were created, in the day that the LORD God made the earth and the heavens.

The key to understanding Genesis 2:4 is the opening Hebrew phrase *tôlĕdōt* (meaning "This is the history of'") as it formulates the structure of the Book of Genesis.[5] A number of scholars recognize that here *tôlĕdōt* serves as a heading that introduces a new section of the narrative.[6] Interestingly, this is the only time *tôlĕdōt* occurs without a personal name, the reason being that "Adam had no human predecessors."[7] The *tôlĕdōt* serves two main purposes in 2:4. First, it "links 2:4–25 with 1:1–2:3. The language of 2:4 looks back to the creation account,"[8] just as the *tôlĕdōt* in Genesis 11:10 looks back to a line of Shem in Genesis 10:1 and 10:21–31. Second, "its main purpose is to shift attention to the creation of man and his placement in the garden."[9] This shift can be seen from the chiastic structure in verse 4 which comes after the *tôlĕdōt*:

> A of the heavens
> > B and the earth
> > > C when they were created
> > > C in the day that the LORD God made
> > B the earth
> A and the heaven

This chiasm shows that verse 4 should not be divided because its "structure evidences a single unit."[10] The unity of verse 4 is evidence that it is not made up of material from two different sources and points to a sole author of the text (Moses) rather than to multiple authors.[11] Those who wish to split up verse 4 into 2:4a and 4b do so "merely to prop up a purely theoretical literary

5. B.S. Childs, *Introduction to the Old Testament as Scripture* (London: SCM, 1979), p. 146.
6. Gordon Wenham, *Genesis 1–15*. Vol. 1, Word Biblical Commentary (Waco, TX: Thomas Nelson, 1987), p. 49; Hamilton, *The Book of Genesis Chapters 1–17*, p. 2–11; Mathews, *Genesis 1–11:26*, p. 26–41.
7. Robert V. McCabe, "A Critique of the Framework Interpretation of the Creation Account (Part 2 of 2)," *Detroit Baptist Seminary Journal* 11 (2006), p. 73.
8. Ibid., p. 75.
9. Ibid., p. 73.
10. Mathews, *Genesis 1–11:26*, p. 191.
11. Critical scholars who hold to the documentary hypothesis argue that Genesis 1:1–2:4a is the product of Priestly source (550–450 B.C.) and 2:4b–4:26 is part of Jahwist source (850 B.C. – Wellhausen; 960–930 B.C. – post-Wellhausen scholars).

analysis."[12] The shift in attention is also reflected in the use of the divine names. In Genesis 1:1–2:3, the divine name used is 'ĕlōhîm, which appears 35 times and focuses on the majesty and power of God. In Genesis 2:4–3:24, however, God's covenant-keeping name YHWH is combined with 'ĕlōhîm, which appears 20 times. The combining of the names is to show that the transcendent God of Genesis 1 is the same as the immanent God of Genesis 2–3 (cf. Exodus 3:14–15; 6:7).[13] Therefore, rather than being a separate and contradictory account of creation, Genesis 2:4–25 focuses on events leading up to and including man in the garden in Eden. Most importantly, Jesus used Genesis 1 and 2 together in Matthew 19:4–5 to make a theological point on marriage. By combining Genesis 1:27b and 2:24 in this way, He showed that He in no way regarded them as separate, contradictory accounts of creation. If Genesis 2 is not historical, it calls into question the meaning and theology of Jesus's point on marriage, because it was based on the history of Genesis being accurate. Genesis 2 is the beginning of the history of mankind.

Furthermore, in Genesis 2:4 the clause "in the day" (bəyōm) is referring to a general period of time (see page 68 on Genesis 2:17). This does not suggest that the days in Genesis 1 are non-literal days (see Exodus 20:11). Key to understanding the length of the days in Genesis 1 is that they are numbered and are used with qualifiers such as "evening" and "morning." These contextual clues help us comprehend their meaning. Similarly, the contextual clues in Genesis 2:4 surrounding bəyōm (i.e., "in the day that the LORD God made the earth and the heavens") serve to indicate that a general time period is in view (i.e., the sixth day of creation week).

❧ Genesis 2:5–9: The Creation of Man

When no bush of the field was yet in the land and no small plant of the field had yet sprung up — for the LORD God had not caused it to rain on the land, and there was no man to work the ground, and a mist was going up from the land and was watering the whole face of the ground — then the LORD God formed the man of dust from the ground and breathed into his nostrils the breath of life, and the man became a living creature. And the LORD God planted a garden in Eden, in the east, and there he put the man whom he had formed. And out of the ground the LORD God made to spring

---

12. Kenneth A. Kitchen, *On the Reliability of the Old Testament* (Grand Rapids, MI: Eerdmans, 2003), p. 428.
13. John Currid, *Genesis. Vol. 1, Genesis 1:1–25:18: An EP Study Commentary* (USA: Evangelical Press, 2003), p. 96–97.

up every tree that is pleasant to the sight and good for food. The tree of life was in the midst of the garden, and the tree of the knowledge of good and evil.

Genesis 2:5 begins the account of mankind's creation in the garden in Eden. Verses 5–7 of the narrative are a distinct syntactical unit in which verses 5–6 "present a series of circumstantial clauses, describing the condition of the land when God formed the first man."[14] Verses 5–6 provide the setting for verse 7. However, it has been noted that verses 5–6 present a problem for understanding Genesis 2 as a more specific account of the events of the sixth day. For example, Old Testament scholar John Walton states:

> If Genesis 2 is read as a recapitulation, Genesis 2:5–6 is confusing. It says that there were no plants when God created humans, yet plants come on day three and humans on day six in Genesis 1. Another sequence problem is that God created the animals first and then humans on day six. In Genesis 2, Adam is formed before the animals. The second problem exists for those who consider the days to be twenty-four-hour days. That the events of Genesis 2 could all take place in a twenty-four-hour day (among them, naming all the animals, which apparently is completed because no helper was found) stretches credulity.[15]

Unfortunately, Walton's objection overlooks the specific details of these verses and the account of creation in Genesis 1. Genesis 2:5–7 is best related to the judgment oracles of Genesis 3:8–24 indicating what the world was like before and after sin.[16] The Hebrew word 'ereṣ (earth) occurs twice in 2:5. Because the context of Genesis 2 is man in the garden in Eden, it is best to view 'ereṣ here as referring to land "since it is the habitat of the first man that is in view."[17] Additionally, the word "ground" ('ădāmâ) in verse 5 has to do with the soil, which is cultivated by human enterprise (Genesis 2:9; 3:17, 23; 4:2; 5:29; 8:21); it is the same substance from which man is made (Genesis 2:7, 19). There is a play on words in verse 5 — "ground" and "man" — indicating that the 'ădāmâ (ground) needs 'ādām (man) to produce a harvest from it. When viewed this way, we find that the "herb" and "plant" of Genesis 2:5 are not the same as the vegetation of Genesis 1:11–12. For example, "plant ['ēśeb] of the field" describes the diet of man which he eats only after the sweat of his labor after sin (Genesis 3:18–19), whereas seed-bearing

---

14. Mathews, *Genesis 1–11:26*, p. 191.
15. Walton, *The Lost World of Adam and Eve*, p. 64.
16. Mathews, *Genesis 1–11:26*, p. 194–195, 252–254.
17. Ibid., p. 194.

plants found in the creation narrative were produced by God for human and animal consumption (Genesis 1:11–12, 29–30; 9:3). These plants reproduce themselves by seed alone, whereas "plant" in Genesis 2:5 requires human cultivation to produce the grain necessary for edible food. It is by means of this cultivation that fallen man will eat his food (Genesis 3:19).

In Genesis 3:18–19, plants ('ēśeb) and bread (lechem) are the product of man's cultivating the ground. These did not exist before the Fall. Thorns and thistles came into existence after Adam sinned (Genesis 3:18, 23). This means that man did not have to cultivate the ground for food before the Fall (Genesis 2:9). Yet, because there was no man around to cultivate God's creation, in 2:7 the text informs us that "the LORD God formed man of the dust of the ground and breathed into his nostrils the breath of life; and man became a living being" (NKJV). The process of Adam's creation is the most crucial part of this debate. Regrettably, for many Christian scholars today who have compromised with evolutionary ideas, there is uncertainty as to how the body of Adam was formed.

John Walton raises a novel objection to the supernatural creation of Adam. Walton objects to a material understanding of the terms yāṣar (formed) and 'āpār (dust). Walton believes the Hebrew term yāṣar is unrelated to a material act but corresponds well to functional creation.[18] Walton wants to reduce the meaning of the term 'āpār to "mortality" and rejects the idea that the text is referring to God crafting the dust as "one shapes clay … [because dust] is impervious to being shaped by its very nature."[19] For Walton, the better alternative to the meaning of 'āpār is found in Genesis 3:19, where "we discover that dust refers to mortality."[20] Walton therefore believes that "dust" in Genesis 2:7 "has the significance of indicating that people were created mortal."[21] This has the theological implication that death is not the punishment for sin (Romans 5:12), but was already in place and was a good thing (cf. Genesis 1:31).

The exegesis of 2:7, however, speaks against the idea of there being an intermediate process in the formation of the first man. It is necessary to understand yāṣar as "forming" and 'āpār as "dust," describing God's forming man from the dust of the ground. First, yāṣar is a perfectly acceptable term to refer to a material act of creation because it is often used to describe the creative activity of a potter (Jeremiah 18:2; Isaiah 45:9). In Isaiah 44:9–20, a satire against idols, the craftsman (verse 12) who makes idols shapes

18. Walton, The Lost World of Adam and Eve, p. 72.
19. Ibid., p. 73.
20. Ibid., p. 73
21. Ibid., p. 74.

(*yāṣar*) his material with a hammer. While *yāṣar* is also used elsewhere to describe YHWH as the one who "formed" the world (Jeremiah 33:2), the reason why *yāṣar* is used instead of *bārā'* (create) is that the man was being made of an already existing material. Second, the meaning of *'āpār*, "dust," has to be established exegetically from the context. Although clay is generally shaped, the term *dust* "may refer to a clay-like mixture such as that used to plaster the walls of a house, as in Leviticus 14:41, 45, where the same term [*'āpār*] is also used."[22]

The forming of the man from the dust of the ground shows that the LORD God formed the body almost immediately without intermediate processes. The act of formation and impartation (the breath of life) are two distinct but inseparable acts — two sides of one creative act. This means that you cannot place minutes, hours, days, or years between those two acts, as they are distinct, inseparable, essentially simultaneous sides of the one creative event. This, therefore, rules out the idea that man developed from a lower form of a pre-existing hominid. The first man, Adam, was created from the dust of the ground, and "dust" can only mean "dust" in the context of Genesis 2–3 because it is to "dust" that Adam will return because of his disobedience (Genesis 3:19; cf. Job 34:15; Ecclesiastes 3:20; 12:7).

Moses obviously understands his work this way, as in Psalm 90:3 he acknowledges that death was a returning (*šûb*, Genesis 3:19) to the dust: "You return man to dust and say, 'Return, O children of man!'" The intention of the phrase "you return man to dust" is to be understood according to Genesis 3:19 and the phrase "children of men" (*běnê-'ādām*) could be translated "sons of Adam."[23] The Apostle Paul also affirmed that Adam was made from the dust of the ground (1 Corinthians 15:47). Dust in Genesis 3:19 cannot be referring to Adam's mortality, as Walton argues, because this "mortality" comes in the context of a curse upon Adam and his wife because of their disobedience. To claim that Adam was created mortal and that death was therefore a natural part of the creation, theologian Gerhard Vos argues that the words of Genesis 3:19 "would have to be wrenched from [their] context.... If they expressed a mere declaration of the natural working out of man's destiny, as created mortal, there would be nothing of a curse in them."[24] According to the Bible, death is not a biological necessity but is the wage for sin (Romans 6:23).

22. Richard Averbeck, "The Lost World of Adam and Eve: A Review Essay," *Themelios* 40, no. 2 (2015), p. 236.

23. Although "dust" (*dakkā'*) is a different word to Genesis 3:19, the verb for return is the same. See Derek Kidner, *Psalms 73–150: A Commentary on Books III, IV and V of the Psalms, Tyndale Old Testament Commentaries* (London: Inter-Varsity Press, 1975), p. 328.

24. Gerhard Vos, *Biblical Theology: Old and New Testaments* (Grand Rapids, MI: Eerdmans, 1948), p. 48.

The place where God formed Adam was "the ground," which "indicates the source whence the dust was taken."[25] After the formation of man from the dust of the ground, he is given human life when God breathes into him the breath of life which is "a clear indication of life — and thereby the life-less body became a living soul, a living being."[26] Adam consists, then, of the material (dust) and the immaterial (breath of life) (cf. Matthew 10:28). It was not until God breathed into Adam that the first human life came into existence. The ground was not only the place of Adam's creation but also his home, and, because of his later disobedience, it would become his grave (Genesis 2:15, 3:19). Adam's value is seen not in what he was made from but rather in the unique way God formed him (cf. Genesis 1:27; Psalm 8:3-4, 139:13–14). The context and language of Genesis 2:7 clearly rule out any evolutionary processes. This is evident from the fact that (1) man is alone, (2) God breathes into his nostrils the "breath of life," and (3) he is formed from the dust of the ground.

In Genesis 2:8, after the creation of Adam, God then continues His work of creating by planting a garden in the east in Eden, where He places the man whom He had formed to live in. Interestingly, based upon the biblical text, because of the similarities between the tabernacle constructed by Moses and the garden in Eden, it has been identified as a tabernacle where Adam functions as a king and a priest (see Genesis 1:28, 2:14–15, 3:24). However, others believe Eden is used to describe something related but different.[27] The tabernacle was a place for the people of Israel to have fellowship with God, but it was in the garden that man first enjoyed that fellowship with God. God "planted" the garden, so He is still working, showing it is the sixth day.

God is someone who works, as He is described as one who "creates" (Genesis 1:1, 21, 27) "makes" (Genesis 1:16, 26), "forms" (Genesis 2:7), "plants" (Genesis 2:8), and "fashions" (Genesis 2:22). This is important to understand, as man who is made in the image of God is also created to work (see pages 66–67). The garden God plants is in the east in Eden and at a relatively high elevation; the river flowing from it divided into four other rivers as it

---

25. Umberto Cassuto, *A Commentary on the Book of Genesis, Part One: From Adam to Noah,* trans. Israel Abrahams (Jerusalem: Magnes Press, The Hebrew University, 1944), p. 106.
26. Ibid., p. s106.
27. Noel Weeks responds to the argument that because the garden was to the east (Genesis 3:24) it relates to the tabernacle: "It is equally plausible that tabernacle and temple open to the east because they have the 'Edenic' character of bringing man into association with God. We would then read temple and tabernacle in terms of the earlier Eden and not vice versa." Noel Weeks, "The Fall and Genesis 3," in *Adam, the Fall, and Original Sin* (eds. Hans Madueme and Michael Reeves; Grand Rapids, MI: Baker Academic, 2014), p. 293, n16.

flowed downhill (Genesis 2:10–14). The high elevation of Eden is noted by the prophet Ezekiel, as he describes Eden as being the mountain of God (Ezekiel 28:13–14). Eden would have been destroyed in the global Flood as the waters covered all the high mountains (Genesis 7:19–20). The meaning of Eden (*ʿēden*) is hard to determine, but it may be related to a term that means "luxury or delight."[28] The Hebrew word for "garden" (*gan*, Genesis 2:8) was later translated in the Greek translation of the Old Testament (LXX) as *paradeisos,* paradise (cf. Luke 23:43; Revelation 2:7). In Genesis 3:23, the LXX relates the word *ʿēden* to the word "delight" (*tryphēs*).[29] The word *paradeisos* is also used later in the prophets to refer to the eschatological paradise (Isaiah 51:3; Ezekiel 28:13). Other texts describe God as the owner of Eden ("garden of the LORD," Genesis 13:10) but even though He is the owner of the garden it is important to recognize that "God does not dwell in the garden; rather it is the place where he meets with man."[30] God dwells in heaven somewhere much greater than an earthly tabernacle (cf. Isaiah 40:22; 66:1). The garden was planted by God to be man's home (Genesis 2:8, 15).

In Genesis 2:9, God makes trees that are pleasant to the sight and good for food as well as in the middle of the garden, the tree of life and the tree of the knowledge of good and evil (cf. Genesis 3:3). These two trees probably stand side by side in the middle of the garden. But how do we explain these two trees? The difficulty is that Moses does not explain the nature of these two trees in the text. However, the narrative does provide clues as to their names. What we do know is that they are real trees not magical ones (the Bible nowhere describes them as magical or symbolic). There are even physical objects in a fallen world that have surprising effects (Number 21:8–9; 2 Kings 6). The trees are as real and historical as Adam and his sin.

The Book of Proverbs sees the tree of life as being able to give man a pleasurable existence (Proverbs 3:18, 11:30, 13:12, 15:4). The Book of Revelation has the tree of life in the eschatological paradise of God, which has been given to the people of God (Revelation 2:7; 22:2, 14). Some believe the presence of the tree of life indicates that eating its fruit results in continued life. In Genesis 3:22, the word "also" seems to suggest that Adam and Eve had not yet eaten from the tree of life.[31] Nevertheless, does the presence

---

28. F. Brown, S. Driver, and C. Briggs., *The Brown-Driver-Briggs Hebrew and English Lexicon* (Peabody, MA: Hendrickson Publishers, 2006), p. 726.

29. In Genesis 3:23 the words "Garden of Eden" are translated by the LXX as *paradeisou tēs tryphēs.*

30. Matthews, *Genesis 1–11:26,* p. 200.

31. Weeks, *The Fall and Genesis 3,* p. 295.

of the tree of life mean that Adam had to eat from it to retain his deathless condition, an implication that Adam was not created immortal? No, this does not necessarily follow. God may have used the tree of life as the means for Adam not to have died, but once he rebelled against God that means was taken away from him so that he would not live forever in a fallen world (Genesis 3:22–23). Had Adam not sinned, he would not have died.

What was the tree of knowledge of good and evil? While there are numerous suggestions as to what it refers to, what can't be denied is that after their disobedience God recognized that Adam and Eve had become like God "knowing good and evil" (Genesis 3:22).[32] But in what way had they become like God? It seems that Adam and Eve in their autonomy tried to obtain knowledge that only God possessed. When King Solomon prayed for the ability to discern between good and evil, he was granted wisdom (1 Kings 3:9–12). In acquiring knowledge through disobedience, they obtained wisdom possessed by God through moral autonomy (Genesis 3:5–6).[33]

It is important to note that Genesis 2:8 identifies the garden as being distinguished from Eden; it is toward the east in Eden. It seems that Eden was a larger geographical area of which the garden was a part. Man's first home was a garden that was planted by God Himself. It is a gracious gift given to them by their creator. Importantly, Moses goes to great length to place Eden within the geography of the pre-Flood world, it is not part of a mythical world (Genesis 2:10–14; 4:16). Once the man, Adam, is placed in the garden, he is given a specific task to do (Genesis 2:15) and commanded what to do and what not to do (Genesis 2:16–17).

❧ The Creation of Adam vs the *Atrahasis Epic*

There are many evangelical scholars today who believe the similarities between Genesis 2:7 and other ANE accounts, such as the *Atrahasis Epic,* show that they provide the conceptual background to the creation of Adam.[34] The *Atrahasis Epic,* for example, says of the creation of man:

> We-ila [a god], who had personality, They slaughtered in their assembly. From his flesh and blood Nintu mixed clay.... After she had mixed that clay She summoned the Anunnaki, the great gods. The Igigi, the great gods, Spat upon the clay. Mami opened her mouth. And addressed the great gods, "You have commanded me a

---

32. Infants do not know the difference between good and evil (Deuteronomy 1:39; cf. Isaiah 7:16).
33. Matthews, *Genesis 1–11:26,* p. 205–206.
34. Longman III, "What Genesis 1–2 Teaches (and What It Doesn't)," p. 106–108, 122; Venema and McKnight, *Adam and the Genome,* p. 111–146.

task, I have completed it; You have slaughtered a god together with his personality. I have removed your heavy work, I have imposed your toil on man."[35]

Many Old Testament scholars today put much emphasis on the similarities between the ANE accounts, like the *Atrahasis Epic*, and they tend not to highlight the significant differences. There is much dissimilarity between the ANE accounts and the Bible. For example, the *Atrahasis Epic* has humans made from both material and divine elements, and there is no suggestion of the gods breathing into man the breath of life as Genesis 2:7 describes; it is the flesh of a slain god that is the source of the "spirit" of man in the *Atrahasis Epic*. Furthermore, in the *Atrahasis Epic* mankind is created to relieve the gods of their heavy work. That is not why God created man in the biblical account of creation, as He creates mankind in His image and graciously blesses them with the delightful garden in Eden. Some argue that the differences can be explained by the biblical writers using a process of demythologizing, such that the author of Genesis "substituted God's breath for either divine spit or blood."[36] However, "the differences are monumental and are so striking that they cannot be explained by a simple Hebrew cleansing of myth."[37] The argument that the Bible is simply demythologizing these pagan myths simply will not work. The significance of the differences between Genesis and the ANE accounts of the creation of man should lead us to conclude that Genesis is not dependent on them.

By using ANE literature to interpret Genesis 1–11, scholars are going outside the Bible, which is committing eisegesis — reading meanings "into" the biblical text as opposed to "out of" the biblical text exegesis, in order to substantiate what they want the Bible to say in order to accommodate those views. In other words, these scholars are over-emphasizing the ANE texts and under-emphasizing the biblical text. There is much dissimilarity between the ANE accounts and the Bible. For example, how does one explain the polytheism, the theogony (creation of the various gods), the cosmic wars, the magic that is at the center of these epics. These are not found in the Bible. The Scriptures on the other hand give a true historical, chronological account of the event. The revelation of God says something completely different from those ANE myths. The accounts in the Bible are not based upon myth (cf. 2 Peter 1:16–21). Far from being domesticated

---

35. As quoted in Hamilton, *The Book of Genesis Chapters 1–17*, p. 157–158.
36. Tremper Longman III, *How to Read Genesis* (Downers Grove, IL: InterVarsity Press, 2005), p. 78.
37. John Currid, *Against the Gods: The Polemical Theology of the Old Testament* (Wheaton, IL: Crossway, 2013), p. 44.

by the background of the ANE texts, Genesis confronts the background, revises the background, and challenges the background of those other texts. In Genesis 2:7 Moses not only gives us the correct account of the origin of mankind (Adam and Eve), but at the same time refutes all other ANE pagan myths regarding the creation of man and the world (i.e., Egyptian, Canaanite, Mesopotamian). Similarities between the Bible and other ANE texts are no surprise, since "Moses was instructed in all the wisdom of the Egyptians…" (Acts 7:22). No doubt Moses knew ANE literature very well and was able to counter myth with history.[38]

🌺 Genesis 2:15–16: Created to Worship

> The LORD God took the man and put him in the garden of Eden to work it and keep it. And the LORD God commanded the man, saying, "You may surely eat of every tree of the garden.…

After the creation of the man, the LORD God takes him from the land from which he was formed and puts him in a garden in Eden, a place with trees, beautiful stones, and flowing rivers (Genesis 2:9–14). The text notes that God "put" Adam in the garden. The word "put" is translated from "… the causative form of the verb *nûaḥ*, 'rest,' and so could be rendered literally 'caused to rest.'"[39] Adam was given the garden so that he could "rest" in the paradise God had created for him. Once the man, Adam, is put in the garden, he is given the specific task, as the steward of Eden, to work the ground (cf. Genesis 2:5). The garden was not a paradise in the sense that Adam could waste away the day by sitting back with his feet up with no interference to his daily schedule. Adam's life in the garden was not one of laziness; he had work to do. Therefore, Adam had a purpose to his existence (just like the rest of mankind would), to glorify God (cf. Isaiah 43:7; 1 Corinthians 10:31).

Work is an essential part of what it is to be human as it was established by God for the benefit of mankind. God worked for six days as a pattern for his people Israel to follow (Exodus 20:8–11). God's works are also to be studied by all those who delight in them (Psalm 111:2). Work is sometimes viewed as a product of the Fall, but this is not the case. Rather, *difficulty* in our work is a product of the Fall (Genesis 3:17–19). Since the Fall made our

---

38. Given that Moses authored the Torah after coming out of Egypt (1446–1406 B.C.) Genesis is written to refute the Egyptian mythology and in general the later Canaanite and Mesopotamian ANE myths the people of Israel would encounter, although Moses probably knew of other creation myths as he would have had access to documents from around the world at the royal Egyptian library.

39. Matthews, *Genesis 1–11:26*, p. 208.

work difficult, and because we are in a fallen state, we naturally want to find a way not to do our work. In our culture, and even in the Church, our fallen state often shapes our attitude toward work. For example, in secular society, human fulfillment is often seen as an escape from work (i.e., early retirement or winning the lottery). On the other hand, for many people work is the center of their life and in effect becomes their idol — their means of personal fulfillment. The Bible warns against both of these mentalities. Scripture condemns slothful and lazy attitudes toward work (Proverbs 18:9, 19:15; 2 Thessalonians 3:6–13). If Christians can work and chose not to then we are worse than an unbeliever (1 Timothy 5:8). The Bible teaches that we should work with all of our hearts as to the Lord (Colossians 3:23) rather than being motivated by our own fulfillment. The goal for the Christian is not a life of leisure but one of work accompanied by rest in which we delight and rejoice in God (Genesis 2:3; Isaiah 58:13–14; Hebrew 4:8–9).

Adam's work in the garden was also not just a means to an end but was a way for him to worship God. The Hebrew words in Genesis 2:15 "work" (ʿaḇaḏ) and "keep" (šāmar) primarily refer to the principal commission of man to take care of their home, yet they also anticipate the Mosaic context of man's worship of God (Exodus 8:1, 20, 9:1, 13) and of his obedience to God's Word (Genesis 17:9, 18:19). The two words also appear together in Deuteronomy 10:12–13 in the context of worshiping God. One of the reasons Adam was put in the garden was to worship God by "working" and "keeping" it, a priestly role (Numbers 3:6-10).

In verse 16 God addresses the man (Adam) and begins the divine fellowship that now exists between God and man. This fellowship between God and man shows that Adam was not created to be autonomous (self-law) as, in His revelation to Adam, God gives him a command (ṣāwâ, Exodus 25:22; cf. Genesis 3:11, 17). Adam has boundaries — he cannot simply do what he wants to do. Adam was not created as an autonomous creature independent from God who can live life according to his own standard. That way of living only ends in tragedy (see Genesis 3). As part of this command, God gives Adam permission to "eat of every tree of the garden" (Genesis 2:16), but He also prohibits him by telling him not to eat of "the tree of the knowledge of good and evil" (Genesis 2:17). Adam could eat from every tree in the garden, but as a test of his obedience, God said he could not eat from one. The test of obedience proved too much for Adam as, unlike Noah, he did not do the things commanded of him by God (see Genesis 6:22, 7:5). It is the consequence of this prohibition that we will now consider more closely.

⚜ Genesis 2:17–20

"but of the tree of the knowledge of good and evil you shall not
eat, for in the day that you eat of it you shall surely die."
Then the LORD God said, "It is not good that the man should be
alone; I will make him a helper fit for him." Now out of the ground
the LORD God had formed every beast of the field and every bird of
the heavens and brought them to the man to see what he would call
them. And whatever the man called every living creature, that was
its name. The man gave names to all livestock and to the birds of the
heavens and to every beast of the field. But for Adam there was not
found a helper fit for him.

In Genesis 2:17 God gives Adam a command: "but of the tree of the
knowledge of good and evil you shall not eat, for in the day that you eat of
it you shall surely die." There are two questions that need to be answered.
First, what does "in the day that you eat of it you shall surely die" imply?
Is it referring to an immediate death sentence? To answer this question, it
is necessary to understand the phrase *bəyōm* (in the day). In this context
the Hebrew phrase *bəyōm* should be understood as a general indication of
time.[40] When *bəyōm* is understood in the light of the Hebrew phrase *môt
tāmût* "you shall surely die," it should not be understood as an immediate
death sentence, as some argue. The phrase *môt tāmût* uses the "infinitive absolute with an imperfect,"[41] which strengthens its meaning. The
phrase "you shall surely die" may be understood as "you are doomed to
die,"[42] meaning that "death will follow as a punishment but not necessarily immediately."[43]

The grammatical construction of 2:17 is very similar to the way Mosaic
law threatened capital punishment: "He will surely die," or "They will
surely die" (see Exodus 21:12; Leviticus 20:9–16). The second question

---

40. Jenni recognizes that "in many cases *yôm* loses the specific meaning "day" and becomes
    a rather general and somewhat vague word for "time," "moment."… The construction
    bəyōm + inf. "on the day when" = "at the time when" = "as/when" is relatively frequent."
    E. Jenni, 'Yom,' in Ernst Jenni and Claus Westermann, *Theological Lexicon of the Old
    Testament*, trans. Mark E. Biddle (Peabody, MA: Hendrickson, 1997), p. 529. Jenni
    identifies Genesis 2:17 as one of these occurrences.
41. Collins, *Genesis 1–4*, p. 118.
42. Robert Alter, *Genesis: Translation and Commentary* (London: W.W. Norton & Company,
    1996), p. 8.
43. David W. Cotter, *Genesis: Berit Olam; Studies in Hebrew Narrative and Poetry*
    (Collegeville, MN: Liturgical Press, 2003), p. 31. Cotter lists a number of examples of
    this: Gen. 20:7; Num. 26:65; Judg. 13:22; 1 Sam. 14:39, 44; 2 Sam. 12:14, 14:14; 2
    Kings 1:4, 6, 16; 8:10; Jer. 26:8; Ezek. 3:18; 33:8, 14.

related to the phrase "you shall surely die" is whether it refers to spiritual or physical death. Old Testament scholar C.J. Collins believes that is referring to spiritual rather than physical death.[44] However, this overlooks the meaning of *bəyōm* and the context of the garden narrative. After disobeying God's command, Adam and Eve are immediately separated from God (Genesis 3:7–9; spiritual death). Yet in Genesis 3:17–19 God places a curse on the ground and tells Adam he will return to it (physical death). Yet, we should not see this as an either-or, as the context clearly indicates that the command includes both spiritual and physical death (Genesis 3:8, 17–19). The Apostle Paul's interpretation of this passage also has spiritual and physical death in view (Romans 5:12, 14; 1 Corinthians 15:21–22, 26). Importantly, Vos says of the words in Genesis 2:17:

> On the basis of these words the belief of all ages has been that death is the penalty for sin, that the race became first subject to death through the commission of the primordial sin. At present many writers take exception to this, largely on scientific grounds.... But, as is frequently the case, strenuous attempts are made to give such a turn to the Biblical phrases as to render them compatible with what science is believed to require, and not only this, some proceed to the assertion that the Scriptural statements compel acceptance of the findings of science. Attempts of this kind make for poor and forced exegesis.[45]

Vos rightly recognizes that those who try to argue on the basis of secular ideas that the words of Genesis 2:17 refer to anything other than physical death are forcing the text to say something it clearly does not mean.

Genesis 2:18 says that the man was alone. Adam was the only human, which shows that it was not yet the end of the sixth day — for part of the reason why creation was declared to be "very good" on day six (Genesis 1:31) was that by the end of that day God had made a helper for the man (Genesis 2:18–22). The problem for scholars like Denis Alexander, John Walton, and C.J. Collins is how could Adam be alone if he represented a Neolithic farmer, an archetype of humanity or the head of a tribe?

The purpose of the formation of the animals in Genesis 2:19 was so that Adam could review all the kinds of animals in order to give them names and find among them a helper corresponding to him so that he would no longer be alone. It has been argued that there is a contradiction here in verse 19, because the creation of animals comes after the creation of man, whereas in

---

44. Collins, *Did Adam and Eve Really Exist*, p. 62.
45. Vos, *Biblical Theology*, p. 47.

Genesis 1 man is created after the animals (Genesis 1:24–25, 27). There are two solutions for this supposed chronological problem in Genesis 2:19. One is to take the verb as a pluperfect (ESV and NIV).[46] The pluperfect tense can be considered as the past of the past — that is, the past in a narration set in the past. This would suggest that the animals brought to Adam had already been made and were not being brought to him immediately after their creation. Alternatively, it is possible to understand it as God having formed these animals after Adam, but that they were a special group of animals formed in the garden.[47] We must remember that the setting of Genesis 2 is the garden in Eden and not the whole world (Genesis 2:8, 15).

Also, Walton's argument (see above) that the events in Genesis 2, specifically the naming of all the animals, could not all take place in a 24-hour day is unwarranted given the fact that no time duration is given in the text concerning what took place on the sixth day. Walton has to assume that a large number of animals were named, but again the text does not say how many animals Adam had to name. Genesis 2:20 tells us that Adam named only the cattle, the beasts of the field, and birds of the air. He did not have to name the sea creatures, the beasts of the earth, or creeping things.[48] Walton also has to discount the fact that God miraculously put Adam to sleep to create Eve, which, for the Creator of the universe, could take no time at all. Adam's naming of these animals reveals that man was created as an intelligent being, a fact that does not fit with an evolutionary model of mankind.

Yet there was no suitable counterpart among the animals for Adam. This was because none of the animals bore the image of God, and an adequate counterpart must bear the image of God just as Adam was made in the image of God. It is claimed that the first unambiguous reference to "Adam" as a personal name does not occur until Genesis 5:1, but the evidence of verse 20 seriously contests that claim, especially as it comes within the context of naming the animals. The phrase *lĕ'ādām* in the Masoretic Text reads as a proper name since it appears without the definite article, which indicates a proper name in Hebrew. Jewish scholar Nahum Sarna comments, "The Hebrew vocalization *lĕ'ādām* makes the word a proper name for the first time, probably because the narrative now speaks of the man as a personality

---

46. Collins argues that the chronological problem in Genesis 2:19 is solved by taking the verb as a pluperfect. C.J. Collins, "The Wayyiqtol as 'Pluperfect': When and Why," Tyndale Bulletin 46, no. 1 (1995), p. 117–240.

47. Cassuto, *A Commentary on the Book of Genesis*, p. 176.

48. Adam may have only named the basic kinds or some of their varieties and not all the individual species that we think of today, making the number much smaller than the modern mind thinks.

rather than an archetypal human."[49] Genesis 2 refers to the individual first man, as the narrative presents Adam as acting and speaking.

🌿 Genesis 2:21–25: The Creation of Woman

> So the LORD God caused a deep sleep to fall upon the man, and while he slept took one of his ribs and closed up its place with flesh. And the rib that the LORD God had taken from the man he made into a woman and brought her to the man. Then the man said,
>
>> "This at last is bone of my bones
>> and flesh of my flesh;
>> she shall be called Woman,
>> because she was taken out of Man."
>
> Therefore a man shall leave his father and his mother and hold fast to his wife, and they shall become one flesh. And the man and his wife were both naked and were not ashamed.

Because Adam cannot find a helper ('ēzer) who corresponds (kĕnegdô) to him from among the animals (Genesis 2:20), the LORD God puts him into a deep sleep (cf. Jonah 1:5–6) and builds (bānâ) a woman, who corresponds to him, from his "rib" (Genesis 2:21). The verb bānâ depicts the LORD God as "building" Eve out of the "rib" of Adam (Genesis 2:22). It is used elsewhere in Genesis for the material building of a city and a tower (Genesis 4:17, 11:4; cf. Amos 9:6). The word rib (ṣēlāʿ) complements the word built (bānâ), as it is a beautiful picture of how the LORD God constructed the first woman. The term built also compliments the craftsman's term "fashion" used for the creation of Adam (Genesis 2:7), as the LORD God is now working with hard material and not soft dust.[50] Eve, unlike Adam, was not created from the ground, but her source comes from a "living creature." There is no way to harmonize Genesis 2:22 with theistic evolution: it is describing supernatural creation!

In Genesis 2:22, Adam finally meets the one who corresponds to him, that the LORD God built to be a helper for him. After meeting the woman, Adam says, "This at last is bone of my bones and flesh of my flesh; she [this one] shall be called woman, because she [this one] was taken out of man" (Genesis 2:23). In Hebrew the three occurrences of the demonstrative pronoun this (zōʾt) in verse 23 show Adam's exclamation of the one who rightly

49. Nahum M. Sarna, *Genesis, JPS Torah Commentary* (New York: Jewish Publication Society, 1989), p. 22.
50. Alter, *Genesis*, p. 9.

corresponds to him. The fact that the woman (*'iššâ*) came from the man (*'îš*) shows that they are made of the same stuff. Adam goes on to name his wife "Eve" because she is to become the mother of all the living (Genesis 3:20). The creation of Eve inspires Adam to poetry, which is a problem for theistic evolutionists, for how could someone be capable of producing sophisticated qualities of poetry if his speech were still evolving at this point?

The woman who was built from the man is now joined to him and they become "one flesh" (Genesis 2:24). This "one flesh" imagery is the basis for marriage being the union of one man and woman in a lifelong covenantal relationship (Matthew 19:4–6). The words "leave" (*'āzab*) and "hold fast" (*dābaq*) depict the fact that marriage is a covenantal relationship (see Deuteronomy 28:20; Hosea 4:10). Marriage is not a social construct but is something that God ordained as a creation ordinance and institution. In the context of marriage there is male headship (Ephesians 5:25-31), which has nothing to do with worth or value as both men and women as image bearers have equal worth and value before God.[51] It has to do with our roles. Male headship is seen in Genesis 2 before the Fall: the woman is made after the man, the woman is made for the man, the woman was made from the man, the woman was brought to the man and the woman was named by the man (cf. 1 Corinthians 11:8–9).

In Genesis 1 and 2, there are several things about the distinction between male and female that are important for us to understand as they are being eroded away today by the neo-pagan worldview (i.e., the denial of distinctions). The distinction between male and female is a biological reality and not something that is socially or self-constructed. What made Adam and Eve "male and female" is that they were told to be "fruitful and multiply and fill the earth" (Genesis 1:28). The fact that the man and woman can procreate tells us what God means by "male and female" as this is what their reproductive systems have been designed to do.

In Genesis 2:18, God told Adam: "It is not good that the man should be alone; I will make him a helper fit for him." When God sought a "helper" fit for Adam, he chose neither an animal nor an exact duplicate of the man, but instead he created a woman — uniquely formed for intimacy, companionship, co-workmanship, and pro-creation (Genesis 2:22). God joined together the first man Adam (1 Corinthians 15:45) and the first woman, who was taken from his side, called Eve (Genesis 3:20). The fact that Adam and Eve are made for each other is indicated in the wordplay of man (*'îš*)

---

51. Male-headship is about being willing to lay down your life for your wife. Just as Christ "gave Himself up" for the Church, by His sacrificial death, so husbands are to do the same because they have a covenantal commitment to their wives.

and woman ('*iššâ*) (see Genesis 2:23). This specific association is a reflection of the fact that when a man and a woman leave their father and mother, they become "one flesh" (Genesis 2:24; cf. Matthew 19:5). Only a female "helper" could help Adam fulfill the command to be "fruitful and multiply" (cf. Genesis 1:28). The "one flesh" aspect of the marriage covenant is a social manifestation of a biological reality, as Eve is able to do what Adam cannot do — in that she can bear children. The distinction between maleness and femaleness is not self-constructed, but rather is constructed by God and is to be celebrated as being very good.

After their creations, Adam and Eve are described as "naked and unashamed" (Genesis 2:25). This shows their original righteous state, as after they disobeyed they are ashamed because of their nakedness. Adam's original righteous state is confirmed in the Old Testament by the author of Ecclesiastes who writes, "That God made man upright" (Ecclesiastes 7:29). In their "nakedness" Adam and Eve enjoyed fellowship with God, which was something that the priests of Israel were forbidden to do in the presence of God (Exodus 20:26, 28:42). As we will see, Adam and Eve's expulsion from the garden (Genesis 3:24) represents a loss of that intimate fellowship they had with God.

The narrative in Genesis 2, which focuses primarily on the sixth day of creation, clearly presents us with the supernatural creation of the first man from the dust of the ground (Genesis 2:7), who was alone (Genesis 2:18) until God made a wife for him (Genesis 2:21–23). The Bible clearly depicts Adam and Eve as being uniquely created by God in His image. Those that have already been convinced of evolutionary origins have managed to adapt and twist the text of Genesis to their interpretation of the creation of Adam and Eve, but they have not derived this from the text of Scripture.

Chapter 4

Genesis 3: In Adam's Fall We Sinned All

The understanding of Adam is vital to many areas of theology, and particularly to the doctrine of the Fall, yet there is an increasing attack upon this today. Without exaggeration it would be safe to say that many evangelical theologians either explicitly or implicitly deny that Genesis 3 teaches the doctrine of the Fall of man, arguing that it is not original to the text but is something that has been forced upon it. Critical scholars have long rejected Genesis 3 as an accurate account of actual events such as the Fall of man. However, in the recent debate over the historical Adam, many professing evangelicals who have adopted the methods and conclusions of critical secular scholarship have argued that the doctrine of the Fall, which includes original sin, is not found in the text of Genesis 3. These scholars see the doctrine of the Fall and original sin as an invention that has been read into the text by the Church Father Augustine of Hippo (see chapter 7). In his book *Saving the Original Sinner*, Karl Giberson, who describes himself as a liberal critic, argues,

> The Hebrew scriptures suggest that Adam passed nothing on to his offspring. Subsequent sin — Cain's murder of Abel, the wickedness of Noah's generation, or the folly at the tower of Babel — is never described as inevitable. Adam's sin is never mentioned again in the Hebrew scriptures. Paul ... embellishes the Adam story in ways that certainly stretch the authorial intent of the writer(s) of Genesis, but Paul nowhere suggests that Adam's unfortunate choice was made by a "pre-Fall" human.[1]

---

1. Karl Giberson, *Saving the Original Sinner: How Christians Have Used the Bible's First Man to Oppress, Inspire, and Make Sense of the World* (Boston, MA: Beacon Press, 2015), p. 51.

In the book *Adam and the Genome*, which rejects a historical Adam, theologian Scot McKnight argues:

> What we call the 'fall' story of Genesis 3 borrows a later Christian term and, more importantly, in borrowing a later category, reads the text in ways that miss what the text meant in the ancient Near East.... In fact, the whole of Genesis 1–3 barely — if ever — makes another appearance in the entire Old Testament; so while many would say Genesis 1–11 is the foundation for reading the whole Bible, that is certainly at least an exaggeration if not a serious error.[2]

It has also been claimed that because Genesis 3 contains none of the language associated with disobedience, such as "sin," "evil," "rebellion," "transgression," "guilt," it therefore cannot be a passage that teaches the doctrine of the Fall.[3] Are these objections valid? Does Genesis 3 say anything about the concept of Adam's Fall from grace by which his descendants were made sinners? Have Christians read something into Genesis 3 that is simply not there? I will argue that the doctrine of the Fall is a biblical concept and can be derived from the biblical text. It is important to defend the biblical concept of the Fall because no doctrine is more important to our anthropology and soteriology. This chapter will show that Genesis 3 does indeed teach an account of the Fall of Adam.

✸ Genesis 3:1: The Tempter

Genesis 3 continues the context of the garden narrative as it part of the same *tôlĕdōt* heading, explaining what happens to the man and woman in their garden paradise (Genesis 2:4-4:26).

> Now the serpent was more crafty than any other beast of the field that the LORD God had made. He said to the woman, "Did

---

2. Venema and McKnight, *Adam and the Genome*, p. 139.
3. James Barr, *The Garden of Eden and the Hope of Immortality* (Minneapolis, MN: Fortress, 1992), p. 6

God actually say, 'You shall not eat of any tree in the garden'?"
(Genesis 3:1).

Genesis 3 begins by introducing us to another character in the narrative,
the serpent, who unexpectedly appears. In Genesis 1–2 there was no mention of the serpent, so the question is: who is he and where does he come
from? The text identifies this new character as "the serpent" (*hannāḥāš*, with
the definite article) a common Hebrew word for serpent in the Old Testament (*nāḥāš*, Exodus 4:3; Numbers 21:7–9). It could have a connection
to the word *nĕḥōšet* (bronze) as in Numbers 21:9 where Moses makes a
"bronze serpent" (*nĕḥaš nĕḥōšet*) which is later referred to by people of Israel
as Nehushtan (*nĕḥuštān*, 2 Kings 18:4).[4] If this is the case, then there may
well have been something attractive about this serpent's appearance that
drew Eve's attention toward it (cf. 2 Corinthians 11:14).[5] The serpent is no
mythological creature but is a real creature, as the words "had made" show
its origins are from the ground (Genesis 2:19; cf. Genesis 3:14 "all the days
of your life"). Yet, there is more to the serpent than just being a creature that
God created. Rather than giving us the identity of the serpent, Moses tells
us two things about his character, that is different from the other creatures
that God has made: 1) it is crafty 2) it can speak.

The serpent is described as being "more crafty" than any other beast of the
field, so it is a creature whom Adam and Eve should have exercised dominion
over (Genesis 1:28). Its characterization as "crafty" (*'ārûm*) is used positively
elsewhere in the Bible ("prudent" in Proverbs 12:16, 14:8) but it is also used
in a negative sense (Job 5:12, 15:5), such as the case in this narrative. The
word "crafty" is the Hebrew word עָרוּם and echoes the word עָרוֹם "naked"
at the end of chapter 2 (Genesis 2:25). This is a deliberate play on words. It
is meant to show the relationship between the serpent's "craftiness" and the
innocence implied by the "nakedness" of Adam and Eve. There is also a difference between "naked" עָרוֹם (*'ārôm*, Genesis 2:25) and "naked" עֵירֹם (*'êrōm*,
Genesis 3:7). The word *'êrōm* reflects Israel's exiles who have been judged
because they failed to trust God's Word (Deuteronomy 28:48). The Fall did
not just make Adam and Eve aware of their nakedness, but that they knew
they were "naked" in the sense that they were under the judgment of God.[6]

---

4. The Philistine champion Goliath is portrayed as being of the evil one (serpent = Satan)
   as he is covered in bronze (the word bronze, *nĕḥšet*, sounds like the Hebrew word for
   serpent). Interestingly, the future king of Israel, David, defeats Goliath by crushing his
   head with a stone, foreshadowing what the Messiah would do to Satan (1 Samuel 17:5–
   6, 49; cf. Genesis 3:15; 1 John 3:8).
5. Hamilton, *Genesis 1–17*, p. 187.
6. Sailhamer, *The Pentateuch As Narrative*, p. 103.

The craftiness of the serpent should prepare us for the fact that it can speak. For people who have been influenced by an enlightenment philosophy (i.e. the denial of the supernatural) the fact that the serpent speaks is evidence that this is a fairy tale or myth, but this is obviously not what is being communicated (the garden in Eden is not the magical land of Narnia).[7] In the garden Adam was able to name the animals (Genesis 2:20) because he was made in the image of God and had both the faculty of thought and speech, but they could not name him as they were not made in God's image and did not possess the ability to speak. So, when the serpent speaks, something is wrong, as Old Testament scholar E.J. Young notes:

> The actions of the serpent, however, constitute a denial that God has made him. The serpent speaks; it does what animals cannot do. Only man, of earthly creatures, possesses the ability to speak. Yet the serpent acts as a man; it raises itself above the beast of the field which the LORD God had made and it elevates itself to an equality with man. There is something wrong and Eve should have recognized this as soon as the serpent began to speak.[8]

The fact that the serpent can speak raises the question: is this creature being used by someone for their own purposes? Although there are numerous explanations for the serpent by commentators, neither Genesis nor the rest of the Old Testament specifically identifies it. The text strongly suggests that there is an instrument of evil behind the serpent, as its speech is directly contradictory to God's Word (Genesis 3:4; cf. 2:17). It is with the progression of revelation in the New Testament that we see the agent behind the serpent is revealed as Satan (see Revelation 12:9).

But who is Satan? The New Testament frequently refers to Satan (Mathew 4:10, 12:26, 16:23; Acts 26:18; Romans 16:20; 1 Thessalonians 2:18) who is also known as the Devil (Matthew 4:1–11, 25:41; John 13:2; 1 Peter 5:8), Beelzebul (Matthew 10:25, 12:24), and Belial (2 Corinthians 6:14).[9] Jesus described Satan as "the ruler of this world" (John 12:31, 14:30, 16:11) and the Apostle Paul says he is the "god of this world" (2 Corinthians 4:4).[10] As such, Satan not only rules over unredeemed mankind (Acts 26:18;

---

7. The only other instance of an animal speaking in Scripture is when God miraculously "opened the mouth of the donkey" that Balaam was sitting upon (see Numbers 22:28). It was obvious to Balaam that donkeys did not normally speak.

8. E.J. Young, *Genesis 3* (Banner of Truth: Great Britain, 1966), p. 18–19.

9. There are those in the Old Testament who are described as being of Belial (Proverbs 6:12, 16:26; 1 Samuel 30:22; 2 Samuel 16:7) or sons of Belial (Judges 19:22, 20:13; 1 Samuel 1:16 [daughter of Belial], 10:27, 25:25).

10. Jesus' death on the cross defeated Satan and his rule over this world. Satan is a defeated foe who is in his last act of rebellion.

Colossians 1:13) but over demons who are fallen angels (Matthew 12:24, 25:41; cf. 2 Corinthians 11:14). His character is that of a deceiver (Revelation 12:9, 20:3), a destroyer (1 Peter 5:8), a liar, and a murderer (John 8:44).

Whereas the New Testament frequently refers to Satan, he is not fully revealed in the Old Testament, although he was active in this period of history (cf. Jude 9).[11] In the Book of Job Satan is mentioned several times in the first two chapters (Job 1:6, 7, 8 ,9, 12; 2:1, 2, 3, 4, 6, 7). However, the Hebrew word in those verses *haśśāṭān* has the article, so it points to a title rather than a personal name ("the adversary" or "the accuser"). Satan is there in a hostile role to oppose God's servant Job, and he shows himself to be an evil being (Job 1:13–19, 2:7). Satan is mentioned again in Zechariah 3:1–2, with the title *haśśāṭān*, as an accuser of Joshua the High Priest. In 1 Chronicles 21:1 we read: "Then Satan stood against Israel and incited David to number Israel." Here the Hebrew word is *śāṭān,* a personal name. In a parallel passage written several hundred years earlier (1 Chronicles is written after the Babylonian exile) we read that "the anger of the LORD was kindled against Israel, and he incited David against them, saying, 'Go, number Israel and Judah'" (2 Samuel 24:1). Who then incited David — was it Satan or the LORD? It was both — God allowed Satan to provoke David to go and number Israel. Interestingly, the passage in 1 Chronicles was not revealed before the exile (Job was probably written at the time of the exile) when there was so much idolatry in Israel, but after the exile when idolatry had effectively been purged out from the nation. So, in 1 Chronicles 21:1 God reveals what happened behind the scenes for David to be incited to number Israel. The New Testament follows up this revelation of Satan, the accuser of God's people.[12]

It probably did not take that long for the creature known as Satan to rebel against his creator and find his way into the garden. Although the Bible does not say how long after creation week the Fall of Satan from heaven took place (Luke 10:18), it most likely was not that long. Since creation was morally "very good" (Genesis 1:31) when God had finished creating on the sixth day and the seventh day was "blessed" and "made holy" (Genesis 2:1–3),

---

11. When God judged the nation of Egypt with ten plagues, he was judging their "gods" (Exodus 12:12; Numbers 33:4). Scripture identifies the gods of the nations as worthless idols (Psalm 96:5) but at the same time behind the idolatrous worship of pagan nations are demons (Deuteronomy 32:8, 17; Psalm 106:37; 1 Corinthians 10:20-21; 1 Timothy 4:1). Satan is the ruler of demons (Matthew 12:24). When God judged Egypt, he also pierced the "dragon" (Isaiah 51:9, Rahab is another term for Egypt, cf. 30:7; Job 26:11–13), and it is Satan who is identified as the ancient dragon (Revelation 12:9).

12. Michael L. Brown, *Job: The Faith to Challenge God* (Peabody, MA: Hendrickson Publishers, 2019), p. 12–13, 340–341.

the Fall of Satan must have occurred after this time. This raises the question of how could creation be "very good" if the serpent (Satan) was there? Unlike Adam, Satan did not have dominion over the creation; the rebellion of Satan did not affect the goodness of the rest of God's creation as Adam's sin did (see Genesis 3:17–19; Romans 5:12, 8:19–22). How Satan became the enemy of God is not clearly described anywhere in the Bible.

Among the people of the ancient world the serpent was both friend (because they offered protection) and foe (because of their power and danger), some were worshiped, and others were seen as incarnations of evil; the latter is the view of the serpent in Genesis 3 as the narrative makes clear. At the time of Moses, the people of Israel, would have seen the serpent as being associated among the unclean animals and as being associated with the judgment of God (Leviticus 11:41–45; Number 21:6) The serpent's craftiness is seen in his very first words: did God actually say?

These words from the serpent misrepresent God's authority and bring doubt to the woman (Eve) by: 1) questioning God's motivation with the subtle addition "really say," 2) using the name "God" rather than the covenant name "Lord" (YHWH), 3) reworking the wording of God's command slightly by adding "not" at the beginning (with "any" expresses absolute prohibition), omits the emphatic "freely," uses the plural "you" rather than the singular in 2:16, and 4) placing "from any tree" at the end of the sentence rather than at the beginning as in 2:16.[13] The serpent's words, which were designed to get Eve to debate God's command, entertained the possibility that God did not know what was best. While God had commanded Adam not to eat from one tree, Satan told Eve it was "any tree in the garden." In other words, Satan presents God as the cosmic killjoy, someone who comes along and likes saying no to everything and everyone. In his temptation, the serpent did not just point to the tree and say, "Go on — eat it," but he described reality in a way that is false. The serpent's first step in deceiving Eve was having her question the truthfulness of God's Word. The serpent speaks as to his nature, falsely (John 8:44). As Adam and Eve found out, there are only tragic consequences when we reject God's Word as the sole authority for our lives.

❧ Genesis 3:2–5: Debating God's Word

And the woman said to the serpent, "We may eat of the fruit of the trees in the garden, but God said, 'You shall not eat of the fruit of the tree that is in the midst of the garden, neither shall you touch it,

---

13. Matthews, *Genesis 1–11:26*, p. 235.

lest you die.'" But the serpent said to the woman, "You will not surely die. For God knows that when you eat of it your eyes will be opened, and you will be like God, knowing good and evil" (Genesis 3:2–5).

Eve's response to Satan's temptation, which is often like ours, was initially appropriate: "We may eat of the fruit of the trees in the garden, but God said, "You shall not eat of the fruit of the tree that is in the midst of the garden'" (Genesis 3:2–3). So far, Eve is telling the truth. But her mistake was to set her sights on what God had commanded not to do rather than on what God had blessed them with (i.e., all the other trees in the garden). The serpent succeeded in getting the woman to reinterpret God's Word. Eve does this by: 1) omitting the words "any" and "freely" from the command, 2) identifying the tree according to its location rather than significance, 3) referring to "God" as the serpent had done, rather than "the LORD," 4) making the command more strict by adding the phrase "you must not touch it," and 5) failing to capture the urgency of certain death "you will [surely] die."[14] The tactic of twisting God's Word is second nature to the serpent (cf. Matthew 4:6). Eve's response, however, entertained the possibility of standing in judgment over God, which leads the serpent to challenge what God had said by telling her, "You will not surely die" (Genesis 3:4). Now, as a result of the deception, Eve has doubt in her mind and has fallen into unbelief. As Christians, we need to be aware of Satan's designs so that we are not outwitted by him (2 Corinthians 2:11).

What Satan promised Eve was partly true, but its ultimate end was a lie. The truth was that by succumbing to this temptation, her "eyes will be opened and you will be like God" (Genesis 3:5).[15] According to God this was true (see Genesis 3:22). On the other hand, it was a total misrepresentation of what God had said. Satan's lie was that "you will not surely die." Adam and Eve's mistake was to believe the lie of Satan over the truth of God and to think that they could determine truth for themselves. For us to try to determine truth apart from God is in fact saying, "I won't accept God's rules. I'll make my own." This determination is the beginning of idolatry. When God becomes too uncomfortable for us, we make our own rules. We fashion other gods, more domesticated gods, which are idols (cf. Romans 1:22–23). Instead of obeying God's Word, Adam and Eve act autonomously, which is to act like God.

---

14. Ibid., p. 235–236.
15. There is debate over how to translate the Hebrew ʾĕlōhîm here (God or gods). However, Mathews rightly notes: "Since Elohim as 'God' occurs earlier in the verse, it is best to retain the singular sense." Mathews, *Genesis 1–11:26*, p. 236.

🌿 Genesis 3:6–7: Pride Comes Before *the* Fall

> So when the woman saw that the tree was good for food, and
> that it was a delight to the eyes, and that the tree was to be desired to
> make one wise, she took of its fruit and ate, and she also gave some
> to her husband who was with her, and he ate. Then the eyes of both
> were opened, and they knew that they were naked. And they sewed
> fig leaves together and made themselves loincloths.

After being tempted by the serpent Eve rebelled against God because she
saw that the tree was (1) good for food, (2) pleasing to the eye, and (3)
desirable for gaining wisdom (Genesis 3:6). These temptations correspond
to John's description of the things of this world: "The desires of the flesh and
the desires of the eyes and the pride of life" (1 John 2:16). This is a pattern
of sin that runs through Scripture: (1) start listening to the creature instead
of the Creator; (2) follow our own impressions instead of God's instructions;
and (3) make self-fulfillment the goal. The prospect of these things seems
good to life, when in fact it leads to death. If you rebel against the God who
gives life, what else is there but death (Proverbs 14:12)?

Eve was deceived by the crafty serpent (1 Timothy 2:14; 2 Corinthians
11:3) and Adam who was with her, also ate the fruit. Was Adam present
during the temptation? It is hard to know for sure, but the plural use of
"you" in Genesis 3:1–5 suggests that he is a witness to the dialogue, as does
the fact that God created the woman to be with the man (Genesis 3:12).[16]
Although the text does not explicitly say why Adam does not intervene, it
seems that Eve was active in being deceived, whereas Adam acts passively.
Another question that comes up, is how could Adam and Eve sin if they
were created morally "very good" (Genesis 1:31) and when did their nature
change? Although it is difficult to give a satisfactory answer to these questions, E.J Young helpfully points out:

> [Adam] was truly a responsible, free being, who acted because
> he wished to. He himself, his nature, disposition and character,
> determine what he will do, and in accordance with that nature, dis-
> position and character he acts. He cannot, however, act or make
> choices which are contrary to his nature, disposition and character.
> God, for example, who is good, cannot act contrary to His nature.
> He cannot lie. Sinful acts proceed from a sinful nature. In sinning,
> Adam showed that he possessed a sinful nature. Inasmuch as he

---

16. Several scholars recognize Adam's presence with Eve in the dialogue with the serpent. See
Mathews, *Genesis 1:11–26*, p. 238; Currid, *Genesis 1:1–25:18*, p.118.

was created good, however, whence came this sinful nature?... It has been held that the mysterious change and the overt transgression are bound up together, so that we cannot necessarily say that the change took place temporally before the act of transgression. It has also been held that when Eve looked at the tree, thus influenced by the subtle suggestion of Satan, that change had already taken place. It is also possible that when Satan first approached her, the change had occurred. It does seem strange that she saw nothing out of place in an animal acting as a man, indeed setting itself above man and on an equality with God. In the light of the superior position which had been assigned to man in 2:19 it is strange that Eve did not react to the approach of the serpent in an unfavourable manner. It is also strange that in her language to the serpent she misrepresented the prohibition of God. On the basis of these two considerations there are those who think that the tragic change in nature may have occurred when the tempter approached and that this change manifested itself almost immediately in Eve's partaking of the forbidden fruit. One thing is surely clear. When she actually partook of the forbidden fruit, Eve acted as an enemy of God. As created, however, she was neither mortal nor sinful.[17]

After disobeying God's command not to eat from the tree of the knowledge of good and evil, both Adam and Eve's "eyes were opened," and they can now see their nakedness. This indicates that they not only know their prior created goodness is now a memory, but that God's judgment is upon them (see above). The eyes of fallen people are closed to spiritual matters and they can only be opened by God (Genesis 21:19; Numbers 22:31; Acts 26:18). Whereas before they were unashamed (Genesis 2:25), they now stand ashamed in guilt because of their nakedness and are exposed to God's judgment. For the Hebrews, nakedness is shameful because it is related with guilt (Genesis 9:22–23). The couple's shame led them to try to solve their own problem by clothing themselves, by sowing fig leaves together and making loincloths. The fact that Adam and Eve see the need to cover their own nakedness is evidence of a change in their condition.[18] They are no longer morally upright (Ecclesiastes 7:29), but their relationship with God is now broken. Like the preacher in Ecclesiastes, Adam and Eve sought wisdom outside of "God's Word" but all they found was vanity and toil (see Ecclesiastes 1:1, 14; 2:21; 4:8).

17. Young, *Genesis 3*, p. 47–48.
18. Collins, *Genesis 1–4*, p. 173.

How long did it take for Adam and Eve to rebel against God? Well, the text does not specifically answer that, however, it could not have been that long after God commanded Adam and Eve to be "fruitful and multiply" (Genesis 1:28), which they would have obeyed before the Fall, so they probably did not wait long to have children. Because their first child Cain killed Abel (Genesis 4:1, 8) the Fall of Adam and Eve was only shortly after (a few weeks?) creation week.

🜪 Genesis 3:8–13: Adam, Where Are You?

> And they heard the sound of the LORD God walking in the garden in the cool of the day, and the man and his wife hid themselves from the presence of the LORD God among the trees of the garden. But the LORD God called to the man and said to him, "Where are you?" And he said, "I heard the sound of you in the garden, and I was afraid, because I was naked, and I hid myself." He said, "Who told you that you were naked? Have you eaten of the tree of which I commanded you not to eat?" The man said, "The woman whom you gave to be with me, she gave me fruit of the tree, and I ate." Then the LORD God said to the woman, "What is this that you have done?" The woman said, "The serpent deceived me, and I ate."

The transcendent God who created the world in Genesis 1 is also the imminent God who meets with man in the garden. The garden was a place where the LORD God came on a regular basis to have fellowship with Adam and Eve when He "walked" (*mithallēk*)[19] with them in the garden; just as He often "walked" in the sanctuary and the camp to have fellowship with the people Israel (Leviticus 26:12; Deuteronomy 23:14). Adam and Eve did not hear the voice of the LORD God (*qôl yhwh 'ĕlōhîm*) speaking or calling, but the sound of Him walking (cf. 2 Samuel 5:24; 1 Kings 14:6). This is why they hid themselves among the trees (if it was God speaking to them then they would not be able to hide from Him as he is omnipresent). This was not the first time the LORD God appeared to Adam, as He previously brought the animals to him (Genesis 2:19, 22). God's coming to earth to meet with man is not uncommon in the Book of Genesis (Genesis 16:7–13; 18–19; 32:24–30; cf. John 1:1, 14). The LORD God's appearing to Adam in human form in the garden would be a theophany (Greek: *theos* = "God" + *phaino* = "appear"), a pre-incarnate appearance of God the Son (Jesus).

---

19. The *hitpael* verb form "walking" (*mithallēk*) in Genesis 3:8 implies this as it stresses habitual aspects of action. See Hamilton, *Genesis 1-17*, p. 192.

However, now in their guilty state, Adam and Eve now fear the sound (*qôl*, Exodus 20:18) of the Lord God walking in the garden and so they hide from His presence among the trees. The innocence and freedom they once enjoyed is now gone. Something is obviously wrong, but it is not God's walking in the garden that is unusual, but the reaction of Adam and Eve. Both Adam and Eve now fear the presence of the Lord God with whom they had once had fellowship in the garden. The fact that Adam and Eve run and hide further indicates the Lord God's physical presence in the garden.

The Lord God calls out to Adam with a question: "Where are you?" Adam is the only one who is addressed by God, probably because he is the one who God first gave the prohibition and was the one responsible for the woman (Genesis 2:16, 22–23). God is not asking the question because He does not know where Adam is, but He is wanting to get him to acknowledge his sin and responsibility (cf. Genesis 4:9). Before reconciliation can take place, their disobedience must be confessed. God cannot simply overlook disobedience, or He would not be just. Adam responds by saying he hid himself because in his nakedness he was afraid of God. When Adam previously heard the Lord's voice, he was unafraid (Genesis 2:17), but now there is fear when the Lord speaks. Adam's guilt can also be seen by his violated conscience when God asks him two further questions, "Who told you that you were naked? Have you eaten from the tree of which I commanded you not to eat?" (Genesis 3:11). The second question God asks is linked to the tree that Adam was commanded not to eat from (Genesis 2:16). Both of "these questions explain to the man that his sense of shame arose from his defiance of God's command."[20] Although the words guilt, disobedience, sin, and transgression do not appear in Genesis 3, this does not mean that the concepts are not there in the passage. The Apostle Paul described Adam as being disobedient and Eve as a transgressor (Romans 5:19; 1 Timothy 2:14). Adam's guilt and disobedience are clearly expressed within the passage.

In response to God's question, Adam is quick to point out to God that it was the woman that He gave to him who is responsible, as she gave him the fruit to eat. Adam was not deceived by the serpent. God asks the woman why she did it, but like Adam, she plays the blame game and points to the serpent. Although neither Adam nor Eve are contrite, Eve's response to God is not like Adam's, as Eve does not blame God for making the serpent or giving Adam to her, but rather, she admits to being deceived by the serpent.

---

20. Collins, *Genesis 1–4*, p. 241.

🌿 Genesis 3:14–19: Judgment Begins

> The LORD God said to the serpent, "Because you have done this, cursed are you above all livestock and above all beasts of the field; on your belly you shall go, and dust you shall eat all the days of your life. I will put enmity between you and the woman, and between your offspring and her offspring; he shall bruise your head, and you shall bruise his heel." To the woman he said, "I will surely multiply your pain in childbearing; in pain you shall bring forth children. Your desire shall be contrary to your husband, but he shall rule over you." And to Adam he said, "Because you have listened to the voice of your wife and have eaten of the tree of which I commanded you, 'You shall not eat of it,' cursed is the ground because of you; in pain you shall eat of it all the days of your life; thorns and thistles it shall bring forth for you; and you shall eat the plants of the field. By the sweat of your face you shall eat bread, till you return to the ground, for out of it you were taken; for you are dust, and to dust you shall return."

Now God is no longer asking questions but pronouncing judgments. The serpent is up first. God speaks to the serpent and sees him as the cause of all the judgments: "you have done this." God curses (*'ārar*) the serpent above all the creatures, indicating that he is doomed (Genesis 4:11, 9:25; cf. Deuteronomy 28:17–18). The serpent's punishment has 3 aspects: 1) consigned to crawl on its belly, 2) the eating of dust "all the days of your life," and 3) its ultimate defeat by the seed of the woman. The serpent's crawling on his belly and eating dust express humiliation and defeat (Psalm 72:9; Isaiah 49:23). The once proud serpent is now humbled. But this is not the end of the punishment, as there will be a great defeat for the serpent to come (see chapter 8).

God then speaks to the woman and pronounces judgments upon her which has two aspects: 1) multiplied pain in childbearing, and 2) her desire will be to rule over her husband (Genesis 3:16). If Eve had children before the Fall there would have been pain (not all pain is bad, i.e., exercise), but because of the Fall that pain is multiplied. The Apostle Paul alludes to this pain when he states, "creation has been groaning together in the pains of childbirth" (Romans 8:22). The desire of the woman to "rule" (*māšal*) over her husband is for control of their marriage. The same noun is used in the next chapter where God tells Cain that sins "desire is contrary to you, but you must rule over it" (Genesis 4:7). Interestingly, unlike the serpent, who was said to be deceptive (Genesis 3:14) and the man, who ate disobediently (Genesis 3:17), there is no cause associated with the woman's suffering. In

God's judgment of the serpent, He curses him (Genesis 3:14) and in the judgment of the man He curses the ground (Genesis 3:17), but there is no curse in the woman's judgment. This may be because the woman was guilty through deception, whereas the serpent and the man were willfully disobedient. In the justice of the woman's punishment there is mercy, as it includes the hope of salvation for fallen mankind (Genesis 3:15).

Finally, God speaks to Adam and pronounces judgment upon him, which has two aspects: 1) lifelong toilsome labor, and 2) death. Just as with the judgments against the serpent and the woman so here the judgments are physical judgments; speaking against the idea that the text here is just speaking of spiritual death (Genesis 3:8). Adam's sin is the cause of the ground being cursed (Genesis 3:17). Adam was created to "rule" creation and therefore as the head over creation it experiences the consequences of his disobedience. The Hebrew words 'ādām (man) and 'ădāmâ (ground) are closely related and show the related consequences of Adam's disobedience on the ground from which he was taken (Genesis 2:7). The ground that was cursed was not just the ground in Eden but the whole earth outside of the Garden from which Adam was taken (before he was placed in the garden —Genesis 2:15, 3:23, 5:29). Adam's disobedience has a ripple effect on the rest of creation (Romans 8:20–22).

The consequence of eating the prohibited fruit now means the work needed to gain food will become a painful matter (Genesis 5:29). As the cursed ground will now produce "thorns and thistles," (Genesis 3:18) and Adam will have to cultivate the ground to eat the plants of the field instead of taking his food from the trees that were pleasant for food (Genesis 2:9). The punishment Adam received for his disobedience is seen in the fulfillment of God's warning that he would die (both physically and spiritually) if he disobeyed His command (Genesis 2:17; 3:7–8, 19). Adam was told that he would return to the dust from which he had been taken, a concept that is referenced by many of the Old Testament writers (Job 10:9, 34:15; Psalm 90:3. 104:29; Ecclesiastes 3:20. 12:7). This demonstrates a mindfulness of the curse and the one who brought this about, namely Adam. When Adam disobeyed, death came not only to him, but also to his descendants. Cain killed Abel, the first human death; but death did not stop there. It impacted everyone, as the genealogies in Genesis reveal: "… and he died … and he died … and he died … etc." (Genesis 5:5, 8, 11, 14, 17, 20, 27, 31). Therefore, the Apostle Paul writes, "because of one man's trespass, death reigned." (Romans 5:17).

Old Testament scholar Peter Enns does not read Genesis 3 as an account of the Fall, and objects to the idea that Adam's disobedience is the cause of our sinfulness. Enns is not questioning whether we are sinful but whether the Old Testament says that Adam is the cause of our sinfulness. Concerning the account of Cain and Abel in Genesis 4, he states:

> Does this story imply that Cain's murder of his brother, Abel, is a consequence of being born in a state of sin due to his father's transgression? Or should Cain's sin be understood, like the sin of his parents, as his own responsibility, his own choice to disobey? In other words, "like father, like son."... We do not read that Adam's disobedience is somehow causally linked to Cain's act.[21]

Enns's objection, however, misunderstands the doctrine of original sin. Of course, Cain had a choice and bore the responsibility for the sinful choice he made, just as we all do. Cain's sin, however, did not come from outside of him but from within him; the mention of him being "angry" and of his "countenance [falling]" suggests this (see Genesis 4:5). The Bible teaches that our sin comes from the corrupt nature we have inherited from Adam (Romans 5:12–19; 1 Corinthians 15:21–22). We are guilty sinners in Adam. When we yield to temptation, we do not become sinners: we already are sinners. This is because we are descendants of Adam. By thinking that there should be some theological statement in the narrative of Genesis 3–4 that expresses that Adam's disobedience is the cause of human sinfulness, Enns disregards how the narrative works. This objection to original sin overlooks the fact that the literature of Genesis 1–50 is historical narrative; therefore, we should not expect the unfolding of the doctrine to look like a collection of theological propositions as we have in Romans 5:12–19. Adam's experience was not like Cain's experience, or even our own, because Adam was not in a state of sin to start with. However, the similarities in the scenes of condemnation of sin in the narratives of Genesis 3 and 4 serve as a model of human sinfulness (see table). Old Testament scholar Gordon Wenham believes that these "similarities between Chapters 3 and 4 confirm that the former should be read as a paradigm of human sin."[22] Genesis 3, then, provides us with an account of the consequences and effects of Adam's disobedience in which humanity is now entrenched.

The consequences for his offspring of Adam's disobedience are felt throughout the remainder of Genesis. They can be seen in the account of Cain slaying his brother, Abel (Genesis 4:8); Lamech (not Noah's father) boasting of murder (Genesis 4:23–24); Lamech's (Noah's father) comments in Genesis 5:29 affirming that the curse of Genesis 3 continued to bring the

---

21. Enns, *The Evolution of Adam*, p. 85.
22. Gordon Wenham, "Original Sin in Genesis 1–11," *Churchman* 104, no. 4 (1990), p. 319.

Genesis 3	Genesis 4
Where are you? (3:9)	Where is Abel your brother? (4:9)
What is this that you have done? (3:13)	What have you done? (4:10)
Cursed is the ground because of you (3:17)	You are cursed from the ground (4:11)
Drove out the man (3:24)	You have driven me ... away from the ground (4:14)
East of the Garden of Eden (3:24)	East of Eden (4:16)

problem of "painful toil"; and the description of the wickedness of man's heart before and after the Flood (Genesis 6:5, 8:21). As the narrative continues to unfold, we read of Noah cursing Canaan (Genesis 9:25) and of the judgment on mankind's pride and deliberate disobedience at Babel against the LORD's command to increase greatly upon the earth (Genesis 9:1, 7; 11:4). These examples show how things became progressively worse from Genesis 3 onward, and how sin and its consequences affected the whole human race. These texts do not need to state that the reason for these things was Adam's sin; the narrative has clearly shown this to be the case. When we read Genesis 3 in its context, it clearly implies the effects of the Fall. Because of Adam's disobedience, God's "very good" creation became a place marked by wickedness, violence, and death. The consequences of Adam's disobedience in Genesis are felt throughout the rest of the Old Testament: Sodom and Gomorrah, Israel's scattering, and the constant human failure are all evidence of the consequences of Adam's sin. While the exact words we use to describe the doctrine of the Fall and original sin are not in the text, the ideas are clearly presented from the very beginning and demonstrated in subsequent inspired writings.

Adam's descendants now start life, unlike him, spiritually separated from God and are in need of His saving grace (Ephesians 2:1–8). Before Genesis 3, there was only blessing (Genesis 1:22, 28, 2:3), but the curses came because of Adam's disobedience. God curses the serpent and the ground (Genesis 3:14, 17) but not the man and the woman, as there is still the hope of blessing.

❧ Genesis 3:20–24: Out of the Garden

The man called his wife's name Eve, because she was the mother of all living. And the LORD God made for Adam and for his wife garments of skins and clothed them. Then the LORD God said, "Behold, the man has become like one of us in knowing good and evil. Now, lest he reach out his hand and take also of the tree of life and eat, and live forever —" therefore the LORD God sent him out from the garden of Eden to work the ground from which he was taken. He drove out the man, and at the east of the garden of Eden he placed the cherubim and a flaming sword that turned every way to guard the way to the tree of life.

Even though God has justly judged the couple, there is still hope for them in the fact that: 1) Adam names his wife, and 2) God provides animal skins as garments. Adam acts in faith to the promise that God has made (Genesis 3:15) and names his wife: Eve (Genesis 3:20). Although at her creation Adam recognized her as a "woman" (Genesis 2:23) here he now gives her a name as an individual. The Hebrew word for Eve is "ḥawwâ" meaning "living" (in Greek Zōē = life). Adam named his wife Eve because she is the mother of all living. Before Adam disobeyed God, he was naked, and unashamed, then after he disobeyed Him, he clothed himself in fig leaves (Genesis 3:7). Now it is God Himself who will make ('āśâ) clothes for Adam and Eve. This is interesting as it shows us that even though God as Creator had finished making things on the seventh day (Genesis 2:1–3), He now makes things as man's Savior.

The skins that God uses is a reference to the first death of any kind mentioned in the Bible. God had to kill animals to clothe Adam and Eve. But why the skins of animals instead of fig leaves? It is hard to say, and we cannot be sure, but it may be because "without the shedding of blood there is no forgiveness of sins" (Hebrews 9:22). The Hebrew words for "garments," kĕthoneth and "clothed" lābaš, are used in the Torah's description of priestly garments (Exodus 28:4, 39–40; 28:41; 29:8). The priest had to be properly clothed before God in his service (Exodus 20:26; 28:42). So the garments would probably have been long covering for the couple (Genesis 37:3). The killing of animals would make sense to the original audience (Mosaic Community) where the skin of an animal was offered to make atonement for sin (Leviticus 7:8). In Genesis 4, Abel knows to bring an animal sacrifice before the LORD (Genesis 4:4). The reason we wear clothes, in a fallen world, is because nakedness brings about shame. God's "clothing" of Adam and Eve is also a reminder that our salvation does not come to us through our own works but by God's grace when He clothes us in His righteousness (Zechariah 3:1–5; Philippians 3:9; 2 Corinthians 5:21).

Now that Adam and Eve are clothed, what is to become of them? Because of their disobedience, God sends them out of the garden. To understand why Adam and Eve are sent from the garden it is important to understand

God's statement: "Behold, the man has become like one of us" (Genesis 3:22). God sees that man has become like Him, in that they now have a knowledge of what belongs to God: good and evil. God's concern now is that Adam and Eve will eat from the tree of life and live forever in a fallen state. The words "and take also of the tree of life" (Genesis 3:22) suggests that Adam had not yet eaten from the tree of life. So God acts by sending (*šālaḥ*, Genesis 21:14; 25:6) Adam out of the garden to work or serve the ground from which he was taken. Adam was created to serve God by tending the garden (Genesis 2:15), but because of his disobedience he will now serve the ground. God "drove" Adam out of the garden, just as He drove Cain out from His presence (Genesis 4:4). To prevent entrance back into the garden, God places the cherubim (plural) to guard its entrance in the east (Genesis 4:14, 11:2). These angelic creatures are associated with the presence of God (Psalm 18:10; Ezekiel 10). Along with the cherubim, God places a flaming sword to guard the tree of life. The sword is independent of the cherubim as it "turned every way" to guard (*šāmar*) the garden. It is a sad reflection on Adam who was created to "guard" (*šāmar*, Genesis 2:15) the garden but it is now he who is guarded from it.

Adam was in Eden and was once upright yet because of his sin he was cast from the garden. Adam and Eve, now expelled from the garden, are away from God's presence and the paradise they once knew is now lost and they will have to survive by themselves in a cursed world. Only by God's grace can we gain entrance back into His presence. In the new heavens and earth with the curse removed, and with Eden restored, the tree of life will bring healing to the nations and the redeemed from every tribe, tongue, and nation will no longer be separated from their God but will see His face (Revelation 22:2, 14, 19; cf. Isaiah 51:3; 65:17, 25).

Chapter 5

The First Adam: The History of Adam's Descendants

The history of Adam begins on the sixth day of creation week when God creates him supernaturally from the dust of the ground (Genesis 2:7). As a result of Adam being created directly by God, he is upright (morally innocent) (Ecclesiastes 7:29). Adam was also created as an intelligent being — his naming of the animals reveals his intelligence and wisdom, or God would not have brought the animals to him to name them (Genesis 2:19–20; cf. Job 15:7–8).

Not only was Adam created upright, and intelligent, but he was meant to live forever (Romans 5:12).[1] Yet in the course of time Adam rebelled against God, who gave him life, and his sin changed and disrupted all creation (Genesis 3:14–19; Romans 8:20). Adam was no longer upright and blameless, but was in a state of shame and would die as God said he would (Genesis 2:17; 3:7, 19). Although Adam was no longer without sin, he was still intelligent, and because of the nature of the death penalty, his death would take time. He died at the age of 930 (Genesis 5:5). The fact of Adam being created this way is reflected in the history of his descendants recorded in Genesis 4–5. In Genesis 4 we have the account of Adam's sons Cain and Abel. Both Cain and Abel are described as real persons, in real geographical locations, who worked as farmers and shepherds (Genesis 4:2–3, 8, 16; cf. Hebrews 11:4; 1 John

---

1. The principle throughout the Bible is that if you sin, you will die (Ezekiel 18:4). Another crucial point that is often overlooked in the Adam–Christ parallel is that Jesus' death was voluntary (John 10:18). Jesus did not die because of His sin. As the Bible teaches, He was without sin (1 Peter 1:19). Jesus was dying for the sins of others (Mark 10:45; 1 John 2:1–2). This indicates that if you do not sin, you will not die. Thus, it can be argued that if Adam had not sinned, then he would not have died.

3:12). After killing Abel, Cain also went on to build the world's first city, to protect himself from those who would want to take vengeance upon him (Genesis 4:17; cf. 11:4). Cain's descendants also kept livestock, made musical instruments, and worked with metal (Genesis 4:20–22). These details are important to know as they have implications for how we understand and interpret the history of Adam's descendants in the rest of Genesis.

For example, how should we understand the long life spans of those who lived pre/post-Flood and even the patriarchs? It is often argued by both critical and a growing number of evangelical scholars that because no one could ever live to 900 or 500 years old that the life spans have been manufactured and are only intended to be symbolic or honorific. Another question is, do the biblical genealogies in Genesis 5 and 11 have gaps in them or are they closed chronological records of ancestors? What about the history of the patriarchs? Is there any evidence for them and do we know when they lived? The biblical background of Genesis 1–3 must inform how we read the rest of Scripture (not Darwinian evolution or ANE concepts of existence). This chapter will try and answer these questions and show that the history in the Book of Genesis is consistent and reliable. It will show that the genealogies do not just have a historical function — to show an accurate list of historical ancestors from Adam to Abraham — but they also present a theological line of ancestors from Adam and Eve that leads to the promised Savior (Genesis 3:15). It will begin by establishing a chronology for the Old Testament.

✹ An Old Testament Chronology

To know when the patriarchs lived and to help establish a date for the Flood it is important to establish an accurate chronology for the Old Testament and to know that the textual data being used has been preserved correctly. In chronological matters, the Masoretic Text (MT) of the Old Testament has been shown to be superior to the Septuagint (LXX).[2] A careful examination of the relevant biblical texts in Genesis 5 and 11 shows that the MT has a superior claim to preservation and a superior chronology to that of the LXX.[3] Based on a straightforward reading of the MT, there are three dates in biblical history that give us great confidence for establishing a dating scheme for the Old Testament: 967 b.c., 1446 b.c., and 1876 b.c. These three dates give a solid foundation for determining the dates for the lives of the patriarchs and for the global Flood.

---

2. Although his focus was on Israel's kingdoms, Thiele has shown this to be true. Edwin R. Thiele, *The Mysterious Numbers of the Hebrew Kings*, Rev. ed. (Grand Rapids, MI: Kregel, 1994), p. 90–94.

3. Lita Costner, and Robert Carter, "Textual Traditions and Biblical Chronology," *Journal of Creation* 29, no. (August 2015), p. 99–105.

The foundation of Old Testament history in establishing a solid chronology is 1 Kings 6:1:

> In the four hundred and eightieth year after the people of Israel came out of the land of Egypt, in the fourth year of Solomon's reign over Israel, in the month of Ziv, which is the second month, he began to build the house of the LORD.

The information in 1 Kings 6:1 uses very precise chronological language (i.e., 480th year, 4th year, the 2nd month) and tells us that the exodus from Egypt took place 480 years before the construction of the temple, signifying an elapsed time of 479+ years. First Kings 6:1 presents two issues that need to be determined: when did the 480 years begin, and should the number 480 be understood symbolically or at face value? It is agreed by scholars who hold to a late (1267 B.C.) and an early date (1446 B.C.) for the exodus, that the 480 years began in May of 967 B.C.[4] The date of 967 B.C. is in exact agreement with the date that archival records of Tyre give for sending material to Solomon for building the temple.[5] There are compelling reasons why the 480 years should be taken at face value, rather than symbolically.[6] In the Old Testament, when numbers are presented in an ascending order such as "eightieth and four-hundredth," the text is giving technical data.[7] In 1 Kings 6:1 the smaller number (80th) is followed by the larger number (400th) and is "intended to be a technically precise figure."[8] Normal hermeneutics give an objective basis for the chronological information in 1 Kings 6:1 that places the exodus in 1446 B.C. (967 + 479 = 1446 B.C.).[9]

---

4. Kitchen, *On The Reliability of the Old Testament*, p. 202–203; Rodger C. Young, "When Did Solomon Die?" *Journal of the Evangelical Theological Society* 46, no. 4 (December 2003): p. 589–603.

5. Rodger Young, "Solomon and the Kings of Tyre," *Bible and Spade* 30, no. 3 (Summer 2017), p. 66–73.

6. The late date for the exodus view (c. 1267 B.C.) holds that the 480 years in 1 Kings 6:1 is symbolic (12 generations of 25 years each; this number more accurately reflects 300 years than 480).

7. Umberto Cassuto, *The Documentary Hypothesis and the Composition of the Pentateuch*, Translated by I. Abrahams (Jerusalem, Israel: Magnes, 1961), p. 62. For other biblical examples of this ascending order see Genesis 11:13, 15, 17; Exodus 12:40–41.

8. Bryant G. Wood "The Rise and Fall of the 13th-Century Exodus-Conquest Theory," *Journal of the Evangelical Theological Society* 48, no. 3 (September 2005), p. 486.

9. This chapter synchronizes biblical history with conventional Egyptian chronology. Conventional chronological dates assigned to Egyptian history are said to be a challenge to the dates for creation (c. 4174 B.C.) and the Global Flood (c. 2518 B.C.) as the first Egyptian dynasty is believed to have begun around 3200 B.C. Although there is debate about Egyptian chronology (it certainly needs to be revised in places; most probably during the pre-dynastic and Old Kingdom periods for which there are little archaeological remains), the dates assigned to the New Kingdom chronologies (18th–20th Dynasties) are the best attested of all the Egyptian dynasties.

Another biblical evidence confirms the 1446 B.C. date for the exodus. The early date for the Israelites in Egypt is affirmed in Jephthah's statement in Judges 11:26:

> While Israel lived in Heshbon and its villages, and in Aroer and its villages, and in all the cities that are on the banks of the Arnon, 300 years, why did you not deliver them within that time?

Jephthah is telling his Ammonite enemies that they have no foundation for their hostility toward Israel as they have been in the land for 300 years. Since the exodus took place in 1446 B.C., and the conquest was 40 years later (1406 B.C.), then Jephthah is communicating with the Ammonites around 1106 B.C. Some try and get around taking the 300 years at face value by arguing that Jephthah's speech was political and therefore was an exaggeration meant for rhetorical effect. The fact that Jephthah was making a political speech does not mean the chronological reference is not accurate. Old Testament scholar Michael Grisanti rightly argues that Jephthah's "point is that Ammon did not have a legitimate claim to the land. The Israelites took it from Sihon the Amorite, who had taken it from Moab. This fits Jephthah's reference to Chemosh (the Moabite god) instead of Milcon (the Ammonite god) and does not totally discredit his chronological statement."[10] There is no good reason to try and explain away the 300 years unless you are trying to fit it with a certain chronological view.

Taken together, 1 Kings 6:1 and Judges 11:26 place the exodus from Egypt in 1446 B.C. (also 1 Chronicles 6:33–37 reveals 19 generations from the exodus to Solomon). Compelling arguments have even been made for the precise date of the exodus on Friday, April 24, 1446 B.C.; synchronizing perfectly with the 18th dynasty of Egypt under the reign of Amenhotep II.[11] After Israel left Egypt, they wandered in the wilderness for 40 years (Numbers 14:34; 33:38; Deuteronomy 1:3). Joshua 5:6 makes it clear that the

---

10. Michael Grisanti, "The Book of Exodus," in *The World and the Word: An Introduction to the Old Testament*, edited by Eugene H. Merrill, Mark F. Rooker, and Michael A. Grisanti (Nashville, TN: B&H Academic, 2011), p. 200.

11. Douglas Petrovich, "Amenhotep II and the Historicity of the Exodus-Pharaoh," *The Master's Seminary Journal* 17, no. 1 (Spring 2006), p. 81–110. Amenhotep II is the only candidate in the fifteenth century B.C. that matches all the autobiographical requirements of the exodus Pharaoh. First, the Pharaoh who preceded the exodus Pharaoh had to have reigned beyond 40 years (Exodus 4:19; Acts 7:23). In the Eighteenth Dynasty (c. 1570–1320 B.C.), only Thutmose III (1504–1450 B.C.) reigned more than forty years. Second, the exodus Pharaoh cannot be a first-born son, nor can his firstborn son have reigned after him (see Exodus 11:4-5). Amenhotep II was not the firstborn son of his father (Thutmose III) and the Pharaoh who proceeded him (Thutmose IV) was also not the first-born. Amenhotep II's oldest son, Amenemhat, did not become Pharaoh.

conquest occurred 40 years after the exodus, meaning 1406 B.C. The conquest under Joshua occurred between 1406–1400 B.C. as the conquest of the seven nations took around seven years (Joshua 14:7–10; cf. Deuteronomy 2:14). The Israelites left Egypt in 1446 B.C., but when did they arrive there? The critical passage for the length of the Israelites' sojourn in Egypt is found in Exodus 12:40–41:

> The time that the people of Israel lived in Egypt was 430 years. At the end of 430 years, on that very day, all the hosts of the LORD went out from the land of Egypt.

Moses, the author of the exodus narrative, explicitly states that Israel lived in Egypt for 430 years, giving strong support to the long sojourn position (cf. Ezekiel 4:6-9).[12] There are several reasons to accept the MT reading of Exodus 12:40.[13] Importantly, the MT reading makes sense of the context. In Exodus 12:40, the LXX adds "and in the land of Canaan" after "in Egypt," but chronologically the patriarchs sojourned in Canaan before Jacob came and settled in Egypt. In Genesis 15:13 God said to Abraham: "Know for certain that your offspring will be sojourners in a land that is not theirs and will be servants there, and they will be afflicted for four hundred years." The land not theirs is probably a reference to Egypt and the 400 years is an approximation for the more precise figure of 430 years. In Genesis 15:16, Abraham is told that his descendants will come back to the land "in the fourth generation" ("generation," is probably best taken as 100 years[14]).

The 430 years can be reconciled with other genealogical lists, if we remember that they contain selective genealogizing (cf. Exodus 6:16–20).[15] Although Abraham and his descendants were sojourners (*gûr*) in Canaan

---

12. In Ezekiel 4:6–9 some scholars regard the total number 430 (40 + 390) as a symbolic reference to the nation of Israel's sojourn in Egypt. Ezekiel is looking forward to the possibility of a new exodus for God's people at the end of this period. See John L. Mackay, *Ezekiel* Volume 1: Chapter 1–24 (Scotland: Christian Focus Publications, 2018), p. 172.

13. The short sojourn view is based upon the LXX reading of Exodus 12:40: "And the residing of the sons of Israel during which they resided in the land of Egypt and in the land of Canaan is 430 years." According to the short sojourn position, this encompasses the patriarch's time in Canaan and Egypt, supposing that the sojourn in Egypt only lasted about 215 years (note the LXX does not mention a 215-year sojourn in Egypt preceded by 215 years in the land of Canaan). Nevertheless, the MT has been shown to be the superior witness to the original text, as the discovery of 4Q14Exod at Qumran dates to the first century B.C. and confirms the reading of Exodus 12:40 found in the MT.

14. Kenneth. A Mathews, *Genesis 11:27–50:26: An Exegetical and Theological Exposition of Holy Scripture, New American Commentary* (Nashville, TN: B&H Publishing Group, 2005), p. 174–175.

15. Eugene Merrill, *Kingdom of Priests: A History of Old Testament Israel*, 2nd ed (Grand Rapids, MI: Baker Academic, 2008), p. 95.

and Egypt (Genesis 12:10; 21:34; 26:3), they were not slaves to them or afflicted by them. In fact, they were treated well. The people of Israel, however, were later slaves and afflicted in Egypt (Exodus 3:17, 4:31). The Book of Exodus focuses on the nation of Israel's time in Egypt not upon their earlier time in Canaan, which was to be their future homeland (Exodus 3:8, 17). Even though Egypt (before the Israelites' affliction) had once been a place of great prosperity for the people of Israel (Genesis 47:7, 27), it was always a foreign land for them. The people named in Exodus 12:40 are called the *běnê yiśrā'ēl* (people of Israel; cf. 1 Kings 6:1), and not Hebrews. Abraham was called a Hebrew (Genesis 14:13) but was never called an Israelite. It is Jacob who is given the name "Israel" after he had striven with God (Genesis 32:28). The *běnê yiśrā'ēl* who sojourned in Egypt cannot refer to the patriarchs (Abraham, Isaac), but must refer to the offspring of Jacob (people of Israel) who came and sojourned in Egypt (Genesis 46:5–27; 50:25; Psalm 105:23).[16] Jacob was the father of the 12 patriarchs, the children of Israel (Acts 7:8, 23). These reasons demonstrate that the short sojourn view, based on the LXX, is not acceptable and the MT should be seen as the accurate witness.

The long sojourn (430 years) is also consistent with the Apostle Paul's sermon, which covered the history of Israel, in the synagogue at Antioch:

> The God of this people Israel chose our fathers and made the people great during their stay in the land of Egypt, and with uplifted arm he led them out of it. And for about forty years he put up with them in the wilderness. And after destroying seven nations in the land of Canaan, he gave them their land as an inheritance. All this took about 450 years (Acts 13:17–20).

Even though these verses do not explicitly address the length of the sojourn, they refer to three events: 1) Egyptian sojourn, 2) the 40 years of wandering in the desert, and 3) the conquest of seven nations in Canaan. Paul states that these three events: "took about 450 years" (Acts 13:20).[17] These three

---

16. Williams points out that the mention of the "people of Israel" (Jacob's descendants) in the LXX of Exodus 12:40 helps clarify the meaning of 430 years, that has been misunderstood: "… the idea of a 215-year sojourn in Egypt preceded by 215 years in the land of Canaan finds no justification in the Septuagint. Though it is an ancient view that Paul used the Septuagint in Galatians 3:17, the Septuagint does not say what people assert it says. The Septuagint probably intends to speak of a 30 year stay of Jacob's children in Canaan, before they went down to join Joseph, and thereafter of a 400-year stay by the descendants of Jacob." Peter J. Williams, "Some Remarks Preliminary to a Biblical Chronology," *Creation Ex Nihilo Technical Journal* 12, no. 1 (April 1998), p. 102.

17. Many scholars agree that the 450 years refers specifically to these three events. See Darrell L. Bock, *Acts: Baker Exegetical Commentary on the New Testament* (Grand Rapids, MI:

events together total, with a 430-year sojourn, 476 years. If Paul is rounding down the sojourn to 400 years, as in Genesis 15:16, then the total comes to 446 years. This timeframe fits perfectly with the long sojourn but not with the short sojourn view.[18]

The date of the exodus (1446 B.C.) along with the length of the Israelite sojourn in Egypt (430 years) helps establish the dates for the patriarchal period (2166–1806 B.C.). This means that Jacob (Israel) and all his sons departed from Canaan and entered into Egypt exactly 430 years before the exodus, in 1876 B.C. (Genesis 46:8–27). Archaeological evidence for the family of Jacob being in Egypt at that time is confirmed by Dr Douglas Petrovich's translation of a caption on Sinai 115, composed by Joseph's son Manasseh: "6 Levantines: Hebrews of Bethel, the beloved." Bethel was the home of Jacob (see Genesis 35:1). This places Joseph's son Manasseh in Egypt in 1842 B.C.[19] If the translation is correct, this would make it the world's oldest extrabiblical reference to the Hebrews (Israelites) in Egypt at the time the Bible places them there. This is in the reign of Sesostris III, who dies two years later (1840 B.C.), after a prosperous reign in Egypt. This fits with Jacob having previously blessed the Pharaoh (Genesis 47:7-10), the only reference in Genesis to the blessing of a foreigner by a patriarch.[20] When Jacob appeared before the Pharaoh (Sesostris III), in 1876 B.C., he was 130 years old (Genesis 47:9), and so Jacob was born in 2006 B.C.[21] His father Isaac, was 60 years old at the time of his birth (Genesis 25:26), indicating Isaac was born in 2066 B.C. The destruction of Sodom takes place between the promise to Abraham and Sarah that they would have a son within a year (Genesis 18:14) and the birth of Isaac (Genesis 21:2). This would place it around 2067 B.C. Abraham was 99 when Sodom was destroyed (Genesis 17:1, 21:5, 2067 B.C.), which would place his birth in 2166 B.C. With the birth of Abraham in 2166 B.C., the genealogies in Genesis 5 and 11 give a basis for determining the date for creation and the Flood.

Baker Academic, 2007), p. 452; Ben Witherington III, *The Acts of the Apostles: A Socio-Rhetorical Commentary* (Grand Rapids, MI: W.B. Eerdmans, 1998), p. 410; I Howard Marshall, *Acts* (Leicester, England: InterVarsity Press, 1980), p. 223. R.C.H. Lenski, *The Acts of the Apostles* (Minneapolis, MN: Augsburg Publishing House, 1961), p. 519.

18. In Galatians 3:17, the 430 years is not referring to the initial promise that God made to Abraham, but when the promise of the covenant was "previously ratified" (προκεκυρωμένην) to Jacob before his descent into Egypt (Genesis 46:1–7).

19. Petrovich, *The World's Oldest Alphabet*, p. 15–29.

20. Douglas Petrovich, *Origins of the Hebrews: New Evidence of Israelites in Egypt from Joseph to the Exodus* (Nashville, TN: New Creation, 2021), p. 29.

21. Jacob died in 1859 B.C.; this is the same year that Sesostris III (Pharaoh of the famine) decided to put his son Amenemhat III on the throne as co-regent.

❧ Genesis 5 and 11

In Genesis 5 and 11 we are given chronogenealogies, genealogies that include both time and personal information. For example, Genesis 5:3 states, "When Adam had lived 130 years, he fathered a son in his own likeness, after his image, and named him Seth." Not all biblical genealogies mention the name of the father at the birth of the next name in a list of descent, so they are irrelevant to determining the chronology of Genesis (cf. Matthew 1:8–9). Although some Christians want to assert gaps in the genealogies in Genesis 5 and 11, there are very good arguments against this, as the age of the patriarch is given when the next man is born.[22] The chronogenealogies in Genesis 5 and 11 intend to communicate an unbroken chronology of Adam to Abraham. The formula expressed throughout these chronogenealogies, "When A had lived x years, he fathered (*yālad*) B," indicates the year in which A "fathered" B, the year in which B became the son of A.[23] The phrase "he fathered" in Genesis 5 and 11 cannot be referring to a distant descendant of the patriarch but is referring to a direct physical descendant (cf. 1 Chronicles 1:34).

In Genesis 5 there is a list of 10 names that links the history Adam to the account of Noah. The *tôlĕdōt* heading (literally "This is the book of the generations of Adam," Genesis 5:1) reveals the historical nature of the chapter, giving us details of historical individuals (Genesis 5:1–32). At the beginning of Genesis 5:3, Adam names his son Seth, who is seen as replacement for Abel (Genesis 4:25). Enosh must be a direct son of Seth because Seth named him (Genesis 4:26, 5:6). Toward the end, in Genesis 5:28–29, Lamech names his son Noah, so there cannot be any gaps between father and son in those places. Furthermore, Noah takes his sons Shem, Ham, and Japheth onto the Ark with him (Genesis 5:32, 6:10, 7:13). A no-gap chronology is even implied by the New Testament authors, as Jude, the half-brother of Jesus, tells us, "Enoch, the seventh from Adam" (Jude 14). When Jude said that Enoch was "the seventh from Adam" he counted inclusively beginning with Adam: Adam, Seth, Enosh, Kenan, Mahalalel, Jared, Enoch. The chronogenealogies in Genesis 5 and 11 give sufficient details (e.g., numerical data) in order to establish an accurate chronology. If we combine the time covered in Genesis 5 and 11 (from the MT) with other chronological information in the Bible, then the six days of creation would have occurred around 6,000 years ago. For example, there is roughly 2,000

---

22. For a persuasive analysis and defense of a no-gap chronology in Genesis 5–11, see Terry Mortenson, "When Was Adam Created?" chap. 5, *Searching for Adam*, (Green Forest, AR: Master Books, 2016).

23. See Jeremy Sexton, "Evangelicalism's Search for Chronological Gaps in Genesis 5 and 11: A Historical, Hermeneutical, and Linguisitic Critique," *JETS* 61.1 (2018), p. 5–25.

years from Adam to Abraham; Abraham lived around 2000 B.C. Then from Abraham to Jesus is roughly another 2,000 years, and from Jesus to today is just over 2,000 years, all totaling about 6,000 years. When the chronogenealogies in Genesis 5 and 11 are taken plainly according to the text, the years from Adam to the Flood is 1656 AM (Anno Mundi = year of the world).

Before the rise of uniformitarian geology and biblical criticism in the 19th century, the Church Fathers and Reformers used the genealogies in Genesis 5 and 11 to determine the age of the world.[24] Theophilus (Θεόφιλος, friend of God), bishop of Antioch (died A.D. 181) discussed the history of the Old Testament from the beginning of the world to his own day, specifically focusing on the genealogies of Genesis 5 and 11. In particular, he argues, "All the years from the creation of the world [to Theophilus's day] amount to a total of 5,698 years" (*Ad Autolyc.* 3:28).[25] Interestingly, Theophilus goes on to write about the chronology of the world set forth by the philosophers Apollonius (Egyptian) and Plato (Greek):

> For some, maintaining that the world was uncreated, went into infinity; and others, asserting that it was created, said that already 153,075 years had passed.... For if even a chronological error has been committed by us, of, e.g., 50 or 100, or even 200 years, yet not of thousands and tens of thousands, as Plato and Apollonius and other mendacious authors have hitherto written. (*Ad Autolyc.* 3:16, 29)

Theophilus rejected the long ages for the world that the Egyptians and the Greeks proposed, clearly regarding the genealogies in Genesis 5 and 11 as accurate and authoritative when it came to the age of the world. The conflict over the age of the earth is not new — it has always been a debate between pagans and Christians (until, that is, Christians in the early 19th century started to believe what non-Christian geologists said about the age of the creation rather than believing God's Word).

It is interesting that the ages of the pre-Flood patriarchs at death are somewhat close to each other. Enoch is the exception. He did not die, as "Enoch walked with God, and he was not, for God took him" (Genesis 5:24).

Genesis 5 ends with Noah and his three sons: Shem, Ham, and Japheth (Genesis 5:32). The account of Noah and his three sons is picked up in Genesis 6. Because of the wickedness of mankind, God warns Noah that He is going to destroy the world through a global Flood (Genesis 6:11–13, 7:19; cf. 2 Peter 2:5, 3:6). By God's grace Noah and his family survive the Flood

---

24. The French Reformer John Calvin (1509–1564) believed that the world had not yet "completed its six thousandth year...." Calvin, *Institutes of the Christian Religion*, p. 90.
25. Theophilus came to this date for creation because he was using the chronology of the Greek translation of the Old Testament, the Septuagint (LXX).

Adam's *tôledot* Gen. 5:1–32	Age at begetting next in line	Age at Death
1. Adam	130	930
2. Seth	105	912
3. Enosh	90	905
4. Kenan	70	910
5. Mahalalel	65	895
6. Jared	162	962
7. Enoch	65	Did not die (God took him)
8. Methuselah	187	969
9. Lamech	182	777
10. Noah	500	950 (Genesis 9:29)

through the provision of the Ark (Genesis 6:18, 7:1). Noah was 600 years old when the Flood waters came upon the earth and 601 when he came out of the Ark (Genesis 7:6, 8:13–15). Now in the new world Noah is given the same creation mandate as Adam and Eve: "Be fruitful and multiply and fill the earth" (Genesis 9:1). Genesis 9:19 states that from Noah's three sons "the people of the whole earth were dispersed."

The genealogy in Genesis 10 (the table of nations) gives the details of that verse as it specifically deals with the descendants of Noah's three sons, Shem, Ham, and Japheth, who spread out across the earth after the Flood (Genesis 10:1, 5, 32). It was from the three sons of Noah that all the nations of the earth emerged; their spreading out over the whole earth was a consequence of God's intervention after they had disobeyed God's initial command to spread across the earth (Genesis 11:9). Genesis 10:1 begins by listing Noah's sons, "Shem, Ham, and Japheth" (cf. Genesis 5:32, 6:10, 9:18). However, the table of nations reverses this structure beginning with Japheth (Genesis 10:2–5). It places the dispersion at Babel between Shem's genealogies and shows that the Babel incident caused the division of languages (Genesis 10:21–31, 11:10–26).[26] The actual time of the division of the nations most likely took place around the end of Peleg's life, as it was in his day that "the earth was divided" (Genesis 10:25; cf. 11:19).[27]

---

26. Mathews, *Genesis 1:1–11:26*, p. 439.
27. The division of the nations connects well with the dispersion and confusion of the languages at Babel, and probably occurred around 340 years (five generations) after the event of the global Flood, at the end of Peleg's life. See Andrew Sibley, "Dating the Tower of Babel Events with Reference to Peleg and Joktan," *Journal of Creation* 31(1) 2017, p. 80–87.

After covering the event of man's disobedience at the Tower of Babel (Genesis 11:1–9), Genesis 11 shifts its focus to "the generations of Shem," which covers a large section of patriarchal history (Genesis 11:10–37:1). The purpose of the chronogenealogy is to not only show structure after a time of confusion but that not even the rebellion at Babel can stop God's purposes being thwarted. God preserves the line of Seth through whom the promise would be fulfilled (cf. Genesis 3:15).[28]

Shem's descendants Gen. 11:10–26[29]	Age at begetting next in line	Age at Death
1. Shem	100	600
2. Arpachshad	35	438
3. Shelah	30	433
4. Eber	34	464
5. Peleg	30	239
6. Reu	32	239
7. Serug	30	230
8. Nahor	29	148
9. Terah	70	205

By adding up the numbers of the ages from Shem to Terah in the MT, when the first son was born, we can establish that Abraham was born around 352 years after the Flood (see Genesis 11:10–26). This considers that Abraham was born when Terah was 130 years old (not 70). This can be seen from the fact that Abraham was 75 when he left Haran (Genesis 12:4), which took place after Terah had died (Acts 7:4) at the age of 205 (Genesis 11:32). Abraham is not Terah's first-born son but is mentioned first in Genesis 11:26 because he is most important in the narrative to follow.[30] This is similar to the preceding chapter where Shem, Ham, and Japheth are listed (Genesis 10:1) in an order unrelated to their age (Ham was the youngest son of Noah, Genesis 9:24). Since Abraham was born 352 years after the Flood in 2166 B.C., this would place the date of the Flood around 2518 B.C., and the date for creation around 4174 B.C. (2518 + 1656 = 4174 B.C., see chart above).

28. Sailhamer, The Pentateuch as Narrative, p. 136.
29. In Genesis 11 the Septuagint includes an extra Cainan, but the name was probably not in the original autographs. See Jonathan Sarfati, The Genesis Account: A Theological, Historical, and Scientific Commentary on Genesis 1–11 (Georgia, USA: Creation Book Publishers, 2015), p. 679, 684.
30. Mathews, Genesis 1:1–11:26, 499n34.

Although the structure of the genealogy in Genesis 11 is like the one in Genesis 5 there is a notable difference. The ages of the post-Flood descendants of Noah have started to rapidly decline. Science may shed some light on the decline of the long lifespans. Adam and Eve were created in a "very good" world (Genesis 1:31) with no genetic mutations; Adam's descendants in Genesis 5 would have only a few harmful mutations allowing them to live long lives. Because Noah had children at an older age (500, Genesis 5:32) we can reason that he would have passed on more mutations to Shem.[31] There also would have been an exponential decay with the population bottleneck after the global Flood (only eight people got on board the Ark, 1 Peter 3:20), leading to progressively shorter lifespans.

☆ Genesis 5 and 11 vs the Sumerian King List

An objection to taking the pre/post Flood lifespans naturally is that other ANE literature has people living for many thousands of years. For example, the Sumerian King List (SKL), with great exaggeration, lists the antediluvian regnal periods (8 kings) as ranging from 43,200 years to 18,600 years, but the postdiluvian regnal years (23 kings) range from 1,560 years to 140 years. However, the last seven reigns of the 23 kings are 1,200 years, 140 years, 305 years, 900 years, 1,200 years, 900 years, and 625 years. There is no similarity in the decay curve between the SKL and Genesis 11. Furthermore, the SKL gives the years of the king's reigns, not lifespans, and it does not include the Sumerian first man or the flood hero. Unless one rejects these long ages a priori (i.e., SKL), then this longevity surely rests on some objective historical basis (cf. Genesis 5:1–32, 11:10–32). The history of the lifespans of the patriarchs are presented to us truthfully in Scripture, but is unreliably echoed in history among other pagan ANE cultures (cf. 2 Peter 1:16, 20–21).

Many scholars today reinterpret the Genesis genealogies because they prioritize ANE evidence over the clear testimony of Scripture. To reject the long lifespans of the post-pre-Flood people because of ANE parallels is clearly a rejection of the supremacy of Scripture when it comes to interpreting the data (cf. 2 Timothy 3:16). If our interpretation of Scripture is controlled by ANE culture, then it is being controlled by a higher authority. ANE culture may illuminate our understanding of the biblical text, but it does not dictate its meaning. The only way to consistently maintain the inerrancy and supreme authority of Scripture is by using Scripture to interpret Scripture. The problem with using ANE literature is that it does not explain, but tries to explain

---

31. Robert Carter, "Patriarchal Drive in the Early Post- Flood Population," *J. Creation* 33(1):110–118, 2019.

away, the specific long lifespans of the patriarchs. The fact of the matter is that there is no convincing symbolic or honorific interpretation of those who lived pre/post Flood or of the lifespans of the patriarchs (see below).

🌿 The History and Lifespans of the Patriarchs

In Genesis 11:27 a new family history begins with the *tôlĕdōt* of Terah, which will concentrate on only one of his sons, Abram. God will later change Abram's name to Abraham (Genesis 17:5). Abraham was born around 2166 B.C. in Ur, northwest Mesopotamia, in modern-day Turkey (Genesis 11:28–32; 24:4, 10).[32] Abraham and his family served various other gods when they lived in Ur (Joshua 24:2). When Abraham lived in Ur, God appeared to him and called him to go to the land of Canaan so that he could worship Him there (Genesis 11:28; Acts 7:2–3; cf. Nehemiah 9:7). Before he went to Canaan, he lived in Haran until his father died and then God removed him from there into Canaan (Acts 7:4). God promised to make Abraham a great nation and that all the families on earth would be blessed in him: "I will bless those who bless you, and him who dishonors you I will curse, and in you all the families of the earth shall be blessed." (Genesis 12:3; cf. Galatians 3:8). It is significant that God calls Abraham after the rebellion at Babel. The people who rebelled at Babel tried to make a name (*šēm*) for themselves (Genesis 11:4), but it is God who promises to make Abraham's name (*šēm*) great (Genesis 12:2).

Abraham was 75 years old (2091 B.C.) when he left Haran to go to the land of Canaan (Genesis 12:4). When Abraham had lived in Canaan for 10 years, because his wife Sarah was still barren, he and his Egyptian servant Hagar conceived Ishmael (Genesis 16:3–4). Fourteen years later, when he was 99 years old, God made a covenant of circumcision with Abraham (Genesis 17:1, 24). Abraham was 100 years old when his son Isaac was born (Genesis 21:5; cf. Romans 4:19). After Sarah's death, Abraham is described as being "old, well advanced in years" (Genesis 24:1; cf. Joshua 23:2), this was because God had blessed (*bārak*) him in all things (Genesis 24:1; cf. 27, 31, 35, 48, 60); old age was a sign of God's blessing (cf. Job 42:12). Abraham was 175 years old when he "died in a good old age, an old man and full

---

32. There is debate as to where Ur is located: southern Mesopotamia in modern-day Iraq (Sumerian) or a city in Haran, northwest Mesopotamia, in modern-day Turkey (Hurrian). There are good reasons to believe Abraham's Ur is in northwest Mesopotamia. For example, when Abraham sent his servant to find a wife for his son Isaac, he told him to "go to my country and to my kindred" (Genesis 24:4), and the servant went "to Mesopotamia to the city of Nahor" (Genesis 24:10). The city Nahor is located near Haran (cf. Genesis 11:24, 11:31–32). See Mathews, *Genesis 1–11:26*, p. 498.

of years" (Genesis 25:7–8). The description "old age" (*bĕśêbâ ṭôbâ*) is used of God's promise to Abraham of long life (Genesis 15:15). Altogether, Abraham lived in the land of Canaan for 100 years and saw his grandchildren's 15th birthday (Genesis 12:4; 21:4; 25:20, 26).

The Egyptian Pharaoh Shoshenq I (Shishak, 1 Kings 11:40, 14:25), invaded the land of Judah/Israel around 925/926 b.c. When he returned to Egypt, he had inscribed on the temple wall at Karnak a list of the places he conquered in his campaign into Canaan. One of those names says it was the fort (or enclosure) of Abraham that he conquered, in a region near the Negev (cf. Genesis 12:1, 13:1, 20:1). This is the only ancient inscription that mentions Abraham.[33]

While he was in Canaan (Negev), Abraham became the father of Isaac when he was 100 years old (2066 b.c.). Isaac was Abraham's unique son, the son of the promise (Genesis 22:2; Hebrews 11:17). In one of the most important accounts in the Old Testament, God tested Abraham's faith by calling him to build an altar on Mount Moriah and offer Isaac upon it (Genesis 22:1–2, 9). This is the same place where the temple of the LORD was built (2 Chronicles 3:1) and the place where king David was told to build an altar to the LORD (1 Chronicles 21:18). Abraham's altar, king David's altar, and King Solomon's temple were all built in the same place, on top of Mount Moriah. After the temple's destruction (587 b.c.) by the Babylonians, Zerubbabel also rebuilt the temple on its original site, Mount Moriah (Ezra 6:7). It was on Mount Moriah that God provided Abraham a ram to sacrifice instead of Isaac (Genesis 22:13–14; Hebrews 11:17–19). When Isaac was 40 years old (2026 b.c.) he married Rebekah (Genesis 25:20) and was 60 years old when the twin boys Esau and Jacob were born (Genesis 25:26). When Isaac, at 136 years old, blessed Jacob, "his eyes were dim so that he could not see" (Genesis 27:1). Poor vision was a sign of old age (see Genesis 48:10). Isaac is described as "old and full of days" when he died at 180 years old (Genesis 35:28–29).

Isaac's son Jacob was born in Beer-lahai-roi (Canaan) (Genesis 25:10–11, 26), after obtaining the "birthright" from his brother Esau, went and lived in Haran for 20 years, marrying two wives, obtaining two concubines, and having 12 sons (Genesis 28:1–31:55; 49:1-27). Later in his life, because of a famine, Jacob went down to Egypt (Genesis 46:5–7). When Joseph presented his father Jacob in front of Pharaoh, the Pharaoh said to Jacob:

> "How many are the days of the years of your life?" And Jacob said to Pharaoh, "The days of the years of my sojourning are 130

33. See "Abraham-The Top Ten Archaeological Discoveries: Digging for Truth Episode 141," August 26th, 2021, Associates for Biblical Research. https://www.youtube.com/watch?v=N4262VGxCYU&t=80s

years. Few and evil have been the days of the years of my life, and they have not attained to the days of the years of the life of my fathers in the days of their sojourning" (Genesis 47:8–9).

Clearly, Pharaoh did not see Jacob's age in an honorific sense, as his question only makes sense if he really was 130 years old. An Egyptian's "ideal age" was 110 years old, so to surpass that would be considered a divine blessing. Jacob's fathers were Abraham who lived 175 years (Genesis 25:7) and Isaac who lived 180 years (Genesis 35:28). Jacob would live another 17 years, as he died at 147 years old (Genesis 47:28; cf. 49:33).

When Jacob and his family settled in the "land of Rameses" (Avaris), they became property owners (Genesis 47:11). In an Asiatic (Semitic) settlement (c. 1876–1560 B.C.) that was discovered at Avaris (Tell el-Dab'a), there is a monumental tomb where archaeologists found fragments of a colossal statue of an Asiatic dignitary that had been broken up. The statue had been deliberately destroyed and defaced. The original statue of the seated official was 150% of life size, approximately 2 m high, made of limestone and carved by Egyptian sculptors. This Asiatic man has a red mushroom-shaped hairstyle, yellow painted skin (traditional color of an Asiatic in Egyptian artwork), a long multi-colored cloak (red, white, and black stripes) which is non-Egyptian, and a throw stick (the Egyptian hieroglyph for a foreigner) held against his right shoulder. There is no name on the statue to identify the person, but the size of the statue indicates a person of great importance. Although some have suggested that this is Joseph, a more plausible explanation is that it is Jacob, the patriarch of the family. The clothing on the statue and its color are Asiatic; Joseph was clothed in Egyptian garments of fine linen (Genesis 41:42). The hairstyle on the statue is distinctly Asiatic; Joseph's hairstyle would have almost certainly been Egyptian given that his brothers did not recognize him when they saw him (Genesis 42:8). Also, a fragment of the statue's base shows that it was inscribed with the Egyptian word *sntr* = incense (a word used on funerary inscriptions), which signifies death. The statue was apparently built to commemorate a dead person. The style of the fragments that come from this statue are in harmony with statuary that came from a facility that produced statues during the reign of Amenemhat III, who came onto the throne the year Jacob died (1859 B.C.).[34] It makes perfect sense that the statue is made to honor Jacob, who was not buried in Avaris but in Canaan (Genesis 47:29–30, 49:28–30).[35]

Jacob's son Joseph was born in Paddan-aram (Mesopotamia) (Genesis 35:24–26) around 1915 B.C. When Joseph was 17, he was sold by his

34. Joseph was still alive during the reign of Amenemhat III and lived beyond him.
35. Petrovich, *Origins of the Hebrews*, p. 46–49; 92–93.

Statue of An Asiatic Man: Image courtesy of Dr. Douglas Petrovich. Copyright 2021 by David E. Graves.

brothers and taken as a slave to Egypt around 1898 B.C. (Genesis 37:2–28). At age 30 Joseph married Asenath, the daughter of Potiphera, and became the second most powerful ruler in the land of Egypt (Genesis 41:45–47). Petrovich translates an inscription (found at Wadi Nasb and dated to 1772 B.C.) on Sinai 376: "The house of the vineyard of Asenath and its innermost room were engraved. They have come to life."[36] If this is the same Asenath (Genesis 41:45, 46:20), it would be a posthumous reference to Joseph's wife, and another piece of evidence that confirms that the Israelites were in Egypt the time the Bible places them there.

The narrative in Genesis portrays Joseph (1915–1805 B.C.) serving as Egypt's vizier (chief administrator) in the court of native Egyptian rulership, not Semitic (Hyksos, "Shepherd Kings" or "Rulers of Foreign Countries"), most likely in their Twelfth Dynasty. Many of the features of Joseph's lifespan reflect this setting: 1) the personal names are Egyptian: Potiphar, Asenath, Zaphenath-paneah (Joseph's Semitic name would not have been changed to an Egyptian name under a Hyksos ruler — Genesis 39:1; 41:45); 2) Joseph shaves himself before seeing Pharaoh, an Egyptian custom not a Semitic one (Genesis 41:14); 3) the embalming process was an Egyptian practice

---

36. Petrovich, *The World's Oldest Alphabet*, p. 65–74.

(Genesis 50:2–3); 4) assuming that Joseph was Egyptian, his brothers spoke Hebrew to one another when they first met him (Genesis 42:23), something they would not do if they supposed he was Hyksos;[37] and 5) Joseph married the daughter of Potiphera priest of On (Heliopolis), as arranged by the Pharaoh (Genesis 41:45). The city of On was the center for the worship of the sun-god Re. Although the Hyksos did not stop the worship of Re, their primary deity of worship was Seth (or Set). If Joseph had lived during the Hyksos period, then he probably would have been given a wife from the family priest of Seth, and not Re.[38]

Those who seek to place Joseph during the reign of the Hyksos (c. 1668–1560 B.C.)[39] offer a couple of arguments for this.

First, it is argued that Hyksos introduced the chariot to Egypt, which makes sense of Genesis 41:43 where both Pharaoh and Joseph are riding in chariots. However, although the Hyksos may have introduced the chariot to Egypt, it was used for war. The chariot given to Joseph by Pharaoh in Genesis 41:43 was not for war. It would not be strange for Egyptian high officials to have chariots in the Twelfth Dynasty under a native Egyptian Pharaoh. In fact, the passage indicates that chariots were a rarity, as the one given to Joseph is called Pharaoh's "second chariot." The implication is that chariots were not common in Egypt, as the only other person who had one was Pharaoh, who outranked Joseph.[40]

Second, it is argued that the Hyksos rule from their capital Avaris (Goshen) in the delta region harmonizes with Joseph placing his father to live in Goshen/land of Rameses (Genesis 45:10, 47:5–11). However, the narrative in Genesis seems to suggest that Goshen is in a part of Egypt other than where the Pharaoh and Joseph lived (see Genesis 45:10, 46:29–31). The narrative in Genesis also has Joseph acting as an intermediary on behalf of his brothers and father when they arrive in Egypt, explaining their customs to Pharaoh and telling his family how to respond to him (Genesis 46:28–34). If the Pharaoh was Hyksos, then it would seem unnecessary for Joseph to have to arrange a diplomatic meeting to introduce his Semitic family to him. The rulers of Egypt in Joseph's day show contempt and prejudice for Semitic visitors to Egypt (Genesis 43:32, 46:34), rather than the cordiality that surely would have been shown to them by Hyksos rulers, who were Semitic settlers.[41]

---

37. Merrill, *Kingdom of Priests*, p. 66–70.
38. Charles F. Aling, *Egypt and Bible History* (Grand Rapids MI: Baker, 1981), p. 45–46.
39. The Turin Royal Canon has the Hyksos ruling for 108 years from their capital at Avaris (c. 1668–1560 B.C.).
40. Charles F. Aling, "Joseph in Egypt — Part IV," *Bible and Spade*, 16 (Winter, 2003), p. 12.
41. Duane Garrett, *A Commentary on Exodus* (Grand Rapids, MI: Kregel Publications, 2014), p. 79.

The narrative in Genesis reveals that Joseph became the second-most powerful man in Egypt (Genesis 41:40). Joseph became Egypt's vizier around 1885 B.C. Petrovich has identified Joseph with Sobekemhat.[42] This was the high official who appointed Ephraim (Di-Sobekemhat) to the position of ruler of Retjenu (the title the Egyptians ascribed to people from Canaan) over the community at Avaris by year 4 of Amenemhat III. This keeps with Joseph's promise to provide for his family (Genesis 50:21). Sobekemhat was buried in an elaborate tomb (mastaba) with various extravagant grave goods. His tomb at Dahshur was built closest to Sesostris III's pyramid, indicating he was the first vizier in his reign. The main burial chamber in the tomb was robbed out in antiquity, which is consistent with the Israelites removing Joseph's remains at the time of the exodus (Exodus 13:19). It seems Joseph served during the reigns of Sesostris II (the abundance Pharaoh) and Sesostris III (the famine Pharaoh).[43]

The specific chronological details regarding Joseph's age help establish the length of his time in Egypt, as Mathews notes:

> The time period between the sale of Joseph (37:2a) and the family's final descent into Egypt (46:1–7) is twenty-two years (Joseph's thirteen yrs. in Egypt (37:2a; 41:46) + seven yrs. of plenty (41:46–49) + two yrs. of famine (45:6–7). Joseph's death at one hundred ten years (50:22, 26) meant he lived ninety-three years in Egypt.[44]

Joseph died at 110 years old (Genesis 50:22, 26; cf. Joshua 24:29), the ideal lifespan for the Egyptian people. But that does not mean Joseph's age at death was any less literal (cf. Matthew 4:1–2; Deuteronomy 8:2–4).[45] In the blessing of old age, Joseph "saw the third generation of Ephraim's

---

42. How do we reconcile this with the Egyptian name that Joseph is given in Genesis 41:45 (Zaphenath-paneah)? Petrovich argues: "Including Joseph's Hebrew name, he apparently had at least five names during his lifetime: (1) He-who-is-called, "He-who-has-set-life-in-order" (Zaphenath-paneah), (2) Son-of-the-god-who-provides-for-Egypt-through-the-life-giving-waters-of-the-Nile (Sa-Sobek), (3) The-king-of-the-gods-is-at-the-forefront (Horemhat) Jr., (4) The-god-who-provides-for-Egypt-through-the-life-giving-waters-of-the-Nile-is-at-the-forefront) (Sobekemhat), and (5) He-increases (Joseph), the Hebrew name that Rachel gave him at birth (Genesis 30:24). Given that every Egyptian king possessed at least five names, seeing Joseph with five names presents no valid objections for anyone trained well in Egyptology or ANE history." Petrovich, *Origins of the Hebrews*, p. 93.

43. Petrovich, *Origins of the Hebrews*, p. 64-73, 94.

44. Mathews, *Genesis 11:27–50:26*, p. 687, footnote 63.

45. Just because a number is used symbolically in some parts of the text does not mean it is not literal in other parts of the text. Jesus' 40 days and nights in the wilderness is parallel to Israel's 40 years of wandering in the wilderness.

children" (Genesis 50:23), referring to his great grandchildren or possibly his great-great grandchildren.[46] This would only be possible if Joseph's age at death is taken naturally.

Moses ends the Book of Genesis with the Hebrew word בְּמִצְרָיִם, which literally means "in Egypt" (Genesis 50:26). By ending Genesis this way, Moses provides the setting for the Book of Exodus. The opening words of Exodus in the MT are וְאֵלֶּה שְׁמוֹת — "And these are the names...."[47] The fact that the text begins this way emphasizes "that the book of Exodus continues the Genesis narrative."[48] Exodus continues the account of God's dealing with the descendants of Jacob (Israel) in the Book of Genesis. It picks up the history of Israel after a silent period of around 275 years (Exodus 12:41). Moses breaks that silence by recounting two important facts: (1) the nation of Israel had experienced tremendous growth (Exodus 1:7); and (2) the Israelites were no longer favored by the Egyptians but were made slaves by a king who did not know Joseph (Exodus 1:8–11). The impressive growth of the Israelites from 70 persons (Exodus 1:5; cf. Genesis 46:27) to a number large enough (Exodus 12:37; Numbers 1:45–46; cf. Psalm 105:24) to concern Pharaoh was the result of providential blessing and protection (Exodus 1:7; cf. Genesis 1:28). This fulfilled God's promise to Jacob (see Genesis 46:3).

The detailed description of the patriarchs ages at crucial moments in their lives are meaningless if they are taken as honorific or symbolically. There is no objective reason to reject the long lifespans of the patriarchs. The only reason to do that is if you are trying to adapt the biblical text to fit with a particular theory (i.e., evolution, ANE conceptual worldview). The fact that Moses continuously highlights the specific years of the patriarchs at key events in their lives precludes taking them in a symbolic or honorific sense. The long lifespans of the patriarchs are distributed throughout Genesis 12–50, not in chronological genealogies (i.e., Genesis 5:1–32, 11:10–26) and show that they should be understood as natural ages that are on the decline.

Those who do not accept the long life spans of the patriarchs raise supposed problems as to why they should not be taken plainly (literally). First, there is a supposed lack of intergenerational contact between the post-Flood people in the Genesis narrative.[49] Second, is that "Noah would thus have been a contemporary of Abraham, and Shem would have even outlived

46. The MT reads great-great grandchildren whereas the variants in the LXX and SP read great grandchildren.

47. The Greek translation of the Old Testament (LXX) gave the book the title *exodou* "a way out," apparently based on Exodus 19:1.

48. T. Desmond Alexander, *Exodus* (Apollos: London, 2017), p. 36.

49. Steven Collins, "Tall el-Hammam is Still Sodom: Critical Data-Sets Cast Serious Doubt on E.H. Merrill's Chronological Analysis," *Biblical Research Bulletin* 13, 2013 no. 1: 17–18.

Abraham by thirty-five years...."[50] Actually, Shem does not outlive Abraham (this assumes Abraham was born when his father Terah was 70 years old and not 130 years old, see page 103). But these reasons are not a problem with the text but is more to do with how modern scholars have been taught to think about the long lifespans of the patriarchs. Why is it rather odd that Shem and Abraham would be contemporaries?[51] There is no objective reason as to why this could not have been the case (Shem died in 2016 B.C., preceding Abraham by 25 years, 1991 B.C., Genesis 11:10–11; 25:7). Shem lived to 600 years (Genesis 11:10–11), and he was 100 years old when he fathered Arpachshad (Genesis 11:10). Abraham was born 350 years after Arpachshad (making Shem 450 years), and Abraham died at 175 years; this means that Shem died 25 years before Abraham.

As well as being unnecessary to the author's purpose, there is a valid reason why we do not hear of intergenerational contact between the post-Flood people (Shem, Eber; Genesis 10:21)[52] who overlapped with the patriarchs. Many of the patriarchs lived in different areas of the ancient world (Ur, Haran, Canaan, Paddan-aram, Egypt), therefore making contact difficult, infrequent, and even unnecessary. But even if there had been contact, what would be the reason for Moses to record such an event? There is none. After Genesis 11, Moses does not need to refer to Shem, as he is the one who connects the pre-Flood history (Genesis 5:32, 11:11) with the patriarchal narrative (Genesis 12–50), which occupies the remainder of Genesis. Shem (*šēm*) whose name means "Name" looks forward to the man whom God would promise a "great name" (*ăgaddēlâ šěmekā*), Abraham. Abraham and his descendants are now the focus of God's redemptive history in Genesis 12–50.

The specific ages of certain Old Testament persons agree with the lifespans and life events of the patriarchs. For example, after his restoration "Job lived 140 years, and saw his sons, and his sons' sons, four generations" (Job 42:16). Modern scholars struggle with the long lifespans of the patriarchs, and the post-Flood people, because of an assumption that people cannot live that long (which is influenced by evolutionary thinking). It is true that people do not live as long today (cf. Psalm 90:10), but this does not mean that it has always been that way as the witness of Scripture testifies against this.

---

50. Craig, *In Quest of the Historical Adam*, p. 130.
51. The LXX and SP add 100 years to the ages of patriarchs from Arpachshad to Serug at the firstborn's birth. This may have been done in order to distance Abraham from Shem.
52. Shem and Eber may be singled out in Genesis 10:21 because they are the two oldest living ancestors of Abraham, who is known as a Hebrew (עִבְרִי; Genesis 14:13) the gentilic form of Eber (עֵבֶר).

Basic Old Testament Chronological Scheme	
4174 B.C.	Creation
2518 B.C.	The Flood
2166 B.C.	Birth of Abram
2091 B.C.	Abram leaves Haran to go to Canaan
2067 B.C.	Destruction of Sodom
1876 B.C.	Jacob moved to Egypt
1446 B.C.	Exodus from Egypt
1406 B.C.	Israelites crossed into Canaan
967 B.C.	Construction of Solomon's Temple
587 B.C.	Jerusalem fell to the Babylonians
445 B.C.	Nehemiah rebuilds the city walls of Jerusalem

✠ Adam, Jesus, and the Canon of Scripture

The history and theology of Adam is not only important in understanding the chronology of the Old Testament but also for the Canon of the New Testament.

We may not think about this very much, but how would first-century Jewish people have viewed the ending of the Old Testament (Hebrew Scriptures)? Did they think it was a complete account? No, the Jewish people of that time did not view the redemptive account of the Old Testament as being complete, but as awaiting completion. As theologian N.T. Wright observes, "The great story of the Hebrew Scriptures was … inevitably read in the Second Temple period as a story in search of a conclusion."[53] It was not until after the death, resurrection, and ascension of Israel's promised Messiah (Jesus Christ) that the conclusion to the great redemptive account of the Old Testament was eventually written down (A.D. 40–90) in the New Covenant documents and read among God's people (cf. 2 Corinthians 3:6; 2 Thessalonians 2:15, 3:14; Revelation 1:11).[54]

There is good reason to believe that the threefold canonical structure of the Old Testament, the Law (Torah), the Prophets (Nevi'im), and the Writings (Ketuvim), was established by the time of Jesus (see Luke 24:44). In Jesus' day, the last book of the Old Testament probably would not have

---

53. N.T. Wright, *The New Testament and the People of God* (Minneapolis, MN: Fortress Press, 1992), p. 217.
54. There is a link between the concept of covenant and written texts being read to God's people (Exodus. 24:7; Deuteronomy 4:13–14).

been Malachi but rather Chronicles, as several scholars have argued.[55] In fact, Jesus' own words point to Chronicles being the last book of the Old Testament:

> Therefore also the Wisdom of God said, "I will send them prophets and apostles, some of whom they will kill and persecute," so that the blood of all the prophets, shed from the foundation of the world, may be charged against this generation, from the blood of Abel to the blood of Zechariah, who perished between the altar and the sanctuary. Yes, I tell you, it will be required of this generation (Luke 11:49–51; cf. Matthew 23:35).

There is good reason to believe that the Zechariah Jesus mentions (in both Luke and Matthew's Gospel) is the martyr "Zechariah son of Jehoiada" from 2 Chronicles 24:20–22. Jesus would be paralleling the first martyr, Abel (Genesis 4:8), with the last person martyred in the final book in the Old Testament, Zechariah (2 Chronicles 24:22). Interestingly, in his commentary on Matthew's Gospel, New Testament scholar John Nolland has noted:

> The dying words of the priest Zechariah in 2 Chronicles 24:22 ("May Yahweh hear and avenge") … match the blood of Abel crying out from the Ground (Gen 4:10). If the right Zechariah has been identified, then the Gospel tradition is probably the earliest indication that, as was true later, 2 Chronicles was placed last in the Hebrew Bible.[56]

To end the Old Testament with the Book of Chronicles would have been very telling. Even though Israel had been brought back from the Babylonian exile into the Promised Land, as Ezra and Nehemiah attest, ending the Old Testament with Chronicles was basically a way of saying that the return from exile was a physical one, but not a spiritual one. God was not finished with Israel; they were still awaiting their ultimate redemption through their promised Messiah. This would have put the first-century Jewish people in a state of anticipation that God's Davidic King was still on his way (Luke 2:25, 38; John 1:41). Seeing Chronicles as the last book of the Old Testament is also significant, as it would mean that the Old Testament begins and ends

---

55. Roger T. Beckwith, *The Old Testament Canon of the New Testament Church and Its Background in Early Judaism* (Eugene, OR: Wipf and Stock, 2008), p. 110–180; Michael J. Kruger, *The Question of Canon: Challenging the Status Quo in the New Testament Debate* (Westmont, IL: InterVarsity Press, 2013), p. 47–77.
56. John Nolland, *The Gospel of Matthew: A Commentary in the Greek Text*, New International Greek Testament Commentary (Grand Rapids, MI: Eerdmans, 2005), p. 947.

with a focus on Adam (Genesis 2:4–3:24, 5:1; 1 Chronicles 1:1). Chronicles was written to the Israelites who returned from the Babylonian exile in the sixth and fifth centuries. For the people who returned from exile, the genealogies in the opening chapters represented the deed of their identity. The purpose, then, of placing Adam at the beginning of Israel's genealogical record is so that "Israel could arrive at an accurate self-perception only by understanding its place in relationship to the first parents and, indeed, to creation itself."[57] Chronicles begins with Adam but focuses on the Davidic reign. Chronicles is a fitting end to the Old Testament because it is still expecting the Davidic King, putting the reader in anticipation of the one who will redeem God's people. This was ultimately fulfilled in the person of our Lord Jesus Christ (Matthew 21:5). It is fitting then that Matthew's Gospel starts with a genealogy focused on David (Matthew 1:2–17), as the only other book in the Bible to start with a genealogy and have a Davidic focus is Chronicles (1 Chronicles 3:1–24).[58]

The theological importance of Adam to the narrative of the New Testament is seen in the opening verse of Matthew's Gospel: "The book of the genealogy of Jesus Christ, the son of David, the son of Abraham" (Matthew 1:1). The words "the book of the genealogy" (Βίβλος γενέσεως, *Biblos geneseōs*) occur only twice in the Greek translation of the Old Testament (LXX), in Genesis 2:4 and 5:1. In their massive technical commentary on the Gospel of Matthew, critical New Testament scholars W.D. Davies and Dale Allison understand Matthew 1:1 to be the title for the entire gospel, in which case γένεσις (genesis) means either "history" or "genesis."[59] Davies and Allison interpret Matthew 1:1 to mean "Book of the New Genesis wrought by Jesus Christ, son of David, Son of Abraham." Commenting on the significance of the words "the book of the generations," they state:

> Gen. 5:1–32 ... recounts in addition the creation of Adam and Eve.... So for those acquainted with the Greek version of Genesis, Βίβλος γενέσεως would likely have brought to mind more than the genealogical table of Adam. It would probably have sent thoughts back to the primeval history in general. This in turn suggests that Matthew might have opened his gospel as he did in order to draw a parallel between one beginning and another beginning, between the

57. Eugene H. Merrill, *Everlasting Dominion: A Theology of the Old Testament* (Nashville, TN: B&H Academic, 2006), p. 167.

58. Michael Kruger, *The Question of Canon: Challenging the Status Quo in the New Testament Debate* (Nottingham: InterVarsity Press, 2013), p. 147–154.

59. W.D. Davies and Dale C. Allison Jr., *Matthew 1–7: International Critical Commentary* (Edinburgh, UK: T&T Clark, 2004), p. 153.

creation of the cosmos and Adam and Eve on the one hand and the new creation brought by the Messiah on the other.[60]

The Gospel of Matthew begins by presenting us with the coming of the last Adam, Jesus the Messiah. Just as the Old Testament begins and ends with Adam, so the New Testament begins (Mark 1:1; John 1:1–3) and ends with the last Adam (Revelation 1–22). The New Testament authors clearly saw the coming of Jesus as corresponding to the creation account in Genesis 1 (John 1:1–5; 2 Corinthians 4:5–6). The Apostle Paul even tells us that those who have been reconciled to God (the Father) through the redemptive work of the last Adam are "new creations" (2 Corinthians 5:17; Galatians 6:15). It is necessary to understand the first Adam before we can properly understand the "last Adam," as the New Testament intentionally ties the two together (see Luke 3:23–38; Romans 5:12–21; 1 Corinthians 15:21–22, 45). The first Adam was supernaturally given life by God, but through his disobedience, he brought death into the world, and the whole creation was cursed (Genesis 2:7, 17, 3:17). But the last Adam came supernaturally into the world and through His perfect life of obedience, even to the point of death, brought life into the world and reconciled creation back to Himself (Romans 5:18–19; Colossians 1:20). Both the first Adam and the last Adam are unique historical individuals who knit the redemptive theme of Scripture together.

---

60. Ibid., p. 150.

Chapter 6

The First Adam: Science and the Origin of Mankind

The Bible clearly teaches that mankind began with just two people — Adam and Eve (Genesis. 1:26–28; Genesis 2:7-22). Since the rise of Darwinian evolution in the 19th century, however, the world has openly ridiculed this biblical teaching. It is not just evolutionary scientists, but also many professing Christians are publicly denying this biblical doctrine. What is even more concerning is that they are urging other Christians to do the same. Theistic evolutionists argue that genetics confirm that mankind came from a population of people rather than a pair. Theistic evolutionists try to support this theologically by arguing that God's "sixty-seventh book" (general revelation) helps us read Scripture (special revelation), so that we can properly understand the history of mankind. There is no reason, however, for Christians to fear science when it comes to the issue of mankind originating from two people. The science of genetics not only confirms the recent creation of Adam, but modern science came about through a belief in a real historical Adam.

❧ Adam and the Rise of Modern Science

Although many in the secular west would see Christianity as being anti-science, in fact science grew out of a Christian worldview. The scientific revolution that began in the 16th century came about in the west because of the Christian belief in creation's uniformity and predictability. This was opposed to the animistic chaos, capricious polytheism, Islamic determinism, or pantheistic spiritualization of nature in other worldviews. For example, the Chinese, who were influenced by Confucian and Taoist philosophies, pursued "enlightenment" over scientific "explanations" of the natural world. The failure of the Chinese to develop science was due to their religious belief. They did not believe in the existence of a divine rational being who ordains nature. The Greeks practiced learning with great enthusiasm, but there was a distance between their speculative philosophy and observation of the natural world. Three things stopped them from pursuing science: 1) their concept of the gods could not permit them to believe in a conscious Creator, 2) their belief that the universe was eternal and uncreated and therefore locked in a cycle of progress and decay, and 3) their religious conceptions transformed inanimate objects into living creatures capable of desires and emotions. In light of this, their speculative philosophy could not be subjected to empirical tests. Although the Islamic world accepted classical scholarship, and progressed in certain sciences (mathematics, astronomy, and medicine) they never established science. Their adoption of the Greek view (Aristotelian) of the natural world prevented any further progress in science, as did the Islamic belief in Allah's (a Monad) determination of all things.[1]

Modern science was pioneered by Christians who described themselves as "thinking God's thoughts after Him" (Johannes Kepler). In his book *For the Glory of God*, professor of social sciences Rodney Stark rightly notes that the origin of science came about because of Christian theology:

> Christianity depicted God as a rational, responsive, dependable, and omnipotent being and the universe as his personal creation, thus having a rational, lawful, stable structure, awaiting human comprehension.…To sum up: the rise of science was not an extension of classical learning. It was the natural outgrowth of Christian doctrine: Nature exists because it was created by God. To love and honor God, one must fully appreciate the wonders of his handiwork. Moreover, because God is perfect, his handiwork functions in accord with *immutable principles*. By the full use of our God-given powers of reason and observation, we ought to be able to discover these principles.[2]

Not only did science come out of a Christian worldview, but scholars also recognize that modern science came from a literal (not literalistic) understanding of the Bible, as Peter Harrison, professor of science and religion at Oxford University, explains: "Had it not been for the rise of the literal interpretation of the Bible and the subsequent appropriation of biblical

---

1. See Rodney Stark, *For the Glory of God: How Monotheism Led to Reformations, Science, Witch-hunts and the End of Slavery* (Princeton, NJ: Princeton University Press, 2003), p. 150–156.
2. Ibid., p. 147, 157.

narratives by early modern scientists, modern science may not have arisen at all. In sum, the Bible and its literal interpretation have played a vital role in the development of Western science."[3] This is interesting given that many would see a literal interpretation of the Bible, especially in Genesis 1–3, as incompatible with science.

Christian Founders of Modern Science	
Physics	Isaac Newton (1643–1727) Michael Faraday (1791–1867) James Clerk Maxwell (1831–1879) William Thomson, Lord Kelvin (1824–1907)
Chemistry	Robert Boyle (1627–1691) John Dalton (1766–1844) William Ramsay (1852–1916)
Biology	John Ray (1627–1705) Carl Linnaeus (1707–1778) Gregor Mendel (1822–1884) Louis Pasteur (1822–1895)
Geology	Nicolas Steno (1638–1686) Georges Cuvier (1769–1832) Adam Sedgwick (1785–1873)
Mathematics	Blaise Pascal (1623–1662) Gottfried Wilhelm Leibniz (1646–1716)
Astronomy	Nicolaus Copernicus (1473–1543) Galileo Galilei (1564–1642) Johannes Kepler (1571–1630)

Francis Bacon (1561–1626), who founded the scientific method (observation, experimentation, analysis) and is often known as "the Father of Science," saw himself as a theologian of the natural world rather than as a scientist who was leaving the things of faith behind him. In his book *The Great Instauration* (1620), Bacon gives us the method of scientific study of the natural world. What is interesting is that the book itself is based upon the Bible. For example, there are six major chapters which, as Bacon says in the preface, are based upon the six days of creation. Not only is the book arranged according to the six days of creation, but Bacon also spends time

---

3. Peter Harrison, "The Bible and the Rise of Science," *Australasian Science* 23, no. 3 (2002), p. 14–15.

in the book coming up with what he believes is a biblical, Christian account for how we can even study the natural order. As a Christian, Bacon realized that we are sinful people, and that the natural world has been corrupted by sin. It was this understanding of the Fall of man that was significant in the advancement of science in the modern Western world. This is because the founders of modern science believed that Adam's Fall weakened his knowledge. The Fall of man affected not only our morality, but also our intellect. It was believed that Adam, before the Fall, had an encyclopedic knowledge and that the founders of modern science (such as Francis Bacon) were trying to recapture some of that knowledge they believed Adam had possessed. Peter Harrison explains:

> For many champions of the new learning in the seventeenth century the encyclopaedic knowledge of Adam was the benchmark against which their own aspirations were gauged. Francis Bacon's project to reform philosophy was motivated by an attempt to determine whether the human mind "might by any means be restored to its perfect and original condition, or if that may not be, yet reduced to a better condition than that in which it now is."[4]

Harrison describes how this came about:

> [I]n the sixteenth century the book of scripture began to be read in a literal, historical sense, [and] it had a major impact on the way in which the book of nature was interpreted. Medieval allegorical readings of scripture had assumed a natural world in which objects symbolised spiritual truths. The demise of the allegory and its replacement by a literal and historical approach called for a reconfiguring of the natural order, the intelligibility of which was no longer seen to reside in symbolic meanings.... [O]ne consequence of that literal turn — the way in which the account of Adam's Fall, now read almost exclusively as an historical narrative rather than an allegory — influenced both theological anthropology and early modern science.[5]

The medieval allegorical reading of Scripture, brought about by the Roman Catholic Church, stifled science as it was influenced by Aristotelian philosophy in its understanding of the natural world. The Protestant Reformation of the 16th century, which emphasized a literal historical reading of the Bible, freed men's minds not only to think correctly about salvation but

4. Peter Harrison, *The Fall of Man and the Foundations of Science* (Cambridge: Cambridge University Press, 2007), p. 1.

5. Ibid., 15.

also to think correctly about the way in which nature was to be interpreted. Rather than being incompatible with science, belief in the supernatural creation of Adam and his Fall played a vital role in the progress of modern science. This belief presupposed that the Bible was accurate when it spoke of a real historical Adam and a real historical Fall from grace. Far from ruling out belief in the supernatural creation of Adam, modern science was founded upon it.

❧ Adam: Special and General Revelation

Throughout Christian history, some people have believed that God revealed Himself to us through two books — nature and Scripture. This concept seems to be increasingly present in origins discussions among Christians who consider how science and faith intersect. Some have even referred to nature as the "sixty-seventh book" of the Bible. But what is behind this "two books" concept? If nature reveals God's attributes to mankind, does that mean it is equal to God's Word as an authoritative source of revelation? How should we read (interpret) these two books? Which "book" should take priority? It's no small matter.

The Bible tells us that the triune God who created the universe has revealed Himself in three specific ways:

1. His written Word: special revelation (2 Timothy 3:16)
2. Creation: general (natural) revelation (Psalm 19:1–6; Romans 1:18–20)
3. God the Son: incarnational revelation (John 1:14; Hebrews 1:1–3)

Each type of revelation has a different role in the way God shares truth with mankind. Christians get into trouble when they take one type of revelation out of context to promote their own agenda. Christians who believe that life evolved over millions of years must go outside God's special revelation in Scripture to find support for their views. So they grant general revelation in nature equal weight with the Bible, calling it one of two books God gave us to understand how He created the world. In the book *Adam and the Genome*, Dr. Dennis Venema uses the two books analogy to ultimately deny that Adam was a historical person:

> If indeed nature and Scripture have the same author, as Christians affirm, then there cannot, ultimately, be any disagreement between what we "read" in one book and what we read in the other.[6]

---

6. Venema and McKnight, *Adam and the Genome*, p. 8.

Since he is certain that his studies of the human genome disprove the possibility of a single human ancestor 6,000 years ago, he concludes that Scripture cannot teach a literal Adam — that would contradict his interpretation of "the book of nature" found in the genetic data. However, it is not the evidence of genetics that discredits a young earth creation or a historical Adam. Rather, it is the naturalistic presuppositions that Venema and other evolutionists use to interpret the evidence and simply accept as fact. If you look closer at all these scientific studies, they are built on unproven (and unprovable) assumptions about the past.

General revelation clearly reveals the existence, attributes, and glory of God. As Psalm 19:1 says, "The heavens declare the glory of God." It even reveals His kindness to all humanity (Matthew 5:45; Acts 14:17). Faced with this evidence, unbelievers are without excuse for not honoring Him as their Creator and God (Romans 1:18–21). But the created world does not reveal all of the Creator's attributes, and it cannot reveal how God's flawless earth functioned before Adam's sin brought corruption and groaning to the whole creation (Romans 8:20–22). Furthermore, key verses on general revelation say nothing about our ability to discern how earth functioned in the unobservable past. General revelation is limited. We must remember that it has a general content and is revealed to a general audience. Everyone has seen the creation's witness to its Creator in nature's incredible design, beauty, and complexity. This does not mean that we cannot learn anything from studying nature. It just means that our interpretation of what we observe must be consistent with the revelation of Scripture. For example, a police detective compares eyewitness testimony with circumstantial evidence to figure out who committed the crime in the unobservable, unrepeatable past. Likewise, the Bible is God's eyewitness testimony that enables us to rightly interpret the present physical evidence so we can reconstruct earth's history since creation. Therefore, it is not biblically sound to equate general revelation to claims and interpretations about evidence from nature.

Whereas God's general revelation in nature is given to all humanity throughout history, His special revelation in Scripture was only given to some people in history. Also, while general revelation is constantly changing, special revelation in the Scriptures has ceased (Hebrews 1:1–2). Furthermore, Scripture speaks directly to God's people who have the Holy Spirit to understand it correctly (1 Corinthians 2:10–16). Special revelation is God-breathed, perfect, right, pure, and profitable for teaching and training believers (Psalm 19:7–9; 2 Timothy 3:16–17). This includes details about the physical creation — how and when it was created (Genesis 1–2; Exodus 20:11; Psalm 33:6–9). It also tells us how the physical creation came to be corrupted (Genesis 3:17; Romans 8:20–22), how it was destroyed in a global catastrophe (Genesis 6:13, 17, 7:19–23), and how God plans to redeem it (Genesis 3:15; Colossians 1:20). All these things were confirmed by God's incarnational revelation through the words of Jesus while He was on earth (Mark 10:6; Luke 17:26–27, 24:44–47). God's special revelation also specifically informs us that the creation itself has been corrupted by the curse and that sin has affected how people view general revelation. The New Testament uses various words to describe the ruin of humanity's intellect: futile (Romans 1:21), debased (Romans 1:28), deluded (Colossians 2:4), and darkened (Ephesians 4:18). Only by having our mind renewed in Christ and our thinking guided by the Holy Spirit can we rightly understand the special revelation of Scripture and then apply that to interpreting general revelation. Theologian Louis Berkhof states, "Since the entrance of sin into the world, man can gather true knowledge about God from His general revelation only if he studies it in the light of Scripture."[7] God has given us special revelation as the eyeglasses that equip us to rightly understand His general revelation.

The most important distinction between the two is that, biblically speaking, special revelation precedes and grounds our understanding of general revelation. For example, in Genesis 1 we read, "And God said, 'Let there be light,' and there was light" (Genesis 1:3). Special revelation brings general revelation into existence. Once creation was completed, God told Adam what to do in the garden He had created (Genesis 2:16–17). Both special and general revelation are complementary concepts: one cannot exist without the other. If we isolate one from the other, we will end up with problems, such as when observations of nature are used to support evolution or millions of years. However, our scientific observations and interpretations of creation are not equivalent to Scripture and cannot be used to modify our understanding of special revelation.

It's important to remember that God's Word offers us direct statements of truth while nature does not speak. As an analogy, nature is like a picture book without words, requiring us to deduce the meaning. The Bible gives us the pictures with the words so we can directly understand the author's intent and rightly interpret the pictures. When we are dealing with an issue like the age of a fossil, the fossil does not speak to us as Scripture does. The Bible gives propositional truth statements that we can directly evaluate. We read explicitly in Genesis 1 that the earth was created before the sun, and birds were created before dinosaurs. Scientific study does not

---

7. Louis Berkhof, *Introductory Volume to Systematic Theology* (Grand Rapids, MI: Eerdmans Publishing, 1932), p. 60.

provide propositional truths about the past, but offers possible explanations based on the evidence we find in nature. Before we "read" the fossil, we must first gather data about the fossil such as the type of rock it is in, the mineral composition, and the structure of the bones. These are aspects of operational science and are generally agreed upon by all observers, whether creationists or evolutionists. Using these pieces of information, we then use our starting assumptions to create a picture of the fossil. From that picture, we construct a story to explain how the creature died and was buried and how long ago it lived, an example of historical science. But this interpretation is still subject to error and isn't a truth statement like statements in the Bible. The evolutionary claims say that the sun was around before the earth and that birds evolved from dinosaurs. We can then evaluate these historical interpretations based on the propositional truth statements given in the Bible.

Since general and special revelation both proceed from God, they cannot ultimately conflict with each other, and they do not conflict when we use special revelation to correctly interpret general revelation. Although Christians who hold to evolution and millions of years call them "two books," we should understand that metaphor is oversimplified. We must interpret general revelation through multiple steps, while we can interpret special revelation more directly. Though a testimony to the Creator's attributes and glory, nature can never be "quoted" as the 67th book in the canon of Scripture. We must always see special revelation as the ultimate authority as we seek to interpret general revelation. If we allow for the "reading" of the book of nature that denies Adam and Eve were the first humans and that the world was created in a very good state over the span of six ordinary days, we undermine the foundation of the gospel message.

🜉 Adam: Observational vs. Historical Science

Important in the discussion over the origin of Adam is the definition of science. The Oxford Dictionary gives the following definition: "The intellectual and practical activity encompassing the systematic study of the structure and behavior of the physical and natural world through observation and experiment."[8] So, basically, science involves the observation of the present physical world. Yet it is necessary to understand a valid distinction between observational science and historical science. Whereas observational science uses repeatable, observable, testable experiments to find out how things in the present world operate so that we can, for example, find cures for diseases, produce new technologies, or make other scientific advancements, historical science seeks to reconstruct the unrepeatable, unobservable past by looking

---

8. See Oxford Living Dictionaries, https://en.oxforddictionaries.com/definition/science.

at the evidence of the past events that produced what we see in the present. Such historical reconstructions are very dependent on a scientist's belief system or worldview. Even evolutionary scientists recognize the validity of this distinction. Harvard professor E.O. Wilson said,

> If a moving automobile were an organism, functional biology would explain how it is constructed and operates, while evolutionary biology would reconstruct its origin and history — how it came to be made and its journey thus far.[9]

However, evolutionists often fail to make the distinction when it comes to the debate over human origins. For example, evolutionary scientist and vocal atheist Sam Harris states, "If you doubt that human beings evolved from prior species, you may as well doubt that the sun is a star."[10] Yet it is through investigation and observation, the basic modus operandi of scientific theory, that we can observe that the sun is a star, but no one has ever observed humans evolving from prior species. Nor is there any biological or paleoanthropological evidence for it. Therefore, when it comes to the debate over the supernatural creation of Adam, we must understand that evolution, the idea that life came about by a common ancestor, is part of historical science and not observational science. The story of the evolution of man (indeed, of the whole universe) is not based on observational evidence but is part of a secular faith (i.e., religion) that denies supernatural revelation.

✣ Adam: What about Supposed Ape-men Ancestry?

In his book *On the Origin of Species* (1859) Charles Darwin avoided the question of the evolution of mankind:

> In the distant future I see open fields for far more important researches.... Light will be thrown on the origin of man and his history.[11]

Darwin went on to apply his paradigm of evolution to mankind in his book *The Descent of Man* (1871), where he proposed that humans evolved from lower animals. Darwin did believe that man had descended from monkeys in Africa (a racist idea):

---

9. Edward O. Wilson, *From So Simple a Beginning: Darwin's Four Great Books* (New York: W.W. Norton, 2006), p. 12.
10. Sam Harris, *Letter to a Christian Nation: A Challenge to Faith* (London: Bantam Press, 2007), p. 68.
11. Charles Darwin, *On the Origin of Species by Means of Natural Selection* (London: John Murray, 185), p. 488, http://darwin-online.org.uk/content/frameset?pageseq=506&itemID=F373&viewtype=side.

The Simiadae then branched off into two great stems, the New World and the Old World monkeys; and from the latter, at a remote period, Man, the wonder and glory of the Universe, proceeded.[12]

It is therefore probable that Africa was formerly inhabited by extinct apes closely allied to the gorilla and chimpanzee; and as these two species are now man's nearest allies, it is somewhat more probable that our early progenitors lived on the African continent than elsewhere.[13]

It was this idea of the evolution of man that directly challenged the Bible's understanding of the creation of man. From that time on, based on the fossil record, evolutionists have historically tried to tie human ancestry to primates — think of the so-called "ape-men" fossils that have been hyped as evidence for human evolution. They have also attempted to buttress this claim with anatomical and physiological comparisons between humans and apes. For example, evolutionists offered many examples of our supposed ape-man ancestry: Neanderthal Man, Nebraska Man, Cro-Magnon Man, and so on.[14]

Neanderthal man was first discovered in 1856 in the Neander Valley in Germany. This specimen consisted of a fossilized skull cap, two femurs, two humeri, and other bone fragments. Neanderthal man was seen by evolutionists as sub-human and primitive because of their characters: prominent eyebrow ridges, low forehead, long narrow skull, a protruding upper jaw, and a strong lower jaw with a short chin. The first Neanderthal skeleton discovered had rickets (vitamin D deficiency) and arthritis. Today we have the fossil remains of approximately 500 Neanderthal individuals from Europe, the Near East, and western Asia.

There are three lines of evidence that show Neanderthals were fully human ancestors of modern humans. First, the study of nuclear DNA has shown that humans and Neanderthals could interbreed and therefore that they were not different species but part of the same humankind. Marvin Lubenow has shown from evolutionary literature that "...the DNA evidence is quite strong that Neanderthals and modern humans have reproduced together in the past.... DNA studies show that about one to four percent of our genes as living humans come from the Neanderthals, and

12. Charles Darwin, *The Descent of Man* (2nd edn; Classic Literature Library, 1874), p. 111, http://charles-darwin.classic-literature.co.uk/the-descent-of-man/ebook-page-111.asp.
13. Charles Darwin, *The Descent of Man*, 2nd ed., John Murray (London, 1890), p. 155.
14. Nebraska man, who was used as evidence at the Scope Monkey Trail (1925), is now discarded because it was in fact reconstructed to look like an ape-man from a pig's tooth!

geneticists are attempting to reassemble the genome of the Neanderthals from those bits and pieces inside us modern humans."[15]

Second, fossil evidence shows that Neanderthals were fully human. The fact that Neanderthals and modern humans have been found buried together (Skhul Cave, Mount Carmel, Israel) strongly suggests that they worked and lived together and even intermarried. Neanderthal anatomy (skeletons) shows that they look like people alive today (stocky, thick bones [muscular], modern human hands and feet). They also have a hyoid bone in their larynx which allows them to speak (apes don't have that).

Third, Neanderthal culture demonstrates that they were fully human as they used stone tools, axes, and spears for hunting, painted in caves, had a controlled use of fire, ground minerals up into powder, buried their dead with ceremonial objects, and sub-divided their caves into partitions.[16] In the biblical creation model, Neanderthals would be a post-Flood people, living in Europe and Asia after the time of the Tower of Babel. Lubenow refers to Neanderthals as "…Homo sapiens neanderthalensis … a sub-species of modern humans, separate from but equal to Homo sapiens sapiens."[17] Far from being sub-human descendants from ape-like creatures, what we now know about Neanderthals show that they are fully human.

Today in museums all around the world and in the media, exhibit A in the attempt to show that humans evolved from an ape-like ancestor is *Australopithecus afarensis* (meaning "southern ape from the Afar triangle of Ethiopia"), one specimen more popularly known as "Lucy." Lucy's bones were found in Ethiopia in 1974 by Dr. Donald Johanson; he and his team found only 47 out of 207 bones, and most of her hands, feet, and skull were missing. Lucy seems to have been a fully grown female primate who would have stood about 3.5 feet tall. Lucy has been dated at 3.2 million years old. However, Lucy's bones (skull, pelvis, and feet) are far from being human; they are more like those of chimpanzees. For example, it is clear from Lucy's pelvis that she was not equipped for sustained, habitual, or efficient bipedal locomotion. The truth is that she was a knuckle-walker, similar to a bonobo or gorilla.[18]

The simple fact is that the supposed evolution of man from an ape-like creature is pure imagination — a faith-based position, and an extraordinary

15. Marvin Lubenow, "Neanderthals: Our Worthy Ancestors," *Searching for Adam* (Green Forest, AR: Master Books, 2016), p. 267.
16. Ibid., p. 263–286.
17. Ibid., 267.
18. David Menton, "Did Humans Really Evolve from Ape-Like Creatures?" *Searching for Adam* (Green Forest, AR: Master Books, 2016), p. 252–256.

one at that. What is really needed to make an ape-man is art and imagination. One of the reasons why the evolution of man has become ingrained in the minds of people in our culture is the iconic image of the transition from ape to man that is based on supposed transitional ape-men fossils. Yet even evolutionists recognize that this famous image is an illusion:

> There is a popular image of human evolution that you'll find all over the place.... On the left of the picture there's an ape.... On the right, a man.... Between the two is a succession of figures that become ever more like humans.... Our progress from ape to human looks so smooth, so tidy. It's such a beguiling image that even the experts are loath to let it go. But it is an illusion.[19]

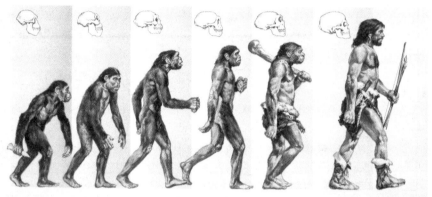

DeAgostini. DeAgostini/Superstock.com

While the image of man evolving from an ape-like creature may seem impressive, the evidence to support it simply is not there. Furthermore, it is impossible for a four-legged creature (quadruped, knuckle-walker) to gradually evolve into a habitual two-legged walker (biped). Professor Stuart Burgess has shown that there are ten design features that are required for human walking and running that could not have evolved step by step:

1. Strong Big Toes: Only humans have feet that have the stiffness necessary for proper two-legged motion. Humans have a very stiff big toe that is orientated straight ahead so that it enables the foot to roll forward in walking. In contrast, the big toe of apes is not stiff and does not point forward.

2. Arched Feet: Only humans have the necessary intricate arched structure in their feet for proper bipedal motion. In contrast, apes

19. Bernard Wood (Professor of human origins, George Washington University), "Who Are We?" *New Scientist* 2366 (26 Oct. 2002), p. 44.

do not have arched feet and instead have flexible feet that are designed to be like hands for gripping branches.

3. Long Legs: Humans have long legs and relatively short arms; apes have short legs and long arms. The fact that humans have long legs emphasizes that there is a clear distinction between the design of a quadruped and biped.

4. Upright Knee Joints: The human knee joint locks in the upright position making standing easy, whereas the knee joint of apes is not fully extendable, and apes cannot stand straight.

5. Angled Femur Bones: Human angled femur bones have the effect of making the knees close together and the feet close together. In contrast, the femur bones of apes drop down vertically, making their knees relatively far apart and the feet far apart.

6. Upright Hip Joints: Humans have unique hip joints that give a fully upright stature. In contrast, the hip joints of apes cannot fully extend to the upright position and apes must always have bent legs, even if they stand on two legs.

7. Upright Back: Humans have an upright back so that the head is directly above the hips. In contrast, the curved back of apes makes their torso project out in front of the hips.

8. Upright Skull: The point at which the spinal cord enters the skull us called the *foramen magnum*. In humans, the foramen magnum is located at the bottom of the skull, so that the most natural position for the human head is looking forward in the upright position. In contrast, apes have a foramen magnum located more to the back of the skull so that the most natural position for the head is looking forward in the horizontal position.

9. Flat Face: Humans have a uniquely flat face that gives them a large field of view that is required for effective bipedal movement. In contrast, apes have a large protruding jaw, and their field of view is much more restricted.

10. Upright Balance: In order to balance on four legs it is only necessary to keep the center of gravity of the body within the four points of contact on the ground, which is a relatively large area. However, when standing on two legs, it is necessary to keep the center of gravity between the two feet and this represents a relatively small area.[20]

---

20. The following points came from Stuart Burgess, "Human Anatomy: Unique Upright Design," *Searching for Adam* (Green Forest, AR: Master Books, 2016), p. 331–345.

These design features of the human body give humans the unique ability to move on two legs with great agility. It also reveals the purposeful design of the human body (cf. Psalm 8:5–8). Professor Burgess notes, "To secular scientists it is a puzzle that out of around 4,000 mammals only humans are bipedal. However, this unique design feature makes complete sense from a biblical perspective."[21] The human body is clearly a wonderful design from the Master Designer and not the product of random evolutionary processes.

Although there have been many attempts to justify an evolutionary view of human ancestry, humans are clearly distinct from apes. The Bible clearly tells us that mankind was made in the image of God in a fully formed mature state (Genesis 1:26–28; 2:7, 21–22). On Day Three of creation week, God created fruit trees already bearing fruit (Genesis 1:11–13). Why? Because three days later He created Adam and Eve, who would need to eat fruit (Genesis 1:29–30). If God had planted seeds and waited for them to grow, Adam and Eve would have gone hungry. Adam and Eve were created as mature adults ready to be fruitful and multiply and subdue creation to begin with (Genesis 1:28). God created a fully formed and functioning creation and not one that evolved over time.

The label of early man as "primitive" comes from a misunderstanding of history. The narrative in Genesis presents Adam and Eve as acting, speaking, and reproducing. Moreover, Adam's descendants were intelligent from the beginning as they were able to forge metal, play musical instruments, farm, and build cities (Genesis 4:17–22). It even gives historical data (dates and events) for Adam's life (see Genesis 5:1–5). There is no suggestion of the evolution of man in the Bible, as theologian Robert Culver observes: "Scripture knows of no evolutionary 'ascent of man' from brute via savage and barbarian to civilized Homo sapiens. Homonids and humanoids of modern 'scientific' imagination are 'nothing in this world,' as Paul declared of the gods and goddesses of ancient heathen imagination."[22]

⚘ Adam and Genetics

To prove humans and apes share a common ancestor, theistic evolutionists often point out that mankind shares 99% of their DNA with chimpanzees. However, it is not true that we share 99% of our DNA with chimpanzees. Even evolutionary research shows we are in fact only 88% identical, which means that humans and chimpanzees differ by nearly 400 million

---

21. Ibid., 344.
22. Robert Culver, *Systematic Theology: Biblical and Historical* (Fearn, Ross-shire: Christian Focus, 2006), p. 290.

(400,000,000) DNA letters.[23] When we understand this difference it no longer makes us sound like we are kissing cousins. Furthermore, a perfectly reasonable alternative explanation to the similarity in DNA would be that we share a common designer. Since God designed the entire world, including all biological life, then we would expect to find that life fits a common design pattern.

Nevertheless, the evolutionary history of man has mankind splitting from chimpanzees around 3 million years ago (evolutionists generally do not believe that man evolved from any ape that is now living) and then modern humans evolving somewhere in Africa around 100,000–200,000 years ago from a population of people. This belief in biological evolution is a determining factor in the rejection by many theologians of Adam as the head of mankind. For example, influential Old Testament theologian John Walton, as well as being dependent on the ANE worldview to interpret Adam, also relies upon the supposed evidence from biological evolution: "Current scientific understanding maintains that there was no first human being because humanity is the result of an evolving population. The evidence of genetics also points to the idea that the genetic diversity that exists in humanity today cannot be traced back to two individuals — a single pair — but that such diversity requires a genetic source population of thousands."[24]

When it comes to the biological evidence, however, we need to keep in mind that theistic evolutionists have a predisposition and an ideology — namely, the theory of evolution — which rules out evidence for the biblical model. The theistic evolutionists claim that genetics prove the nonexistence of Adam and Eve (or the non-existence of a first couple) fails as it does not test the evolutionary assumptions they have built their argument upon (see the following table). In effect, theistic evolutionists have to assume evolution happened in order to prove evolution is true. The reasoning is entirely circular and therefore invalid.

Theistic evolutionists have also failed to look seriously at an alternative theory, such as testing the biblical model of a single pair, to see whether it fits with the data. When the biblical model of a single pair, the population bottleneck at the time of the Flood, and the dispersion of people groups at Babel is taken into account, genetic evidence confirms that the human race descended from a single pair. For example, we have strong genetic

23. Nathaniel Jeanson and Jeffery Tomkins, "Genetics Confirms the Recent, Supernatural Creation of Adam and Eve," *Searching for Adam* (Green Forest, AR: Master Books, 2016), p. 296. Jeanson and Tomkins show this to be true from published scientific papers by evolutionists.

24. Walton, *The Lost World of Adam and Eve*, p. 183.

Evolutionary assumptions	Biblical assumptions
Deep time (millions of years).	Adam and Eve (as the original pair).
Common ancestry (humans split from chimpanzees 3 million years ago, then modern humans evolved somewhere in Africa around 100,000–200,000 years ago from one single woman who was part of a population of people).	The global Flood (population bottleneck at the time of the Flood when only eight people got on board the Ark).
Mutations (seen as the driving force behind evolution).	Tower of Babel (partitioning of the genes that were formerly on board the Ark).

confirmation of a female ancestor living around 6,000 years ago even in evolutionary literature:

> Researchers have calculated that "mitochondrial Eve" — the woman whose mtDNA was ancestral to that in all living people — lived 100,000 to 200,000 years ago in Africa. Using the new [mitochondrial DNA] clock, she would be a mere 6,000 years old. No one thinks that's the case.[25]

Based on the mitochondrial DNA clock, our most recent female ancestor in the evolutionary framework, lived 6000 years ago. This genetic data has been tested and still confirms this.[26] The evidence from mitochondrial DNA contradicts the evolutionary scenario, so it is rejected, but it is consistent with what biblical creationists believes about the origin of mankind.

Despite the argument from theistic evolutionists that modern genetics is incompatible with a historical Adam and Eve, they have never tested the biblical model. The argument from theistic evolutionists is that too many genetic differences separate modern humans from each other. Therefore, they claim that two people could not have given rise to millions of DNA differences in just 6,000 years. This claim would be true, only if we assume that all genetic differences are the result of mutations from the distant past. But is this assumption true? No. It also assumes that when God created Adam and Eve that they had no genetic differences to begin with. If Adam

25. Ann Gibbons, "Calibrating the Mitochondrial Clock," *Science* 02 Jan 1998 Vol. 279, Issue 5347, p. 28–29.
26. See Nathaniel Jeanson, "A Young-Earth Creation Human Mitochondrial DNA 'Clock': Whole Mitochondrial Genome Mutation Rate Confirms D-Loop Results," Published on September 23, 2015, *Answers Research Journal* 8 (2015): p. 375–378.

and Eve's DNA had no genetic differences to begin with, then their fulfillment of be fruitful and multiply (Genesis 1:28) would have occurred by
the process of cloning. This is an awkward position to maintain. Geneticists Dr. Nathaniel Jeanson and Dr. Jeffrey Tomkins have suggested a more
likely scenario:

> A very simple alternative hypothesis resolves the conundrum
> and also makes straightforward scientific sense: God could have cre-
> ated Adam and Eve with genetic differences from the start. In fact,
> all of us possess not just 3 billion letters of DNA in our cells. With
> few exceptions such as red blood cells, the cells of our body possess
> *two versions* of our 3 billion letters, which means that each of our
> cells has 6 billion letters. Each parent passes on only 3 billion in
> sperm or egg, keeping the total of 6 billion letters constant across
> generations. Going back in time, Adam would likely have had the
> same cellular arrangement — two versions of his 3 billion letters
> — and the same would have been true of Eve. This arrangement
> makes sense of the DNA differences that exist in the world today.
> Before the Fall and after the Fall, the two different copies of Adam
> and Eve's DNA would have been reshuffled via at least two processes
> termed *recombination* and *gene conversion*, making each offspring
> unique and leading to diversity within the human race. After the
> Fall, mutations (perhaps at a rate of 60 mutations per generation)
> would have occurred and added to the genetic diversity in their chil-
> dren, and leading to the production of diverse offspring (in contrast
> to cloning). Calculations within the parameters of this model match
> the worldview DNA diversity that we observe today. Thus, to claim
> that the millions of DNA differences that separate each person from
> another somehow invalidates the clear teaching of Scripture about
> the origin of mankind from two people about 6,000 years ago is
> scientifically unsupportable. In fact, this type of creation model is
> considerably more supportive of the genetic paradigm of human
> diversity than the evolutionary model....[27]

Adam and Eve were created with the appearance of having had human parents. In other words, God created their DNA mature, thereby giving them the
ability to immediately produce diverse offspring. In short, God created Adam
and Eve with millions of DNA differences from the beginning. Again, theistic
evolutionists have never tested this hypothesis. The biblical creationist position passes the gold standard of science in that it makes testable predictions.

27. Jeanson and Tomkins, *Searching for Adam,* p. 310.

These predictions fit exactly with what we observe today. Biblical creationist research confirms the existence of a historical Adam and Eve.

✄ Adam: Other Sons and Daughters

Theistic evolutionists suggest another supposed difficulty that arises if one believes humans began with only two initial people. This is the age-old question "Where did Cain get his wife?" Theistic evolutionist generally object to the possibility that she was the sister of Cain. However, if we start with Scripture as the foundation for our thinking there was one man and one woman to begin with (Genesis 2:7, 18, 21–22; 3:20). The 19th century Old Testament scholar and Hebraist Franz Delitzsch (1813–1890) comments on this issue:

> ... the actual unity of the human race is a fundamental doctrine of Scripture which is never broken through, and intends the descendants of Adam to be regarded as the entire human race. In any case we must regard Cain's wife as a daughter of Adam (v.4).[28]

It is interesting that the objection raised by theistic evolutionists was answered by Delitzsch a long time before they wrote (1888)! Genesis 4:17 says nothing about Cain's marriage. It simply assumes that the marriage has taken place and even though Cain's wife is not named she must be one of the daughters of Adam (Genesis 5:4). Delitzsch commented on the idea that this was incest:

> It is quite unjustifiable ... that Cain's marriage with his sister involves the origin of mankind in incest. If the human race was to be propagated from a single pair, such closely related marriages were unavoidable. The notion of incest was originally limited to the reciprocal relation of parents and children, and afterwards extended in proportion as the possibility of conjugal connections was diversified.[29]

The problem of incest is a modern idea, and it was not until the time of Moses (Leviticus 18) that brother and sister relationships were forbidden. The fact that Cain, after killing Abel, fears being recognized beyond Eden presupposes that only the family of Adam existed (Genesis 4:13–14). The view of many theologians that Adam is anything other than the first man who existed is not only contradicted by the clear witness of Scripture, but by evidence from science. Christians have nothing to fear from science — when it is correctly interpreted it will confirm what is written in God's Word.

---

28. Delitzsch, *A New Commentary on Genesis*, p. 190.
29. Ibid., p. 190.

Chapter 7

The First Adam: Original Sin — How Original Is It?

The debate over whether Adam was supernaturally created by God is not an unimportant matter: it is a biblical fact with huge theological implications. The logical consequences for denying the supernatural creation of Adam are that the Bible's metanarrative of creation, Fall, redemption, and new creation need to be told in a very different way. Once this metanarrative goes, so do vital doctrines of the Christian faith. If we reject the supernatural creation of Adam, some important biblical doctrines will be eroded or redefined with it, such as the doctrine of original sin.

The idea that Adam's sin did not bring physical death into the world is not new. In the fourth century, a fierce debate broke out in the early church between a British monk by the name of Pelagius (c. A.D. 360–420) and the African theologian Augustine of Hippo (A.D. 354–430). Pelagius believed that Adam's sin did not result in the corruption of his nature, nor did it result in physical death, as Adam was created mortal. According to Pelagius, Adam's descendants did not inherit physical death, but they died because they too were mortal. Adam's Fall injured himself alone, not mankind as they were born into the world as sinless as Adam. For Pelagius, there was no connection between Adam's sin and ours and, therefore, Adam's transgression bore no consequences for the essential nature of mankind. Man was born in a state of righteousness. In the year A.D. 418, the Council of Carthage condemned the teachings of Pelagius, as did the Council of Ephesus in A.D. 431. The Council of Carthage even stated: "Whosoever says that Adam was created mortal, and would, even without sin, have died by natural necessity, let him be anathema."

In our modern culture, to pronounce someone to be anathema sounds bizarre and even unchristian. However, when these early church councils pronounced people to be anathema, they were using terminology from Paul in Galatians 1:8: "But even if we or an angel from heaven should preach to you a gospel contrary to the one we preached to you, let him be accursed [anathema]." The Council of Carthage saw this issue as central to the Christian gospel. Although those early church councils condemned Pelagianism, it raised its ugly head again in the 16th century, at the time of the Reformation, in a form of rationalism known as Socinianism, which openly denied the doctrine of original sin.

Pelagianism is not a dead heresy but is alive today in "progressive Christianity." Progressive Christians, like Pelagius, are "false brothers" among God's people (Galatians 2:4), who believe that we are all inherently good people (cf. Romans 3:12). Therefore, the gospel basically becomes a self-help message (i.e., moralism) telling people what they need to do for them to be the best version of themselves. The whole idea of grace being the very foundation of salvation is thus circumvented (see Ephesians 2:8–9). This is a false gospel of good works (Galatians 2:16) that rejects the truth of the gospel of God's grace (Galatians 1:6, 15; 2:5). We need to understand that, as fallen descendants of Adam, Pelagianism appeals to us, whereas the gospel is a lot harder to believe. The Apostle John said, "And this is the judgment: the light has come into the world, and people loved the darkness rather than the light because their works were evil" (John 3:19). If the problem is that I am dead in trespasses and sin, a hater and enemy of God, and that he is my enemy (Romans 1:30, 5:10; Ephesians 2:1), then we need a more radical solution and a more radical Savior than the pop culture Jesus (meek and mild, or a social liberator) who helps us to discover our best life now or free society from oppression.

People tend to think, "I just can't buy that negative view of mankind." But the Bible teaches that sin corrupts the entire person (throat, tongues, lips, mouth, feet, paths, and eyes) and is universal in its scope (see Romans 3:9–19).[1] If we don't understand how great our sin is, we will never understand how great a Savior Jesus is. Sadly, "progressive Christianity" is just a rebranding of classic liberalism with new paraphernalia, and in doing so promotes a different religion. In the early 20th century, theologian J. Gresham Machen criticized protestant liberalism for basically being Pelagian. Machen argued that liberalism had exchanged a serious view of the human problem

---

1. The Apostles Paul's point in quoting from the Old Testament passages (Psalms 14:1–3; 53:1–3, Proverbs 1:16; 3:15–17; Ecclesiastes 7:20, Isaiah 59:7–8) in Romans 3:9–18 is to show that Jewish people as well as people from the nations are all under the power of sin (Romans 3:19).

for a more sentimental view of human nature and consequently saw Jesus as simply a good example to be followed:

> Here is found the most fundamental difference between liberalism and Christianity — liberalism is altogether in the imperative mood, while Christianity begins with a triumphant indicative; liberalism appeals to man's will, while Christianity announces, first, a gracious act of God.... Liberalism regards [Christ] as an Example and Guide; Christianity, as a Savior: liberalism makes him an example for faith; Christianity, the object of faith.[2]

Jesus is not just a moral example to be followed, someone who shows us that we can be all that we can be. Rather, Jesus is the one who has come to save us from being all that in fact we have been (Matthew 9:13). The reason we need saving is because, just as Jesus taught, sin is not first and foremost a deed that is committed, but is a heart condition we have inherited (Matthew 15:19–20; cf. 19:8). Mankind's problem is that the heart is corrupt (Jeremiah 17:9), which is why a new one is needed (Deuteronomy 30:6; Ezekiel 36:26; cf. John 3:3–5).

❧ Original Sin

The doctrine of original sin, the belief that we are guilty sinners in Adam, has always been controversial and had critics. This may be due to mankind's optimistic view of human nature, which is based on the idea that mankind is not inherently sinful but inherently good (Romans 3:10–12; Colossians 1:21). However, there are other reasons suggested by scholars for reinterpreting or not accepting this doctrine. Christian philosopher and apologist Dr. William Lane Craig (WLC) in his book *In Quest of the Historical Adam,* states:

> It is, however, dubious that the doctrine of original sin is essential to the Christian faith. The doctrine enjoys slim scriptural support, to put it mildly; not to be found in the account of Gen 3 of the curses following the fall, the doctrine depends entirely on one biblical passage, Rom 5:12–21, and that passage is vague and open to multiple interpretations.... Thus, while the doctrine of original sin depends crucially on the fact of a historical Adam, Christianity need not embrace the traditional doctrine of original sin but may content itself with affirming the universal wrongdoing of human beings and their inability to save themselves.[3]

---

2. J. Gresham Machen, *Christianity and Liberalism* (Grand Rapids, MI: W.B. Eerdmans Publishing Company, 1985), p. 47, 96.
3. Craig, *In Quest of the Historical Adam,* p. 5–6.

WLC can only say these things because his interpretation of Scripture is influenced by evolutionary thinking and critical ideologies used by biblical scholars. It is not being controlled by the biblical text. It is also notable that to reject the traditional understanding of original sin WLC rejects the doctrine of the sufficiency of Scripture (i.e., Romans 5 is vague and open to multiple interpretations).[4] On the other hand, Karl Giberson, who once professed belief, but is now a liberal critic, rejects the doctrine of original sin because of his belief in evolution. In his book *Saving the Original Sinner*, he argues that Christians should also reject this doctrine:

> Christianity emerged in a different time and must be prepared to evolve like everything else.... In the Christian tradition, humanity's problem is referred to as *sin*, blamed on Adam. ... such a viewpoint is no longer tenable, and we must learn to get along without it. There is no original sin and there was no original sinner.[5]

Because of his evolutionary view of humanity, Giberson must redefine the meaning of sin. Rather than being disobedience to God's law (1 John 3:4), he sees it as nothing more than wrongdoing.[6] Sin, however, cannot simply be reduced to wrongdoing because the biblical understanding of sin is profoundly deep in its teaching on the condition of mankind (see Genesis 6:5; 8:21; Jeremiah 17:9; Matthew 12:34–35; John 3:19; Ephesians 2:1–3). Nevertheless, Giberson also rejects the doctrine of original sin as not being original to the text of Romans 5:12. He and others see the doctrine of original sin as an invention of the pre-enlightenment, and more specifically an invention of the church Father Augustine of Hippo who is said to have greatly influenced the Western church with this belief. Giberson states:

> Shaped forcefully by Augustine in the fourth century, this notion — original sin — would become the dominant view in the Christian West.... Prior to Augustine, however, no such consensus existed and many Christians viewed Adam simply as Everyman, the first of our species, like us in many ways, tempted by Satan as we are. Adam, however, was weak and gave in to temptation, but his failure was his, and his alone. We can do better.[7]

Although the term original sin (*peccatum originis*) may have been employed by Augustine to refer to our collective human guilt and corruption, this does

---

4. These multiple interpretations that WLC cites in his book come from critical, neo-orthodox, Roman Catholic and Protestant scholars.
5. Giberson, *Saving the Original Sinner*, p. 176.
6. Ibid., p. 176–177.
7. Ibid., p. 29.

not mean that it was invented by him. Augustine was the great defender of original sin, but he was not the inventor of the doctrine. There is an outline of the teaching of original sin in the Patristic theology of Irenaeus (A.D. 130–202), Basil (A.D. 329–379), and Ambrose (A.D. 339–397).[8] For example, Ambrose the bishop of Milan, in his eulogy to his brother Satyrus, said: "In Adam I fell, in Adam I was cast out of Paradise, in Adam I died; how shall the Lord call me back, except he find me in Adam; Guilty as I was in him, so now Justified in Christ" (*On the Death of Satyrus*, 2.6). According to Ambrose, to be justified is the opposite of being guilty in Adam (cf. Romans 5:1). It was not just many of the early church fathers who believed the doctrine of original sin, but Jewish people at the time of the first century believed that sin was derived from Adam. Possibly the clearest text that refers to original sin resulting from the first man Adam is found in the first century Jewish text 2 Esdras 3: 7, 21–22:

> And you laid upon him one commandment of yours; but he transgressed it, and immediately you appointed death for him and for his descendants. From him there sprang nations and tribes, peoples and clans without number....
>
> For the first Adam, burdened with an evil heart, transgressed and was overcome, as were also all who were descended from him. Thus the disease became permanent; the law was in the hearts of the people along with the evil root; but what was good departed, and the evil remained ... in everything doing just as Adam and all his descendants had done, for they also had the evil heart.

The author of 2 Esdras understood the connection between Adam's action and the sin that came from it corrupted mankind. The nation of Israel understood that she was "in Adam" and that the effects of his first disobedience were entrenched within Israel's understanding of their own disobedience. This concept of cooperate solidarity is foreign to many in the western church with an individualistic theory of human rights, but it was basic to the biblical worldview of Israel (see Joshua 7; 1 Samuel 17).

✵ Romans 5:12–19

The question we must ask is this: does Romans 5:12–19 teach that we are guilty sinners in Adam and that physical death came about through him? This text is important as it contrasts the actions of Adam and Jesus:

8. See Peter Sanlon, "Original Sin in Patristic Theology," in *Adam, The Fall, and Original Sin: Theological, Biblical, and Scientific Perspectives* (Grand Rapids, MI: Baker Academic, 2014), p. 85–107.

Therefore, just as sin came into the world through one man, and death through sin, and so death spread to all men because all sinned — for sin indeed was in the world before the law was given, but sin is not counted where there is no law. Yet death reigned from Adam to Moses, even over those whose sinning was not like the transgression of Adam, who was a type of the one who was to come. But the free gift is not like the trespass. For if many died through one man's trespass, much more have the grace of God and the free gift by the grace of that one man Jesus Christ abounded for many. And the free gift is not like the result of that one man's sin. For the judgment following one trespass brought condemnation, but the free gift following many trespasses brought justification. For if, because of one man's trespass, death reigned through that one man, much more will those who receive the abundance of grace and the free gift of righteousness reign in life through the one man Jesus Christ. Therefore, as one trespass led to condemnation for all men, so one act of righteousness leads to justification and life for all men. For as by the one man's disobedience the many were made sinners, so by the one man's obedience the many will be made righteous.

One of the main themes in Romans is that there is no distinction between Jewish people and people from the nations, as all have sinned and fallen short of the glory of God (Romans 3:20–23). All need salvation through the one man Jesus Christ. Therefore, Paul contrasts the salvific work of the Lord Jesus with the condemning effects of Adam's action (Romans 5:12–21). At the end of Romans 4, Paul declares that Jesus' Resurrection from the dead demonstrates that our justification has been obtained (Romans 4:25). This leads Paul, in Romans 5:1–11, to state that justification by faith is a completed act whereby we have peace with God (Romans 5:1).[9] This peace we have with God is both objective, it comes through Christ's atoning death (Romans 3:25), and subjective, the Holy Spirit bears witness with our spirit that we are children of God (Romans 8:15–16). In Romans 5:11, Paul describes the reconciling work of God's love in Christ on behalf of sinners.

---

9. There is a textual variant in Romans 5:1. Some manuscripts read "let us have" (ἔχωμεν, echōmen, subjunctive), urging people to have peace with God, whereas other manuscripts read "we have" (ἔχομεν, echomen; present indicative) which declares that we already have peace with God. The earliest manuscript witness to Romans 5:1 has the indicative (0220^{vid}, third century). Also, the internal theological evidence points to the indicative as it lists the present benefits of justification. See Philip W. Comfort, *New Testament Text and Translation Commentary* (Carol Stream, IL: Tyndale House Publishers, 2008), p. 443–444.

Those who trust in Christ are both justified (legal aspect) and reconciled (relational aspect) by His death. This leads us to the controversial words over the doctrine of original sin in Romans 5:12: "Therefore, just as sin came into the world through one man, and death through sin, and so death spread to all men because all sinned."

Paul contrasts (*dia touto*, "therefore") the work of Adam and Jesus by opening his discussion in verse 12 stating that "sin came into the world through one man," which of course is an allusion to Adam's disobedience in Genesis 3. Adam's sinful act released the power of sin into the world, making people slaves to sin (Romans 6:6–7, 10–13). Paul does not stop there, as he adds that the entrance of sin brought death into the world. The punishment that God promised in Genesis 2:17 was fulfilled, and death came into the world. In the context of Genesis 3, this is both spiritual (verse 8, i.e., estrangement from God) and physical death (verse 19). Paul's point therefore is that the nature of the death that entered the world was both physical and spiritual death (see below). This leads to Paul's focus in Romans 5:12–21: the reign of death. The power of death came through Adam's sin, and that power affects all people: "thus death spread to all men." This, as Paul states, is "because all sinned." It must be recognized that these words "because all sinned" (*eph' hō pantes hemarton*) are "fiercely contested and difficult to understand."[10] This does not mean, however, they are impossible to understand. If we will allow Paul's theology to stand, we will see how they function in his argument in this passage.

It is becoming increasingly popular for evangelical theologians to argue that the doctrine of original sin is not only an invention of the church father Augustine but is also not original to the text of Romans 5:12.[11] Theistic evolutionist Dr. Denis Alexander believes Romans 5:12 does not speak of sin as being inherited from Adam but rather coming through our own individual acts of sin. He argues:

> The error arose from a mistranslation of the Greek construction eph' ho (i) (ἐφ᾽ ᾧ) as "in whom" rather than its correct meaning in this context of "because." So Augustine read the last phrase to mean that sin was transmitted from Adam to "all men," whereas Paul's

10. Thomas Schreiner, "Original Sin and Original Death: Romans 5:12–19," in *Adam, the Fall, and Original Sin,* eds. Hans Madueme and Michael Reeves (Grand Rapids, MI: Baker Academics, 2014), p. 273.
11. See David Instone-Brewer, an honorary senior research fellow at Tyndale House Cambridge, "Why Christians Should Ditch the Concept of Original Sin," *Premier Christianity,* 28 October 2021. https://www.premierchristianity.com/regular-columnists/why-christians-should-ditch-the-concept-of-original-sin/3425.article .

meaning is quite different, as NIV has it…. So Paul is saying here that spiritual death spread to all people on account of their own sinning. Once Romans 5:12 is correctly translated it does then bring its teaching into line with the rest of Scripture, which is insistent that each person is responsible for his or her own sin. It is not guilt that is inherited from Adam but a propensity to sin, so that as a matter of fact everyone does in a sense repeat the sin of Adam.[12]

As Alexander argues the translation of Romans 5:12 as "because all sinned," it seems to indicate that individuals are subject to death because of their own personal sin. Whereas the translation "in whom all sinned" would mean that people are subject to death not because of their individual sin but because of Adam's. While Augustine may have been in error over the translation of the Greek in Romans 5:12, the theological point he brought out is correct, as the text goes on to explain. Yet it is not necessary to view Romans 5:12 as either teaching that our sin is the result of Adam's disobedience or that it is because of our own individual sin. It should be recognized that the text indicates that there is a primary and a secondary cause, as New Testament theologian Thomas Schreiner acknowledges:

> Paul does not deny in this text that the sin of individuals lead[s] to death. What he affirms … is that individuals come into the world condemned and spiritually dead because of Adam's sin. The latter part of 5:12 must not be separated from the first part of the verse. Sin and death entered into the world through Adam, and hence people sin and die both because of Adam's sin and their own sin, though the sin of Adam is fundamental and foundational.[13]

Therefore, the primary cause would be Adam's disobedience, when death entered the world, and the secondary cause is the sin of individuals who through their own disobedience bring death upon themselves.

After noting the effects of Adam's action, Paul responds to a possible objection ("how can sin have entered the world through Adam, when sin cannot be not known if there is no law to define it") by stating: "for sin indeed was in the world before the law was given, but sin is not counted where there is no law. Yet death reigned from Adam to Moses, even over those whose sinning was not like the transgression of Adam, who was a type of the one who was to come" (Romans 5:13–14). In focusing on the time between Adam and Moses, Paul is limiting himself to specific era in salvation history. Those who lived between the time of Adam and Moses were

---

12. Alexander, *Creation or Evolution*, p. 343–344.

13. Schreiner, *Original Sin and Original Death*, p. 280.

accountable for their sin and were judged for violating God's unwritten law (Romans 2:12).[14] Adam disobeyed a specifically revealed commandment when sin came into the world through him (Genesis 2:17). As the first man, Adam plays an important typological role, just as Christ does. Therefore, those who sinned between Adam and Moses (Cain, Lamech, the Flood generation, and the people at Babel, etc.) did not have the same significance as Adam's sin. Adam's sin is unique as it brought the world under the reign of death (Romans 5:17). But even those who lived between Adam and Moses and did not have a specific commandment revealed to them died, because death reigned over them, and because of their personal sin. The difference being is that their sin did not have the same impact as Adam's, as he transgressed a specific command, and therefore it was not counted against them in the same way it was counted against Adam. As the head of mankind, Adam's sin had a unique impact over the world, as it was the spring for all the sin that followed.[15]

In Romans 5:14 Paul refers to Adam as a type (*typos*) of the one who was to come (Jesus). Theologian Robert Strimple points out that: "In the Bible a type is always an historical person, action, or event appointed by God to be a foreshadowing, a pointer, to the fulfillment, yet to come in history in Christ. To speak of a type is to speak in terms of redemptive history. A type is not merely an allegory but an historical reality."[16] Paul speaks this way of the nation of Israel's sin and God's judgment of it: "Now these things took place as examples [*typos*] for us, that we might not desire evil as they did" (1 Corinthians 10:6). God's judgment upon the nation of Israel because of her sins is a "type" of judgment the Corinthians should expect if they do not hear Paul's warning and continue in their sin. Adam is a "type" of Jesus in that his action affected all people in him just as Christ affects all those in Him. In the verses that follow (Romans 5:15–19) Paul highlights these differences before completing his assessment of the actions of Adam and Jesus.

In verse 15 Paul begins contrast the effects of Adam's action and Christ's action. Instantly, he states: "But the free gift is not like the trespass." Paul's describes Christ work as a gift, something freely and graciously given, which is not like Adam's trespass (transgression). The "trespass" Paul is referring to is Adam's disobedience of God's command (Genesis 2:17). The consequences of Adam's disobedience means that "many died." Schreiner notes

---

14. This is not to say that these people were not condemned because of Adam's sin, but that Genesis states they were judged for their own sin (cf. Genesis 4:7; 6:5, 11).

15. See Schreiner, *Original Sin and Original Death*, p. 279–281.

16. Robert Strimple, "Was Adam historical?" Westminster Seminary California (2010), http://wscal.edu/resource-center/resource/was-adam-historical.

that, "The word "many" (πολλοί) here certainly means "all," as subsequent verses attest. No room is allowed for exceptions. All of humanity, apart from the Christ, died because Adam sinned."[17] Whereas all mankind has been affected by Adam's trespass, Paul then goes on to marvel at God's grace in Christ which liberates those who receive His abundant provision of grace.

In verse 16 Paul continues to contrast the result of Adam sin and the gift in Christ: "And the free gift is not like the result of that one man's sin." In Adam's case, Paul states, "the judgment following one trespass brought condemnation...." After Adam sinned God pronounced a judicial verdict, judgment (Romans 2:2–3, 11:33), upon him for his sin (cf. Genesis 3:17–19). This judicial verdict led to "condemnation" (*katakrima*, Romans 5:18, 8:1), which "does not denote merely a pronouncement of guilt ... but the adjudication of punishment."[18] The punishment handed out to Adam for his disobedience was death (cf. Romans 5:12, 17). What stands out is that the condemnation is not limited to Adam but extends to all mankind (Romans 5:18). All mankind is not condemned because of their own sin (although they will give an account for their sin), but because of what Adam did. Paul does not give an apology for this or a defense of it, he simply states it. What he does, is contrast the judgment brought about by Adam, with the generous gift that brought about justification, which comes about through Christ's atoning death on the Cross (Romans 3:25). Those who trust in Christ are right before God.

Paul continues to show the differences between the actions of Adam and Christ in verse 17. Adam's trespass brought about the reign of death, which the genealogies in Genesis 5 reveal: "and he died" (Genesis 5:5, 8, 11, 14, 17, 20, 26, 31). But death is not just something that happens to us at the end of life but is a state in which we live. As will be shown below, death is both physical and spiritual. People do die because of their own sin, as has already been made clear (cf. Romans 5:12), but Paul goes back to the beginning cause of death and sin. Death has entered creation because of the trespass of one man, Adam. In Genesis 1:28 Adam, as head of mankind, is told to rule over creation, but because of his sin death reigned instead. Whereas, through the actions of Adam "death reigned" (aorist tense) in the world, because of the abundance of grace and the free gift of righteousness, in Jesus Christ, people will reign (future tense) in life.

In verse 18 Paul reasons from what he has argued in the previous verses, as is seen from the words "therefore, as one trespass led to condemnation for

---

17. Schreiner, *Original Sin and Original Death*, p. 282.
18. Walter Bauer, *BDAG: A Greek-English Lexicon of the New Testament*, 3rd Edition (Chicago, IL: The University of Chicago Press, 2000), p. 518.

all men, so one act of righteousness leads to justification and life for all men." Paul has already stated that Adam's sin brought condemnation (Romans 5:16), but here he adds "for all men." All people are condemned before God because of the trespass of Adam. Schreiner comments: "If they are condemned before God because of Adam's sin, then they are guilty for Adam's sin. They can hardly be condemned for Adam's sin if they are not guilty for the sin he committed. Paul offers no apologetic here, nor does he defend the justice of what God has done. He asserts the facts of the case, claiming that Adam's sin spells our condemnation."[19] In contrast, the one act of righteousness by Christ (His atoning sacrifice) leads to our justification, our being declared to be right before God. It not only leads to our justification but to "life"; this is for those who have received God's abundant provision of grace and gift of righteousness (Romans 5:17). The consequence of justification is future life, in the age to come.

In verse 19, Paul concludes his argument regarding the actions of Adam and Christ: "For as by the one man's disobedience the many were made sinners, so by the one man's obedience the many will be made righteous." Paul now focuses on Adam's disobedience and Christ's obedience. Adam disobeyed God by disregarding his command (Genesis 2:16–17), but Jesus obeyed God by becoming obedient to death on the Cross (Philippians 2:8). The result of Adam's disobedience is that "many were made sinners." The word "many" (*polloi*) refers to all people (cf. Romans 5:12). Because both death and condemnation come from Adam, people are counted (*kathistemi*)[20] as sinners by virtue of Adam's disobedience. Therefore, as New Testament scholar Douglas Moo recognizes, "Paul is insisting that people were really 'made' sinners through Adam's act of disobedience."[21] On the other hand, the result of Christ's obedience is that "many will be made righteous." Whether we are counted as sinners or righteous depends on who represents us, Adam or Christ.

Throughout Romans 5:15–19 Paul contrasts the sin of the one (Adam) and the righteousness of the one (Jesus). The whole argument of Romans 5:15–19 is the unity of all sinners in Adam and the unity of the redeemed in Christ. All throughout these verses Paul speaks of the sin of one man and not individuals as the cause of the problem. In fact, five times in verses 15–19 judgment and death are attributed to Adam's one sin and affirm that his guilt is imputed to all mankind.[22]

---

19. Schreiner, *Original Sin and Original Death*, p. 285.
20. The Greek verb καθίστημι in the New Testament can mean "count" or "appoint" (see Matthew 24:45, 47: 25:21, 23; Titus 1:5; Hebrews 5:1; 7:28; 8:3).
21. Douglas Moo, *The Epistle to the Romans: NICNT* (Grand Rapids, MI: W.B. Eerdmans, 1996), p. 345.
22. Schreiner, *Original Sin and Original Death*, p. 276, 282–286.

Adam	Jesus
many died through one man's trespass — v.15	grace of one man abounds for many — v. 15
one man brought condemnation — v.16	one man brings justification — v.16
death through one man's trespass — v.17	righteousness through the one man — v.17
trespass led to condemnation for all men — v.18	one act of righteousness leads to justification for all men — v.18
by one man's disobedience the many were made sinners — v. 19	by one man's obedience the many will be made righteous — v.19

In Romans 5 there is an emphasis on the singularity of the one man (Romans 5:12, 15, 17, 18, 19) as there is in 1 Corinthians 15:45 where again Paul states that Adam was "the first man." Paul's theology of the "one man" is used in his apologetic in Acts 17, where he explains to the Greek philosophers on Mars Hill of the "one man" (Adam) from whom God made every nation on the earth (Acts 17:26). Paul's gospel presentation makes no sense if he is trying to teach that one man, Adam, is archetypal and the other, Jesus, is historical (Acts 17:31). Paul's argument in Romans 5:12–21 is fatally undermined if Adam is merely an archetype, a representation for mankind. If it was not by one man that sin, condemnation, and judgment came upon all, then how can it be by one man, Jesus Christ, that salvation comes? The parallel is broken and the analogy does not work if Adam is a metaphor for mankind. Paul's argument requires both Adam and Jesus to be two distinct historical individual men.[23] Paul, as an Apostle in the New Testament, gives us inspired, theological insights and explains the significance and meaning of Adam. The Old Testament gives the information that speaks of the Fall of humanity due to Adam's disobedience. Paul looks back with theological reflections in Romans 5 (and 1 Corinthians 15), teaching an inseparable tie between the historical reality of Christ's work of redemption and the historical reality of the Fall in Genesis 2–3. In the New Testament, Paul is giving a theological justification for the consequences of Adam's Fall in Genesis 3.

It is because of Adam's disobedience that all of mankind are considered sinners. Adam's sin is the reason that mankind is described as "by nature children of wrath" (Ephesians 2:3), which is describing the nature of our

---

23. Of course, this does not mean that Paul does not also see Adam and Jesus as "archetypal" in the sense that they are both representatives of two humanities — those "in Adam" and those who are "in Christ" (cf. 1 Corinthians 15:22).

being. The Fall brought about a fundamental change in our human nature so that post-Fall mankind is opposed to God and inclined toward things of the flesh (Romans 8:5–8; Galatians 3:3). The epistemological consequences of Adam's sin are that mankind in their unrighteousness "suppress the truth" of God's self-revelation in creation (Romans 1:18–20). Consequently, they become "futile in their thinking" (Romans 1:21) and "Claiming to be wise, they became fools" (Romans 1:22).

🦋 What Does It Mean to Be "In Adam"?

The expression "in Adam" is used by the Apostle Paul in 1 Corinthians 15:21–22, "For as by a man came death, by a man has come also the resurrection of the dead. For as in Adam all die, so also in Christ shall all be made alive." To be "in Adam" means "to be part of the group which finds in Adam its representative and leader, which finds its identity and destiny in Adam and what he has brought about for his people."[24] The Bible clearly lays out the fact that Adam is the head of fallen mankind and Jesus is the head of a redeemed mankind. Mankind "in Adam" is spiritually dead, walks according to the course of this world, and therefore is alienated from the life of God (Ephesians 2:1–2; 4:17–18). Mankind is not born innocent and then sins somewhere along the way, but we are all naturally born sinners (Ephesians 2:3). Those who are "in Adam" are spiritually dead and do not understand the truth of God's Word, "The natural person does not accept the things of the Spirit of God, for they are folly to him, and he is not able to understand them because they are spiritually discerned" (1 Corinthians 2:14).

From a human point of view, death is understandably not a nice subject to think about, and many people in today's secular Western culture try and shield themselves from it, but its existence should remind us of the fact of mankind's being "in Adam." But unlike those "in Adam," those "in Christ" have been made alive by the grace of God (cf. Ephesians 2:4, 8). In Christ, believers are no longer "in Adam" but have been reconciled to God and have peace with Him (Romans 5:1, 11). Nevertheless, because we were born "in Adam," our present mortal bodies still suffer the effects of sin and will one day die, but in the future, they will be raised in glory and be fully redeemed (1 Corinthians 15:43; Romans 8:23).

Some have argued that in 1 Corinthians 15:22 Paul teaches universalism (the idea that all people in the end will be saved) because of the words "in Christ shall all be made alive." But the "all" who will be made alive are those

24. Roy E. Ciampa and Brian S. Rosner, *The First Letter to the Corinthians: The Pillar New Testament Commentary* (W.B. Eerdmans, Publishing Company: Grand Rapids, MI, 2010), p. 763.

"who belong to Christ" (1 Corinthians 15:23). Paul has already said that the gospel is folly to those who are perishing, but it is the power of God to those who are being saved (1 Corinthians 1:18). When he was on Mars Hill, in Athens, he argued that the Resurrection of Jesus is proof that there is a future day of judgment coming (Acts 17:30–31).

This idea of being "in Adam" brings up a common objection to the teaching of original sin, which Giberson raises: "What justice permits you and me to be punished for something with which we had nothing to do?"[25] Of course, the view that we are guilty sinners in Adam is repulsive to our self-serving individualistic Western world. However, this overlooks the corporate dimension to human life and the biblical concept of federal headship (one individual representing an entire group — see Joshua 7:10–26). The idea of federal headship is seen throughout the Old Testament, for example, when David fights Goliath; both men represent each nation (1 Samuel 17). Adam is our federal head. In the Garden of Eden, Adam was not simply acting for himself but for all those he represents. God appointed Adam to act not only for himself but also for his descendants. Never have we been more perfectly represented than when we were represented through Adam. Yet, the real reason many reject the idea of inherited sin from Adam is stated by the late James Montgomery Boice:

> I am convinced that the major reason why the liberal scholars want to regard the opening chapters of Genesis as mythology is that they do not want to face the reality of the fall of the race in Adam or the guilt that flows from it.[26]

As fallen human beings, there is a vigorous protest within our hearts against the belief in the imputation of guilt from one person to another. What is more, for the Christian who does not like this teaching, then consistently you would have to reject any representation of you by Christ. There is a deliberate break in Paul's comparison of Adam and Christ in Romans 5:12 in order to clarify what is meant by "because all sinned." Theologian John Piper argues that if we read, "Through Adam sin and death entered the world, and death spread to everybody because all sinned individually," then the comparison with the work of Jesus would probably be, "So also, through Jesus Christ, righteousness and life entered the world, and life spread to all because all individually did acts of righteousness."[27]

---

25. Giberson, *Saving the Original Sinner*, p. 25.

26. James M. Boice, *Romans, vol. 2. The Reign of Grace (Romans 5–8)* (Grand Rapids, MI: Baker, 1992), p. 583.

27. John Piper, *Counted Righteous in Christ* (Leicester, England: InterVarsity Press), p. 92

Our justification then would not come through the imputed righteousness of Christ's righteousness to us but through our doing individual acts of righteousness with Christ's help.[28] We would not want to find ourselves in this situation, because Scripture makes it abundantly clear we cannot save ourselves apart from divine grace (Ephesians 2:8–9). Jesus, the last Adam (1 Corinthians 15:45), came to succeed where the first Adam had failed in keeping the law of God (Matthew 3:15; John 8:29, 55). Jesus had to do what Adam failed to do to fulfill the required sinless life of perfection. Jesus did this so that His righteousness could be transferred to those who put their faith in Him for the forgiveness of sins (2 Corinthians 5:21; Philippians 3:9).

❧ Evolution and Romans 5:12–19

Theistic evolutionists recognize that the doctrine of original sin is incompatible with evolution. This is because the Bible teaches that physical death came into the world through one man, Adam, whereas evolution demands that physical death has always been in the world. Theistic evolutionists therefore must reinterpret the meaning of death in Romans 5:12 as being spiritual (see Alexander page 142). But what did Paul mean by "death" (*thanatos*) when he stated, "sin came into the world through one man, and death through sin" (Romans 5:12). Although some have argued that it refers to only spiritual death, this view is contrary to the context of Genesis 2–3. Furthermore, in Jewish thought there is no distinction between physical and spiritual death, as they both characterize our separation from our Creator (see Genesis 3:8–9, 17–19). In Romans 5:12, Paul had both physical (verses. 14, 17) and spiritual death (verses 16, 18, 21) in mind, which might be called "total death"[29] the penalty earned for sin.

In fact, in Romans 6, Paul continues to refer to the effects of Adam's sin on our lives. In Romans 6:21 Paul argues that the "fruit" (*karpos*) of sinful living leads to shame (*epaischynomai*) and death (*thanatos*). The Greek words Paul uses here are also found in Genesis 2–3 (LXX). In the garden in Eden Adam and Eve were once not ashamed (*aischunomai*, LXX Genesis 2:25), but their eating the fruit (*karpos*, LXX Genesis 3:2–3, 6) led them to die (*apothnēskō*, LXX Genesis 3:3–4). Paul concludes in Romans 6:23 by stating

---

28. Ibid., 93.

29. New Testament scholar Douglas Moo rightly recognizes that "Paul frequently uses 'death' and related words to designate a 'physical-spiritual entity' — 'total death,' the penalty incurred for sin." Douglas Moo, *The Epistle to the Romans*, p. 320. See also: Colin G. Kruse, *Paul's Letter to the Romans: The Pillar New Testament Commentary* (Nottingham, England: Apollos, 2012), p. 242–244.

"the wages of sin is *the* death" (*ta gar opsōnia tēs hamartias thanatos*). Paul is not saying "the wages of our sins is death" but "the wages of *the* sin is death." In Romans 5:12, the term "the sin" (*tēs hamartias*) refers to the power of sin. It acts like a master who pays wages, namely, the power of sin that came into the world through Adam enslaved us all.[30] In the context of Romans 6:21, Paul is referring to physical death (cf. Romans 6:16, 7:5), but it also includes eternal death as its opposite is eternal life (Romans 6:22–23).

Paul's theology not only in Romans 5 but in 1 Corinthians 15 links the entry of the physical death (*thanatos*) of mankind to Adam (1 Corinthians 15:21–22). Paul understood death (*thanatos*) to be an enemy, an unnatural part of the creation (1 Corinthians 15:26). In 1 Corinthians 15, for example, Paul's emphasis is on Christ's physical Resurrection from the dead, with spiritual consequences. However, if the consequences of Adam's disobedience were only spiritual death, then the question would be why did Christ have to die a physical death? The question for theistic evolutionists is, if physical death has always been present in the world, then given Paul's argument that physical death came into the world because of Adam's sin, what difference did one more death (i.e., Jesus) accomplish? Moreover, those who reject a historical Fall are left with a serious theodicy problem. The Greek word *theodicy* is made up of the two words *theos* (God) and *dike* (justice) and has to do with the justification of God's goodness in the face of evil. Madueme rightly points out:

> Sin's origin in the world must be traceable to an earlier free choice of one of God's creatures. Otherwise, good and evil are eternal co-principles (dualism), or God is both good and evil (monism) — that is, God is the author of sin.[31]

Genesis 1 refutes both dualism and monism as God is not only distinct from His creation but declares His original creation to be morally "very good" (Genesis 1:1, 31). The Bible also makes it very clear that evil is not a part of God (cf. 1 John 1:5). Without the explanation of Adam falling, as the Bible describes, this would mean that God is responsible for the origin of suffering and evil in the world. Too many theistic evolutionists are either unaware of this problem or unfortunately simply do not care.

---

30. See Lita Sanders, "The fruit of sin vs the fruit of sanctification: a Pauline allusion to Genesis 3 in Romans 6 Perspective" *Journal of Creation* 30(2):4–5, August 2016.
31. Hans Madueme, "The Most Vulnerable Part of the Whole Christian Account: Original Sin and Modern Science," in *Adam, the Fall, and Original Sin* (eds. Hans Madueme and Michael Reeves; Grand Rapids, Michigan: Baker Academic, 2014), 232.

The first man, Adam, is vital to many areas of theology, yet there is one doctrine that he is essential to: the doctrine of original sin. Because many Christians are synthesizing evolutionary thinking with the Bible, this doctrine is being eroded. Theistic evolution doesn't just undermine the doctrine of original sin, but it also undermines the doctrine of salvation and our only hope of being rescued from our sinful condition: the gospel of our Lord Jesus Christ.

Chapter 8

The Last Adam: His Humanity

For the last couple of the centuries much of the church's focus on the person of Jesus has been on His divinity, to the point that aspects of His humanity are often overlooked. This can lead to a lack of understanding regarding such a critical part of His human nature. It is important, therefore, to understand why Jesus took on flesh and dwelt among us (John 1:14).[1] As a human, Jesus lived approximately 34 years on this earth. The four canonical gospels (Matthew, Mark, Luke, John) only give us a snapshot of his life (cf. John 21:25); very little is known about Jesus early life. Matthew briefly focuses upon Jesus as a young child (*paidion*, Matthew 2:1–12) and Luke records his birth as a baby, (*brephos*, Luke 2:1–21) and contains a section on him as a 12-year-old boy in the temple in Jerusalem (Luke 2:41–52), but the focus on Jesus is when He begins His ministry when He was about 30 years old (Luke 3:23).

Yet, despite His brief time on the earth there are several important questions that arise regarding Jesus' humanity: Why did Jesus take on a human nature? Did Jesus' human life require sinfulness? In His incarnation did Jesus empty Himself of His divine nature? These are important questions to consider, as Jesus' birth is meaningless without His sinless life, and His sinless life is meaningless without His death and Resurrection from the dead. This chapter will aim to answer these questions, but it will begin by looking at whether Jesus was a real person, the promise of His coming in the Old Testament, and timing of His birth.

---

1. In the first century, the Apostle John had to deal with the false teaching of the docetists (from *dokeo*, "to appear"), who believed Jesus only appeared to be human (see 1 John 1:1–3, 4:1–3).

⚹ Was Jesus a Real Person?

There are some sceptics today who question whether Jesus was in fact a real person (i.e., Jesus mythicists). These people bring a radical scepticism to any source that mentions Jesus. However, if this sceptical view of history is consistently applied it would mean we could not trust any historical document from the ancient world. The fact of the matter is that the four canonical gospels (which are in the historical genre of Greco-Roman biography) give us accurate eyewitness historical biographical accounts of the life of Jesus of Nazareth (see chapter 9).

When it comes to the crucifixion of Jesus it is not only early Christian sources that testify to it (1 Corinthians 15:3; cf. Matthew 27:32–56; Mark 15:21–41; Luke 23:26–49; John 19:17–30), but Jewish and Roman historians and even critical scholars today all agree that Jesus died on the Cross. The first century Jewish historian Josephus (A.D. 37–100) in his book *Antiquities of the Jews* (A.D. 93–94) in book 18 chapter 3 said that Jesus was crucified by Pontius Pilate: "And when Pilate at the suggestion of the principal men amongst us, had condemned him to the cross, those that loved him at the first did not forsake him; for he appeared to them alive again on the third day...."[2] Like Josephus, the Roman historian Tacitus, writing in the second century, also referred to Jesus death on the Cross under Pontius Pilate in his final work, *Annals* (A.D. 116) in book 15 chapter 44 wrote "Christus, from whom the name had its origin, suffered the extreme penalty during the reign of Tiberius at the hands of one of our procurators, Pontius Pilatus...." It is not only first and second century historians that agree that Jesus was crucified but even today critical scholars do. The leading critic of the New Testament today, Dr. Bart Ehrman, an agnostic, has said: "One of the most certain facts of history is that Jesus was crucified on orders of the Roman prefect of Judea, Pontius Pilate."[3] If Jesus was crucified, He existed, and since we know He was crucified He obviously existed. Those who say He did not exist are just wrong. There is no logical reason to dismiss Jesus as a historical person unless you are committed to a philosophical bias that explains away the evidence.

⚹ The Promise of a Savior

The reason the Son of God (Jesus) came into the world does not start in the New Testament but begins from the Old Testament. In Genesis 3:15,

---

2. It is highly unlikely that Josephus' mention of Jesus crucifixion is a later interpolation by Christians.
3. Bart Ehrman, *The Historical Jesus: Lecture Transcript and Course Guidebook*, Part 2 of 2 (Chantilly VA: The Teaching Company, 2000), p. 162.

after Adam and Eve's disobedience of God's command not to eat from the tree of knowledge of good and evil, we read of a promise made concerning the seed of the woman:

> And I will put enmity between you and the woman, and between your seed and her Seed; He shall bruise your head, and you shall bruise His heel (NKJV).

This passage is famously known as the *protoevangelium* because it is the first proclamation of the good news (gospel). God promised to deal a mortal blow to the serpent (Satan) through the offspring of the woman (Eve). Many scholars today, however, reject this messianic interpretation of Genesis 3:15 and instead see it either etiologically (i.e., human misery as a result of sin)[4] or symbolically (mankind's constant struggle over the forces of evil).[5] These views reject the belief that the serpent in Genesis 3 represents Satan (cf. Revelation 12:9). It is argued the text says nothing about an individual coming Savior, the Messiah. Even among many theologians today, who have a high view of Scripture, the understanding that Genesis 3:15 as a messianic prophecy has almost disappeared. So how should we understand Genesis 3:15 — etiologically, symbolically, or messianically? It is important to keep in mind that for Jesus the whole Old Testament should be read as pointing to Him, a messianic text that points to the hope of a future Messiah (cf. Luke 24:44–45; John 5:45). As a historical text, Genesis 3:15 begins the messianic hope of the Old Testament in seed form. Therefore, Moses gives the first allusion to the coming Redeemer in Genesis 3:15 and then uses the rest of the Torah to identify Him as the coming Messiah.[6]

Theologian Michael Rydelnik offers three preliminary considerations for viewing Genesis 3:15 as a messianic text. First, salvation during judgment is a common theme in the early chapters of Genesis. After murdering his brother Abel, God gave Cain a mark to protect him (Genesis 4:15), God spared Noah and his family from the judgment of the global Flood (Genesis 6:18), and the judgment at Tower of Babel (Genesis 11:1–10) was followed by the call of Abram (Genesis 12:1–9). It would be expected then that with God's first pronouncement of judgment that there is the hope of salvation. Second, the serpent should be seen as something other than just a mere snake, i.e., an animal animated by an evil power (snakes cannot talk). Snakes are not inherently evil, as God made everything "very good" (Genesis 1:31), and a mere snake, apart from an evil power animating it, would not be able to tempt mankind. Also,

---

4. Craig, *In Quest of the Historical Adam*, p. 95.

5. John Walton, *Genesis: NIVAC* (Grand Rapids, MI: Zondervan, 2001), p. 226, 234.

6. Michael Rydelnik, *The Messianic Hope: NAC Studies in Bible & Theology* (Nashville, TN: B&H Publishing Group, 2010), p. 135.

it is the serpent himself (not his offspring) who will be crushed by the woman's seed (offspring), indicating a longevity not normal to mere snakes. Third, ancient Jewish interpreters also explained Genesis 3:15 in a messianic sense. This can be seen in the Greek translation of Genesis 3:15 (Septuagint, LXX, c. 250 B.C.), and in pre-Christian Jewish rabbinical literature (non-canonical) in the Targumim *Pseudo-Jonathan, Neofiti,* and *Onkelos.*

Targum *Neofiti* on Genesis 3:15 states, "And I will put enmity between you and the woman, and between your children and her children. And it will come about when her children keep the Torah, and do the commandments, they will aim at you and smite you on your head and kill you, but when they abandon the commandments of the Torah, you will be aiming at him and will bite him on the heel, and will make him deathly ill. But there will be healing for his son, but for you, O serpent, there will not be healing, for they will make appeasement at the last, in the day of the King Messiah."

Moreover, even post-Christian Jewish people still saw Genesis 3:15 as messianic. The Midrash Genesis Rabbah 23:5 states: "Rabbi Tanchuma said, in the name of Rabbi Samuel: Eve had respect to that seed which is coming from another place. And who is this? This is the King Messiah." These ancient Jewish interpreters surely understood and read Genesis 3:15 carefully.[7]

To understand Genesis 3:15 as a messianic text it is important not only to recognize the immediate context but the surrounding and overall context of Genesis. In Genesis 1–2 God has created a world without sin and death. Then in Genesis 3, after the serpent's temptation Adam and Eve Fall from the original righteous state they were created in into sin and separation from God. After listening to the confessions of Adam and Eve, God then judges the serpent. In Genesis 3:14 God directs His judgment to the serpent (not the animated force behind it) by cursing it. But why curse an amoral creature? Rydelnik points out: "The purpose of cursing the animal is for it to become a perpetual reminder of the devastating destruction caused by the role of the serpent in the sin of Adam and Eve."[8] As part of the curse the serpent is to crawl on its belly and eat dust, which is a sign of their perpetual humiliation (Psalm 72:9; Isaiah 49:23). The serpent is cursed above all the animals. The prophet Isaiah even says that when the future effects of the cursed are reversed in God's kingdom the curse on the serpent shall remain forever (Isaiah 65:25).[9] This shows that "the serpent

---

7. For a fuller treatment of these three points see Rydelnik, *The Messianic Hope,* p. 135–137.
8. Ibid., p. 138.
9. Motyer comments: "The only point in the whole of the new creation where there is no change…is in the curse pronounced on sin, which still stands (*cf.* Gn. 3:14)." Alec Motyer, *The Prophecy of Isaiah: An Introduction & Commentary* (Downers Grove, IL: InterVarsity Press, 1993), p. 531.

will remain an eternal outward symbol of the spiritual defeat of the dark force behind the fall."[10]

In Genesis 3:15, God turns His attention to address the evil power that is controlling the serpent. Since animals don't talk and can't contradict what God has said, the serpent is surely being controlled by someone who is later revealed as Satan. God said that there will be "enmity" (*'êbâ*) between the tempter and the woman. In the Old Testament, the word "always refers to enmity between moral agents (persons, not animals)."[11] This enmity is between the woman and tempter who was controlling the serpent. The enmity that exists would not just be between the woman and tempter but would extend to their collective "offspring" (*zera'*) as well. The enmity between the offspring of the serpent and the woman does not take long, as wicked Cain, whose deeds were of Satan (1 John 3:12), killed his righteous brother Abel (Genesis 4:8; cf. Matthew 23:35). Cain and Abel were from the same physical offspring (Adam and Eve) but belonged to different spiritual offspring (Cain was of Satan and Abel was of God).[12] When God confronts Cain, He uses the same language, "you are cursed from the ground" (Genesis 4:11) that He used of the Serpent, "cursed are you above all livestock" (Genesis 3:14a), suggesting that the Serpent is Cain's spiritual Father (cf. Genesis 9:25, 27). In Genesis 4, after Cain kills Abel, God responds by giving Eve another offspring, Seth. In Genesis 4:25, Eve's commentary on God's provision of another offspring uses terminology found only in Genesis 3:15.

Genesis 3:15	Genesis 4:25
I will put [*śît*] enmity between you and the woman [*'iššâ*], and between your offspring [*zera'*] and her offspring; he shall bruise your head, and you shall bruise his heel."	"And Adam knew his wife [*'iššâ*] again, and she bore a son and called his name Seth [*šēt*][13], for she said, "God has appointed [*śît*] for me another offspring [*zera'*] instead of Abel, for Cain killed him."

The word "wife" in Genesis 4:25 is the same word for "woman" in Genesis 3:15. Furthermore, Eve's declaration "God has appointed" uses the same word for "put" in Genesis 3:15, "I will put enmity." In Genesis 4:25 Eve says that God has appointed for her another offspring (Genesis 3:15). Eve interprets

10. Rydelnik, *The Messianic Hope*, p. 138.
11. Ibid., 139. See Numbers 35:21-22; Ezekiel 25:15; 35:5.
12. Some argue that the word for "offspring" (*zera*) only refers to physical offspring, but this is not true as it can have a symbolic meaning, i.e., referring to spiritual offspring (Malachi 2:15; Isaiah 57:4).
13. The Hebrew word "*šēt*" (Seth) sounds like the word "*śît*" ("I will put" / "appointed").

"her offspring" not in a collective sense, but as speaking of an individual who will defeat the serpent.[14] Genesis 3:15 refers to a singular descendant of the woman. This can be seen from the fact that the term "offspring" is used with singular verbs and adjectives, and particularly with singular pronouns.[15] The surrounding pronouns show a singular individual is in view: "*He* shall bruise your head, and you shall bruise *His* heel" (Genesis 3:15; NKJV).[16] The resulting battle leads to the tempter's own head being "bruised" (*šûp*) by a specific descent of the woman, in other words it will receive a violent blow (cf. Job 9:17). The victory over the tempter is won by a descendant of the woman, but it comes at a cost as he will suffer and die for it, as the tempter bruises the heel of this descendant. This is not a purposeless suffering, as the death of the descendant of the woman destroyed the power over death that the tempter once held (Hebrews 2:14).

Nevertheless, to fully understand Genesis 3:15 as a messianic text it must be read not only in the light of the rest of the Book of Genesis but the rest of the Torah, as it is one book (the book of Moses; cf. Mark 12:26). The hope of the appointed offspring is unveiled progressively through the birth to Eve of Seth (Genesis 4:26, 5:1–32), Noah's offspring (Genesis 9:9), and the offspring of Abraham (Genesis 12:1–3, 7). Genesis continues to trace the offspring of Abraham through his sons Isaac (Genesis 21:12, 26:24) and Jacob (Genesis 28:13–14) and the twelves sons of Jacob (Genesis 46:7, 48:19). God also promised Abraham that kings would come from him (Genesis 17:6–7) and this same promise was also made to Jacob (Genesis 35:11). Significantly, in what is a messianic prediction, the promise is narrowed to a specific descendant of Jacob, Judah, whose descendant will be a royal Messiah who will rule the peoples (Genesis 49:9–10; cf. Psalm 2). The future descendant of the woman in Genesis 3:15 will not only be royal and rule all people but he will bless the nations (Genesis 22:17–18).

The author of the Torah, Moses, refers to these promises in the prophecies of Balaam in Numbers 24. There Jacob is promised that "Water shall flow from his buckets, and his seed shall be in many waters" (Numbers 24:7). The next line in the verse describes Jacob's seed as "his king" whose "kingdom shall be exalted" (Numbers 24:7). Then in Numbers 24:9 this seed is identified as a lion who comes from the tribe of Judah (cf. Genesis 49:9–10). This same person will also be blessed (Numbers 24:9), as was

---

14. See Seth D. Postell, Eithan Bar and Erez Soref, *Reading Moses Seeing Jesus: How the Torah Fulfills Its Goals in Yeshua* (Lexham Press: Bellingham, WA, 2017), p.66.

15. Collins, *Genesis 1–4, p.* 156.

16. The term "offspring" often refers to a singular individual (Genesis 4:25; 15:3; 16:10; 21:13; 22:18; 24:60; 38:8-9).

Adam (Genesis 1:28), and those against him will be cursed (Numbers 24:9), even as the serpent was cursed (Genesis 3:14). This prophecy regarding the messianic king is eschatological as it is said to take place "in the last days" (Numbers 24:14; cf. Genesis 49:1). In the next prophecy of Balaam there is another promise of a messianic king: "a star shall come out of Jacob, and a scepter shall rise out of Israel" (Numbers 24:17). A thematic link to Genesis 3:15 exists in Numbers 24:17 as this messianic king will crush the forehead of the enemies of Israel (Moab), which would remind Israel that the offspring of the woman would crush the head of the enemy.[17] The messianic king will also exercise dominion just as Adam did (Numbers 24:19; cf. Genesis 1:28), which will be over all the earth (Psalm 72:8; cf. Daniel 7:14). His enemies will "lick the dust" (Psalm 72:9) just as the serpent is told "on your belly you shall go, and dust you shall eat" (Genesis 3:14).

The rest of the Old Testament traces this person, whose kingdom will last forever, who will rule with righteousness and wisdom, whose people will be blessed in Him (2 Samuel 7:12-13; Psalm 72; Isaiah 11:1, 4; 65:23, 25), and whose enemies will be made a footstool for his feet (Psalm 110:1, 6; cf. Genesis 3:15). The promised offspring finds its fulfillment in the New Testament, where Paul identifies Jesus as the "offspring" and fulfillment of the promises made to Abraham (Galatians 3:16). The Apostle John tells us, "The reason the Son of God appeared was to destroy the works of the devil" (1 John 3:8).

The examination of the details of the text of Genesis 3:15 and the way those details are used and alluded to in the rest of Genesis and the Torah illuminates that it is indeed a messianic text that speaks of a particular descendant of the woman who will crush the head of the tempter (Satan).

✄ Born of a Woman

Accurate chronology is important in relationship to the gospel of Jesus as the Christian faith is dependent upon God working in history to redeem the world. God uses history as a canvas to paint His plan and purpose of redemption. The promise of a coming redeemer who would crush the head of the serpent took place in history when Jesus was born of the virgin Mary in the city of Bethlehem (Luke 2:1–6). The Apostle Paul recognized that the birth of Jesus occurred, in God's plan, exactly at the right time:

---

17. Rydelnik notes that: "Although Num 24:17 uses different words than Gen 3:15 for both the blow struck and the head that is crushed, the thematic literary allusion is plain. The expectation is that when the messianic king arrives, he will crush the heads of Israel's enemies, reminding the readers of the promise that Eve's offspring would crush the head of the enemy." Rydelnik, *The Messianic Hope*, p. 144.

But when the fullness of time had come, God sent forth his Son, born of woman, born under the law, to redeem those who were under the law, so that we might receive adoption as sons (Galatians 4:4–5).

There are several Greek words for *time* that the Apostle Paul could have used. One word that he uses elsewhere is the Greek word, *kairos*, a word which can indicate an ideal time, or even eschatological time (1 Corinthians 4:5). In an interesting twist, Paul doesn't use that word here as he uses the word *chronos*, which indicates calendar time, or linear time. This was the right time for the "Son" to be sent into the world. As the one sent into the world, the Son took on a human nature when He was born of a woman (cf. Romans 8:3).[18] The Apostle Paul also notes that Jesus was born for a purpose: redemption. In the ancient world, the act of redemption involved the paying of a price to set someone free from slavery. Jesus came to give Himself as a ransom for sin so that we could be set free from our slavery to sin (Mark 10:45; John 8:32). The eternal Son of God took on a human nature so that humans could become adopted sons of God (Romans 8:14–15).

The Old Testament prophet Micah predicted that the Messiah, the Son of David, would be born in Bethlehem in Judea (Micah 5:2; cf. Matthew 2:1–6). But when did this take place? The gospel of Luke, read alongside of Matthew, dates the birth of Jesus to both the reign of Herod the Great (Luke 1:5, cf. Matthew 2:19–22) and a census under Quirinius, governor of Syria. (Luke 2:1–2). The date of Jesus' birth is directly related to the date of the death of Herod the great (Matthew 2:15). Herod's death is conventionally dated to 4 B.C., but this is based on the wrong consular year that the Jewish historian Josephus gave for Herod's enthronement as king by the Romans. It is now argued that the evidence strongly suggests that Herod died in 1 B.C.[19] This means that the birth of Jesus was in early 2 B.C. (or late 3 B.C.). If this is the case, then we can confidently date Jesus' death and Resurrection to A.D. 33. Jesus was crucified on "the day of Preparation" (John 19:31), the Friday (*paraskeuē*), before the Sabbath of Passover week (Mark 15:42). The night before, on Thursday evening, Jesus ate the Passover meal with His disciples (Mark 14:12). The Passover was always on the 14th day of Nisan (Exodus 12:6). In A.D. 33, the 14th of Nisan was on April 3rd. Jesus' birth in early 2 B.C. would have made him around 30–31 in Tiberius Caesar 15th year (Luke 3:1) in A.D. 29, making Him "about 30" when He started His ministry (Luke 3:23).[20]

---

18. Since the Son took on a human nature, this presupposes his pre-existence.

19. See Andrew E. Steinmann and Rodger C. Young, "Evidences That Herod the Great's Sons Antedated Their Reigns to a Time before Herod's Death," *Bibliotheca Sacra*, April 7, 2020; John H. Rhoads, "Josephus Misdated the Census of Quirinius", *JETS* 54.1 (March 2011), p. 65–87.

20. If Jesus was born in 4 B.C., He would be 34–35 years of age when He began His ministry and that is hard to reconcile with Him being "about 30" years of age as Luke reports.

❧ Jesus's Human Nature

There is no doubt that the New Testament claims that Jesus was truly God (John 1:1–3, 18; Romans 9:5; 10:9, 13; 1 Corinthians 8:6; Philippians 2:5–11; Colossians 1:15–16; 2:9; Titus 2:13; Hebrews 1:1–3; 2 Peter 1:1). Yet it also tells us that Jesus was truly human: Jesus was wrapped in ordinary infant clothing (Luke 2:7), grew in wisdom as a child (Luke 2:40, 52), became weary (John 4:6), was hungry (Matthew 4:4), was thirsty (John 19:28), was tempted by the devil (Matthew. 4:1–11), was sorrowful (Matthew 26:38a), and, after his Resurrection, still had a human body (Luke 24:39).

The belief that Jesus is both truly God and truly man is known as the Hypostatic Union (the union of two *ousia* [natures], divine and human, in the one *hypostasis* [person] of Jesus Christ). The relationship of the divine and human nature within the person of Christ was debated in early church history.

The Council of Chalcedon (A.D. 451) made a declaration to combat heresies at the extremes of the debate.[21] Eutychianism taught that the human nature of Jesus was swallowed up and lost in the divine nature, while Nestorianism taught that the human nature of Jesus was separated from His divine nature. Against this position, the Council affirmed that Jesus had two distinct natures, divine and human, and that these two natures were indivisible and belonged to one person, the Lord Jesus Christ. On the other hand, Apollinarianism taught that the divine mind of Christ took the place of the human mind: Christ was a divine mind in a human body (Apollinarianism was condemned at the Council of Constantinople in A.D. 381). If Jesus was not truly man, then He could not redeem humanity (Hebrews 2:14–17).

The biblical teaching is that Jesus was truly God and truly man in the one person. Jesus is in fact the God-man forever (Matthew 26:29; Luke 24:39–43; Acts 1:11; 1 Timothy 2:5; cf. Colossians 2:9). Jesus' humanity should be

---

21. "Therefore, following the holy fathers, we all with one accord teach men to acknowledge one and the same Son, our Lord Jesus Christ, at once complete in Godhead and complete in manhood, truly God and truly man, consisting also of a reasonable soul and body; of one substance with the Father as regards his Godhead, and at the same time of one substance with us as regards his manhood; like us in all respects, apart from sin; as regards his Godhead, begotten of the Father before the ages, but yet as regards his manhood begotten, for us men and for our salvation, of Mary the Virgin, the God-bearer; one and the same Christ, Son, Lord, Only-begotten, recognized in two natures, without confusion, without change, without division, without separation; the distinction of natures being in no way annulled by the union, but rather the characteristics of each nature being preserved and coming together to form one person and subsistence, not as parted or separated into two persons, but one and the same Son and Only-begotten God the Word, Lord Jesus Christ; even as the prophets from earliest times spoke of him, and our Lord Jesus Christ himself taught us, and the creed of the fathers has handed down to us."

viewed as an addition to His divine nature and does not subtract anything from His divine nature.

The question we need to ask is, why did Jesus add humanity to His divine nature (John 1:1, 14)? The opening of two of the gospels clearly teach the unique virgin conception of Jesus (Luke 1:26–31). In his gospel account, Matthew sees the birth of Jesus as a fulfillment of the messianic prophecy given to the house of David from Isaiah 7:14:

> Behold, the virgin shall conceive and bear a son, and they shall call his name Immanuel (which means, God with us) (Matthew 1:23).[22]

The child conceived in Mary was by the Holy Spirit (Matthew 1:20). The purpose of Jesus' virginal conception was probably not the cause of His sinlessness (Hebrews 4:15), but rather it was the means whereby the eternal Son of God took into union with His divine nature our human nature. The virgin conception, therefore, answers the question of how Jesus became the God-man.[23]

Much of Christian teaching focuses, rightly, on the death of Jesus. However, in focusing on the death of Christ, we often neglect the teaching that Jesus lived a life of perfect obedience to the Father (John 8:29). Jesus not only died for us, but He also lived for us. If all Jesus had to do was to die for us, then He could have descended from heaven on Good Friday, gone straight to the Cross, risen from the dead, and ascended back into heaven. Theologian R.C. Sproul points out the importance of Jesus' life of righteousness:

> Jesus not only had to die for our sins, but He had to live for our righteousness. If all Jesus did was die for your sins, that would remove all of your guilt, and that would leave you sinless in the sight of God, but not righteous. You would be innocent, but not righteous because you haven't done anything to obey the Law of God which is what righteousness requires.[24]

Jesus did not live for approximately 34 years for no reason. While on earth, Christ did the Father's will (John 5:30) by taking specific actions, teaching, working miracles, and obeying the Law to "fulfill all righteousness"

---

22. The Hebrew word *'almâ*, used in Isaiah 7:14, clearly has the meaning of virgin in the Old Testament (see Genesis 24:43; Song of Solomon 1:3, 6:8; Proverbs 30:19). The LXX translated the word *'almâ* as *parthenos* which referred to virginity (cf. Matthew 1:23). Although, the baby was called Jesus, the name Immanuel is a symbolical description of His throne title. King David's son was called Solomon, but his royal title was Jedidiah (2 Samuel 12:24–25).
23. See Robert Reymond, *A New Systematic Theology of the Christian Faith*, 2nd ed. (Nashville, TN: Thomas Nelson, 1996), p. 552.
24. R.C. Sproul, "Jesus Is Our Righteousness," Ligonier Ministries, October 2017, https://www.ligonier.org/blog/jesus-our-righteousness/.

(Matthew 3:15). Jesus, the Last Adam (1 Corinthians 15:45), came to succeed where the first Adam had failed in keeping the law of God (cf. Genesis 2:16–17). Jesus had to do what Adam failed to do to fulfill the required sinless life of perfection. Jesus did this so that His righteousness could be transferred to those who put their faith in Him for the forgiveness of sins (2 Corinthians 5:21; Philippians 3:9; cf. Isaiah 53:4–6). Although God provided an atonement for Adam's sin through an animal sacrifice in the garden (Genesis 3:21), the blood of animals is ultimately insufficient to deal with sin (Hebrews 10:4), which is why Jesus, the Last Adam, gave Himself as a sacrifice for sin (Hebrews 2:17, 9:11–14). Jesus became our sympathetic High Priest (Hebrews 2:18, 4:15) who now stands before the Father as our mediator (Hebrews 9:15; 1 Timothy 2:5).

🦋 Did Jesus' Humanity Require Sinfulness?

In His humanity, Jesus was subject to everything that humans are subject to, such as tiredness, hunger, and temptation; but does this mean that like all humans He was subject to sin? It is important to keep in mind that being human does not make one sinful, as "sin is not an essential component of human nature."[25] We must remember that God created Adam at the beginning of creation as sinless and with the capacity not to sin. Adam became a sinner because he broke God's Law. Moreover, the incarnation of Jesus shows sin not to be essential to being human.

The reason humans sin is because we are guilty as sinners in Adam (Romans 5:12, 19; 1 Corinthians 15:22). Mankind is guilty in Adam by the fact that he represents us as our federal head. Jesus was sinless in the life He lived, keeping God's law perfectly (Luke 4:13; John 8:29, 15:10; 2 Corinthians 5:21; Hebrews 4:15; 1 Peter 2:22; 1 John 3:5). Jesus was confident in His challenge for His opponents to convict Him of sin (John 8:46). Even the Roman governor, Pilate, found no guilt in Him (John 18:38), and Pilate's wife recognized Jesus as a righteous man (Matthew 27:19). One of the criminals on the cross also recognized that Jesus had done nothing wrong (Luke 23:41), and even Judas after betraying Jesus admitted he had betrayed innocent blood (Matthew 27:4). We must remember that Jesus was a "lamb without blemish and without spot" (1 Peter 1:19). Jesus' sinless life qualifies Him to be a sacrifice for the sins of others (Isaiah 53:7–10).

But how did Jesus, as a true human, not fall into sin? Some believe it was because of the bond between His divine and human nature. Answering the question of whether Christ was able to sin or not (impeccability), theologian

---

25. John Frame, *Systematic Theology: An Introduction to Christian Belief* (New Jersey: P&R Publishing Group, 2013), p. 889.

Louis Berkhof states: "[this] means not merely that Christ could avoid sinning, and did actually avoid it, but also that it was impossible for Him to sin because of the essential bond between the human and divine natures."[26] On the other hand, theologian Bruce Ware believes that:

> The answer Scripture suggests to us is this: Jesus did not sin, not because his divine nature overpowered his human nature, keeping him from sinning, but because he utilized all of the resources given to him in his humanity. He loved and meditated on God's Word ... he prayed to his Father; he trusted in the wisdom and rightness of his Father's will and Word; and, very significantly, he relied on the supernatural power of the Spirit to strengthen him to do all that he was called upon to do.[27]

In his Gospel, Luke, a trustworthy historian (Luke 1:1–4), traces Jesus' genealogy to the first man and father of all humanity — Adam (Luke 3:38). Luke then focuses on Jesus' temptation by Satan (4:1–13). This is interesting as unlike Adam, who is called the son of God (Luke 3:38), who sinned, Jesus overcame His temptation by Satan. Luke tells us that before Jesus went into the wilderness to be tempted by Satan, He was filled with the Holy Spirit and was led by Him into the wilderness (Luke 4:1). Moreover, after His temptation and at the time when He began His ministry, Jesus returned in the power of the Spirit (Luke 4:14; cf. Isaiah 11:1–3). In fact, when Jesus went into the synagogue in Nazareth on the Sabbath, He opened the scroll of the prophet Isaiah (61:1–2) to the place where it said, "the Spirit of the Lord is upon me," which Jesus said had been fulfilled in Him (Luke 4:18–21).

In His life and ministry, Jesus was empowered by the Holy Spirit (Acts 10:38). Not only was Jesus empowered by the Holy Spirit, but He also relied on the Word of God to defeat the Satan (the devil) in his temptations (Luke 4:4, 8, 12). Jesus overcame the Satan's temptations by quoting Scripture, saying to him, "It is written," which has the force of or is equivalent to "that settles it"; and Jesus understood that the Word of God was sufficient for this. Furthermore, when Jesus was in the Garden of Gethsemane and was facing the temptation of giving up on going to the Cross (Luke 22:42), He was committed to pray to the Father (Luke 22:42–44).[28] Jesus fought and

26. Berkhof, *Systematic Theology*, p. 318.
27. Bruce Ware, *The Man Christ Jesus: Theological Reflections on the Humanity of Christ* (Wheaton, IL: Crossway, 2013), p. 84.
28. The cup Jesus refers to in the garden is a metaphor for the suffering He will face on the Cross (see Matthew 20:22–23) by enduring the wrath of God (Isaiah 51:17, 22; Jeremiah 25:15, 17, 28).

Temptation	Genesis 3 (ESV)	Luke 4 (ESV)	1 John 2 (ESV)
Physical	"Has God indeed said, 'You shall not eat of every tree of the garden'?" (3:1)	"If you are the Son of God, command this stone to become bread." (4:3)	Lust of the eyes (2:16)
Personal Gain	"You will not surely die." (3:4)	"...lest you dash your foot against a stone." (4:11)	Lust of the flesh (2:16)
Power	You will be like God (3:5)	"All this authority I will give You..." (4:6)	Pride of life (2:16)

struggled with temptation (Luke 22:44), yet He was always victorious. We must remember that Jesus in His humanity was not superman but a real man. The humanity of Jesus and the deity of Jesus do not mix directly with one another. If they did, then that would mean that the humanity of Jesus would become super-humanity; and if it is super-humanity, it is not our humanity; and if it is not our humanity, He cannot be our substitute since He must be like us (Hebrews 2:14–17).

Jesus' humanity is an example for believers, as it has to do with how we live our lives. The Christian life should be an imitation of the life of Jesus (see John 13:34, 15:12). We are called to live our lives as He lived His (1 Peter 2:21). Just as Jesus was tempted, endured suffering, and faced hatred, so as Christians we will also face those things in this world (John 15:18–20). The apostle John also warns us not to "love the world or the things in the world" (1 John 2:15), noting three things in particular: the desires of the flesh, the desires of the eyes, and the pride of life (1 John 2:16). Interestingly, these were the elements in Satan's temptation of Eve and of Jesus.

Satan, who has sway over the world (1 John 5:19), will use the desires of the world that he used on Eve and Jesus in order to tempt Christians. Nevertheless, the way we overcome this battle with the world is by looking to the one who has already overcome the world (John 16:33). Jesus' life of obedience and faithfulness is an example to us when we face temptation, since we have the same resources that Jesus relied on to fulfill His ministry: the Word of God (Ephesians 6:17), prayer (Ephesians 6:18), and the Holy Spirit (Ephesians 5:18).

In His Humanity Could Jesus Err?

In His humanity, Jesus was subject to everything that humans are subject to, such as tiredness, hunger, and temptation. But does this mean that like all humans He was subject to error? It is argued by some theistic evolutionists that because in His humanity Jesus was not omniscient that this limited knowledge would have made Him capable of error. It is also believed that Jesus accommodated Himself to the prejudices and erroneous views of the Jewish people of the first century A.D., accepting some of the untrue traditions of that time. This, therefore, nullifies His authority on critical questions. For the same reasons, it is not only certain aspects of Jesus's teaching, but also those of the apostles that are seen as erroneous. Writing for the theistic evolutionist organization BioLogos, Kenton Sparks argues that because Jesus, as a human, operated within His finite human horizon, then He would have made errors:

> If Jesus as a finite human being erred from time to time, there is no reason at all to suppose that Moses, Paul, John [sic] wrote Scripture without error. Rather, we are wise to assume that the biblical authors expressed themselves as human beings writing from the perspectives of their own finite, broken horizons.[29]

To believe our Lord was able to err — and did err in the things He taught — is a severe accusation (even heretical) and needs to be taken seriously. To demonstrate that the claim that Jesus erred in His teaching is itself erroneous, it is necessary to evaluate different aspects of Jesus' nature and ministry. First, I will look at the divine nature of Jesus and whether He emptied Himself of that nature. Then I will examine the importance of Jesus' ministry as a prophet and His claims to teach the truth.

❧ In the Incarnation Did Jesus Empty Himself of His Divine Nature?

A question that needs to be asked is whether Jesus emptied Himself of His divine nature in His incarnation. In the 17th century, German scholars debated the issue of Christ's divine attributes while He was on earth. They argued that because there is no reference in the gospels to Christ making use of all of His divine attributes (such as omniscience) that He abandoned the attributes of His divinity in His incarnation.[30] These scholars found support for this in Philippians 2:7, and argued for a *kenotic* theology:

> ... but emptied [*ekenosen*] himself, by taking the form of a servant, being born in the likeness of men.

Because of Christ's self-emptying in Philippians 2:7, it was believed that Jesus was limited essentially by the opinions of His time. It is critical,

29. Kenton Sparks, "After Inerrancy, Evangelicals and the Bible in the Postmodern Age," BioLogos, Part 4. 2010, p. 7 http://biologos.org/uploads/static-content/sparks_scholarly_essay.pdf.
30. Alistar McGrath, *Christian Theology: An introduction*, 5th ed (Oxford, United Kingdom: Blackwell Publishing Limited, 2011), p. 293.

therefore, to ask what Paul means when he says that Jesus emptied Himself. Philippians 2:5–8 says:

> Have this mind among yourselves, which is yours in Christ Jesus, who, though he was in the form of God, did not count equality with God a thing to be grasped, but emptied himself, by taking the form of a servant, being born in the likeness of men. And being found in human form, he humbled himself by becoming obedient to the point of death, even death on a cross.

There are two key words in these verses that help in understanding the nature of Jesus. The first key word is the Greek *morphē* (form). The parallel phrases (form of God and form of a servant) show that *morphē* refers to outward appearance.[31] In Greek literature, the term *morphē* has to do with "external appearance" which is visible to human observation.[32] The word *morphē* in the Old Testament (LXX) refers to something that can be seen (Judges 8:18; Job 4:16; Isaiah 44:13). Christ did not cease to be in the form of God in the incarnation, but taking on the form of a servant He became the God-man.[33]

The second key word is *ekenosen* from which we get the *kenosis* doctrine. Modern English Bibles translate Philippians 2:7 *differently*:

> New International Version/Today's New International Version: "rather, he made himself nothing by taking the very nature of a servant, being made in human likeness."

> English Standard Version: "but emptied himself, by taking the form of a servant, being born in the likeness of men."

> New American Standard Bible: "but emptied Himself by taking the form of a bond-servant, and being born in the likeness of men."

> New King James Version: "but made Himself of no reputation, taking the form of a bondservant, and coming in the likeness of men."

> New Living Translation: "Instead, he gave up his divine privileges; he took the humble position of a slave and was born as a human being. When he appeared in human form...."

---

31. Moises Silva, *Philippians, Baker Exegetical Commentary on the New Testament,* 2nd edn. (Grand Rapids, MI: Baker Academic, 2005), p. 101

32. J. Behm, "μορφή", in G. Kittel (ed.), *Theological Dictionary of the New Testament,* Vol. 4 (Grand Rapids, MI: Eerdmans, 1967), p. 742–743.

33. In Philippians 2:6 the present participle "was" or "existed" (ὑπάρχω *huparcho*) points to Jesus' eternal existence in the "form of God."

It is debatable from a lexical standpoint whether "emptied himself," "made himself of no reputation," or "gave up his divine privileges" are even the best translations. The New International Version/Today's New International Version translation "made himself nothing" is probably more supportable.[34] Philippians 2:7, however, does not say that Jesus emptied Himself of anything in particular; all it says is that He emptied Himself. New Testament scholar George Ladd comments:

> The text does not say that he emptied himself of the *morphē theou* [form of God] or of equality with God.... All that the text states is that "he emptied himself by taking something else to himself, namely, the manner of being, the nature or form of a servant or slave." By becoming human, by entering on a path of humiliation that led to death, the divine Son of God emptied himself.[35]

It is pure conjecture to argue from this verse that Jesus gave up any or all His divine nature. Jesus may have given up or suspended the use of some of His divine privileges, perhaps, for example, His omnipresence or the glory that He had with the Father in heaven (John 17:5), but not His divine power or knowledge. Jesus humbling Himself is seen in that "as man" (*hos anthropos*) "he humbled himself by becoming obedient to the point of death, even death on a cross" (Philippians 2:8).

The fact that Jesus did not give up His divine nature can be seen when He was on the Mount of Transfiguration and the disciples saw His glory (Luke 9:28–35) since here there is an association with the glory of God's presence in Exodus 34:29–35. In the incarnation, Jesus was not exchanging His deity for humanity but suspending the use of some of His divine powers and attributes (cf. 2 Corinthians 8:9). Jesus' emptying of Himself was a refusal to cling to His advantages and privileges as God. We can also compare how Paul uses this same term, *kenoō*, which only appears four other times in the New Testament (Romans 4:14; 1 Corinthians 1:17, 9:15; 2 Corinthians 9:3). In Romans 4:14 and 1 Corinthians 1:17, it means to make void, that is, deprive of force, render vain, useless, or of no effect. In 1 Corinthians 9:15 and 2 Corinthians 9:3 it means to make void, that is, to cause a thing to be seen to be empty, hollow, false.[36] In these instances it is clear that Paul's use of *kenoō* is used figuratively rather than

---

34. G. Walter Hansen, *The Letter to the Philippians, Pillar New Testament Commentary* (Grand Rapids, MI: Eerdmans, 2009), p. 149; Silva, *Philippians*, p. 105.

35. George E. Ladd, *A Theology of the New Testament*, ed. Rev. D. A. Hagner (Cambridge: Lutterworth Press, 1994), p. 460.

36. J.H. Thayer, *Thayer's Greek–English Lexicon of the New Testament*, 8th ed. (Peabody, MA: Hendrickson, 2007), p. 344.

literally.[37] Additionally, in Philippians 2:7 "to press for a literal meaning of 'emptying' ignores the poetic context and nuance of the word."[38] Therefore, in Philippians 2:7 it is perhaps more accurate to see "emptying" as Jesus pouring Himself out, in service, in an expression of divine self-denial (2 Corinthians 8:9). Jesus' service is explained in Mark 10:45: "For even the Son of Man came not to be served but to serve, and to give his life as a ransom for many." In practice, this meant in the incarnation that Jesus:

1. Took the form of a servant
2. Was made in the likeness of men
3. Humbled Himself becoming obedient to death on the Cross.

In His incarnation Jesus did not cease to be God, or cease in any way to have the authority and knowledge of God.

❧ Jesus as a Prophet

In His incarnation, part of Jesus' ministry was to speak God's message to the people. Jesus referred to Himself as a prophet (Matthew 13:57; Mark 6:4; Luke 13:33) and was declared to have done a prophet's work (Matthew 13:57; Luke 13:33; John 6:14). Even those who did not understand that Jesus was God accepted Him as a prophet, (Luke 7:15–17, 24:19; John 4:19, 6:14, 7:40, 9:17). Furthermore, Jesus introduced many of His sayings by "amen" or "truly" (Matthew 6:2, 5, 16). New Testament scholar I. Howard Marshall says of Jesus:

> [Jesus] made no claim to prophetic inspiration; no "thus says the Lord" fell from his lips, but rather he spoke in terms of his own authority. He claimed the right to give the authoritative interpretation of the law, and he did so in a way that went beyond that of the prophets. He thus spoke as if he were God.[39]

In the Old Testament, Deuteronomy 13:1–5 and 18:21–22 provided the people of Israel with two tests to discern true prophets from false prophets. First, a true prophet's message had to be consistent with earlier revelation. Second, a true prophet's predictions always had to come true.

Deuteronomy 18:18–19 foretells of a prophet whom God would raise up from His own people after Moses died: "I will raise up for them a prophet like you from among their brothers. And I will put my words in his mouth,

---

37. Silva, *Philippians*, p. 105
38. Hansen, *The Letter to the Philippians*, p. 147.
39. I.H. Marshall, *The Origins of the New Testament Christology* (Downers Grove, IL: InterVarsity Press, 1976), p. 49–50.

and he shall speak to them all that I command him" (Deuteronomy 18:18). This is properly referred to in the New Testament as having been fulfilled in Jesus Christ (John 1:45; Acts 3:22–23, 7:37). Jesus' teaching had no origin in human ideas but came entirely from God. In His role as prophet, Jesus had to speak God's word to God's people. Therefore, He was subject to God's rules concerning prophets. In the Old Testament, if a prophet was not correct in his predictions he would be stoned to death as a false prophet by order of God (Deuteronomy 13:1–5, 18:20). For a prophet to have credibility with the people, his message must be true, as he has no message of his own but can only report what God has given him. This is because prophecy had its origin in God and not man (Habakkuk 2:2–3; 2 Peter 1:21).

In His prophetic role, Christ represents God the Father to mankind. Jesus came as a light to the world (John 1:9, 8:12), to show us God and bring us out of darkness (John 14:9–10). In John 8:28–29 Jesus also showed evidence of being a true prophet — that of living in close relation with His Father, passing on His teaching (cf. Jeremiah 23:21–23):

> When you lift up the Son of Man, then you will know that I am He, and that I do nothing of Myself; but as My Father taught Me, I speak these things. And He who sent Me is with Me. The Father has not left Me alone, for I always do those things that please Him (NKJV).

Jesus had the absolute knowledge that everything He did was from God. What He said and did is absolute truth because His Father is "truthful" (John 8:26). Jesus only spoke that which His Father told Him to say (John 12:49–50), so it had to be correct in every way. If Jesus as a prophet was wrong in the things He said, then why would we acclaim Him as the Son of God? If Jesus is a true prophet, then His teaching regarding Scripture must be taken seriously as absolute truth (see chapter 10).

✤ Jesus' Teaching and Truth

Theologian Robert Letham says of Jesus' teaching:

> Since God himself is the measure of all truth and Jesus was co-equal with God, he himself was the yardstick by which truth was to be measured and understood.[40]

In John 14:6 we are told that Jesus not only told the truth but that He was, and is, truth. Scripture portrays Jesus as the truth incarnate (John 1:17). Therefore, if He is the truth, He must always tell the truth and it would have

---

40. Robert Letham, *The Work of Christ: Contours of Christian Theology* (Downers Grove, IL: InterVarsity Press, 1993), p. 92.

been impossible for Him to speak or think falsehood. Much of Jesus' teaching began with the phrase "Truly, truly I say...." If Jesus taught anything in error, even if it was from ignorance, He would not be the truth.

To err may be human for us. Falsehood, however, is rooted in the nature of the devil (John 8:44), not the nature of Jesus who speaks the truth (John 8:45–46). The Father is the only true God (John 7:28, 8:26, 17:3) and Jesus taught only what the Father had given to Him (John 3:32–33, 8:40, 18:37). Jesus testifies about the Father, who in turn testifies concerning the Son (John 8:18–19; 1 John 5:10–11), and they are one (John 10:30). The gospel of John shows emphatically that Jesus' teaching and words are the teaching and words of God. Three clear examples of this are:

> And the Jews marveled, saying, "How does this Man know letters, having never studied?" Jesus answered them and said, "My doctrine is not Mine, but His who sent Me. If anyone wills to do His will, he shall know concerning the doctrine, whether it is from God or whether I speak on My own authority" (John 7:15–17).

> I know that you are Abraham's descendants, but you seek to kill Me, because My word has no place in you. I speak what I have seen with My Father, and you do what you have seen with your father.... But now you seek to kill Me, a Man who has told you the truth which I heard from God. Abraham did not do this (John 8:37–38, 40).

> For I have not spoken on My own authority; but the Father who sent Me gave Me a command, what I should say and what I should speak. And I know that His command is everlasting life. Therefore, whatever I speak, just as the Father has told Me, so I speak (John 12:49–50).

According to D.A. Carson, in referring to John 12:49–50, "Not only is what Jesus says just what the Father has told him to say, but he himself is the Word of God, God's self-expression (John 1:1)."[41] The authority behind Jesus' words are the commands that are given to Him by the Father (and Jesus always obeyed the Father's commands; John 14:31). Jesus' teaching did not originate in human ideas but came from God the Father, which is why it is authoritative. Jesus' very own words were spoken in full authorization from the Father who sent Him. The authority of Jesus' teaching then rests upon the unity between Himself and the Father. Jesus is the embodiment,

---

41. D.A. Carson, *The Gospel According to John, Pillar New Testament Commentary* (Grand Rapids, MI: Eerdmans, 1991), p. 453.

revelation, and messenger of truth to mankind, and it is the Holy Spirit who conveys truth about Jesus to the unbelieving world through believers (John 15:26–27, 16:8–11). Again, the point is that if there was error in Jesus' teaching, then He is a false and unreliable teacher. However, Jesus was God incarnate, and God and falsehood can never be reconciled with each other (Titus 1:2; Hebrews 6:18).

The fatal flaw in the idea that Jesus' teaching contained error is that, if Jesus in His humanity claimed to know more or less than He actually did, then such a claim would have profound ethical and theological implications concerning Jesus' claims of being the truth (John 14:6), speaking the truth (John 8:45), and bearing witness to the truth (John 18:37). The critical point in all of this is that Jesus did not have to be omniscient to save us from our sins, but He certainly had to be sinless, which includes never telling a falsehood. If Jesus in His teaching had pretended or proclaimed to have more knowledge than He actually had, then this would have been sinful. The Bible tells us that those "who teach will be judged with greater strictness" (James 3:1). Scripture also says that it would be better for a person to have a millstone hung around his neck and to be drowned than to lead someone astray (Matthew 18:6).

Jesus made statements such as "I do not speak on my own authority, but the Father who dwells in me" (John 14:10) and "I am…the truth" (John 14:6). Now if Jesus claimed to teach these things and then taught erroneous information (for example, regarding Creation and the Flood), then His claims would be falsified, He would be sinning, and this would disqualify Him from being our Savior. The falsehood He would be teaching is that He knows something that He actually does not know. Once Jesus makes the astonishing claim to be speaking the truth, He had better not be teaching mistakes. In His human nature, because Jesus was sinless, and as such the "fullness of the Deity" dwelt in Him (Colossians 2:9), then everything Jesus taught was true; and one of the things that Jesus taught was that the Old Testament Scripture was God's Word (truth) and, therefore, so was His teaching on creation (see chapter 10).

Chapter 9

The Last Adam: His Deity

At a crucial point in His ministry, Jesus asked His disciples, "Who do people say that the Son of Man is?" (Matthew 16:13). The disciples answered Jesus by telling Him what the people said: "Some say John the Baptist, others say Elijah, and others Jeremiah or one of the prophets" (Matthew 16:14) But then Jesus asked the disciples "But who do you say that I am?" (Matthew 16:15). The answer to this question is more important than anything else because if we deny the deity of Jesus then we do not know the Father and, therefore, we do not have eternal life (1 John 2:23, 5:20; cf. John 5:23).[1]

Today, just as in Jesus' day, when Christians ask people the question "Who do you say Jesus is?" there are various answers given concerning His identity. Many people in western society see Jesus as nothing more than a good teacher, someone who came to help the weak and poor in society (an economic liberator as in Liberation Theology). For example, many Progressive Christians see Jesus not as a divine Savior but as a human moral guide who had a "divine" quality. In a similar manner, all major world religions reject the deity of Christ: Islam, Judaism, Hinduism, and Buddhism. Muslims believe Jesus was just a great prophet, whereas Orthodox Judaism sees Jesus as a false prophet. It's not only the world's major religions that deny the deity of Christ, but so do all major cultic groups: Mormons, Oneness Pentecostals, Unitarians, Jehovah's Witnesses, Inglesia ni Cristo,

---

1. The Bible teaches that there is only one true and living God (Deuteronomy 6:4; cf. 1 Corinthians 8:6). The divinity of Jesus is part of the doctrine of the Trinity, which states that within the one Being who is God, there exists eternally three co-equal and co-eternal persons, the Father, the Son, and the Holy Spirit. Each is a distinct person, yet each is identified as God: the Father (1 Corinthians 8:6), the Son (John 1:1–3, 18), and the Holy Spirit (Acts 5:3–4).

and Christadelphians. These cultic groups "claim" the Bible as their authority but each in their own way teach that Jesus is a created being.

In the first century, the early churches confession that Jesus is Lord (Acts 2:21, 10:36; Romans 10:9; Philippians 2:11) is evidence that the deity of Jesus was not controversial. It was not really until the second century and after that there arose heretical groups that attacked and denied the deity of Jesus: Ebionitism and Arianism. One of the first attacks on the deity of Jesus came in the second century from Judaizing Christian influences that held very similar beliefs to the opponents Paul battled in the Book of Galatians (cf. Acts 15:1). The Ebionites (the "poor ones"), were Christ followers but refused to abandon observance of the Jewish Law (circumcision, dietary laws, etc.). The Ebionites accepted the authority of the Old Testament, used a modified gospel of Matthew, and saw the Apostle Paul as an apostate from the Law. While they accepted Jesus' Messiahship, based solely as a human person who justified Himself by keeping the Law, they rejected His deity and virgin conception. The Ebionites accepted a more "adoptionistic" Christology. The view known as "adoptionism" taught that Jesus was not divine, but that God (the Father) gave Jesus powers and then adopted Him at His baptism or birth.[2]

Probably one of the most well-known heresies that the early Christians had to deal with was that of Arianism. In the early fourth century, Arius (256–336), an Alexandrian Presbyter, claimed that Jesus was a created being. In fact, the reason for the Council at Nicaea (A.D. 325) was to debate Arius's views. Arius did believe Jesus was divine, but he believed "Jesus was like the Father in that he existed before creation, played a role in the origin of creation, and was exalted over all creation. Yet the Son himself was a *creature*."[3] Although many in our historically illiterate times claim Jesus' divinity was invented at the Council of Nicaea the real issue at the Council was to determine "*how* not *if* Jesus was divine."[4] Arianism was defeated at Nicaea but it was revived by the Socinians (1500s), assumed in Protestant Liberalism (1800s), taught explicitly by the Jehovah's Witnesses (1870s), and is still very much around today in Progressive Christianity.

The claim that Jesus is the God-man is not only affirmed by Scripture but by statements of the early Church. For example, the early church Father Ignatius Bishop of Antioch (died A.D. 108), who was a disciple of John the Apostle, taught the pre-existence and divinity of Jesus:

2. Michael J. Kruger, *Christianity at the Crossroads: How the Second Century Shaped the Future of the Church* (London: SPCK, 2017), p. 113–116.
3. J. Ed Komoszewski, M. James Sawyer, and Daniel B. Wallace, *Reinventing Jesus: How Contemporary Skeptics Miss the Real Jesus and Mislead Popular Culture* (Grand Rapids, MI: Kregel Publication, 2006) p. 208.
4. Ibid., 212.

> There is one Physician who is possessed both of flesh and spirit; both made and not made; God existing in flesh; true life in death; both of Mary and of God; first possible and then impossible, even Jesus Christ our Lord.... But our Physician is the only true God, the unbegotten and unapproachable, the Lord of all, the Father and Begetter of the only-begotten Son. We have also as a Physician the Lord our God, Jesus the Christ, the only-begotten Son and Word, before time began, but who afterwards became also man, of Mary the virgin.[5]

The fact that early Christians believed in Jesus' deity was even recognized by the Roman lawyer and magistrate Pliny (A.D. 61–113) who said of his encounter with Christians:

> Others named in the document said they were Christians but later denied it saying they had been, but that they had ceased three years ago, or many years ago, or even as much as twenty … they said that this had been the full extent of their guilt or error: they had been accustomed to meet on a fixed day before dawn and to sing antiphonally a song to Christ as to a god.[6]

Pliny who called Christianity a "wretched cult," recognized those second-century Christians who were martyred, met early on a Sunday morning, the first day of the week (Acts 20:7; 1 Corinthians 16:1–2; cf. Revelation 1:10) to worship Jesus as God.

❧ Gospel Witness

New Testament scholars identify the genre of the four canonical gospels as Greco-Roman biographies, "lives" (*bioi*), as they are like the accounts of Plutarch, Suetonius, or Xenophon. These biographies primarily narrate the account of a character. As biographies, the gospels are meant to inform us about Jesus and His message. However, the gospels are not just biographies, history, but are, in fact, redemptive history, as they continue the history of redemption in the Old Testament. In that sense, they are covenant documents, like the Book of Exodus. As covenant documents, they focus on the life of the covenant mediator, the inauguration of a new covenant, and deliver a new law by the covenant mediator.

The structural elements between Exodus and the gospels can be seen in two ways. First the Moses-Exodus typology can be seen throughout

---

5. The Epistle of Ignatius to the Ephesians, Chapter VII, "Beware of False Teachers," http://www.earlychristianwritings.com/text/ignatius-ephesians-longer.html.

6. Pliny the Younger, ca. A.D. 111; Letters 10.96

the gospels: Jesus is depicted as the new Moses (Matthew 5:1; John 5:46); He leads a new exodus (Matthew 2:13, 4:1-17; Mark 1:1–13; Luke 3:4-6); He gives a new law (Matthew 5-7); He supplies bread from heaven (John 6:32-34); He offers a new/final Passover (Matthew 26:26; Mark 14:22; Luke 22:19). Second, much of Jesus' teaching fits into the language of covenantal texts: Jesus' self- declarations as the God of the covenant (John 6:35, 8:12, 8:51), condemnation of Israel's covenant breaking (Matthew 21:40–41; Mark 12:9), teachings on how to live within the covenant community (Matthew 5–7), blessings and curses of the covenant (Luke 6:20–26; Matthew 23), and even covenant discipline (Matthew 16:18–19, 18:15–20).[7] New Testament scholar Michael Kruger notes the significant implication of the gospel as covenant documents: "the Gospels are authoritative not by virtue of some later ecclesiastical court, nor by virtue of the fact that the human authors are reliable eyewitnesses (though they are), but because the Gospels are, from their very inception, a legal and divine witness on behalf of covenant-keepers and against covenant-breakers."[8] To read the gospels as covenant documents keeps the redemptive history of the Bible as its focus and allows us to see Jesus as the fulfillment of that history.

Contrary to the claim of many sceptics today, there are numerous reasons to believe that the Gospels are reliable and that what we are now reading in them is what the apostles wrote down:

- The four canonical Gospels are the earliest we have and the only ones that can be dated to the first century (the gnostic gospels [i.e., Gospel of Thomas, Gospel of Peter] date from the 2nd–8th century).

- The four canonical Gospels were written at a time when there were still eyewitnesses alive who had seen these things happen (written by the apostles or a companion who had access to the information — Matthew 9:9, 10:3; Mark 1:16, 16:7; Luke 1:1–4; John 21:24).

- The canonical Gospels were recognized as authoritative Scripture (cf., 1 Timothy 5:18) within the first century, and the testimony of the patristic authors (e.g., Irenaeus and Clement of Alexandria) confirm this.

People may object to these reasons by stating, "You no longer have the original manuscripts!" But even though we do not have the original manuscripts,

---

7. For the above points see Michael Kruger, "What is a "Gospel" Anyway? A Few Thoughts on Gospel Genre and Why it Matters," July 19th, 2021. https://www.michaeljkruger. com/what-is-a-gospel-anyway-a-few-thoughts-on-gospel-genre-and-why-it-matters-2/#more-9223.

8. Ibid.

we do have the original text of Scripture, which is important, as it is the words that are inspired and not the ink on the parchment. The original text can exist without the original manuscripts. It can be preserved and rendered from the multitude of manuscripts we do have (through the process of textual criticism).[9] If you want to know about the historical Jesus, then the places to look are Matthew, Mark, Luke, and John. God has preserved the text of the Gospels in such a way that we can have confidence that what we are reading is what was written by the original authors. The four canonical gospels can be trusted as accurate historical accounts of the life and teaching of Jesus.

⚑ Did Jesus Claim to Be God?

It is clear that the gospel writers and the authors of the epistles believed Jesus was God (Matthew 1:23, 28:20; Luke 1:32, 2:11; John 1:1–3, 18; 1 Corinthians 2:8, 8:6; Colossians 1:16, 2:9; Philippians 2:5–8; Hebrews 1:1–3; James 2:1; 1 Peter 3:15; 2 Peter 1:1, 11). The question that we need to ask, however, is this: Did Jesus claim to be divine? By this, we do not mean that Jesus went around Israel saying: "Hi, I am Jesus, and I am God." The reason Jesus did not do this is that He came to reveal the Father (cf., Matthew 11:27; John 1:18, 14:9), and, in a monotheistic culture (Mark 12:29) He would not want people to think that He was saying He was the Father. Another question that needs to be asked is, "What would represent a claim to being divine?" For Jesus to view Himself as divine would be to attribute to Himself words, actions, names, offices, and functions from the Old Testament that would be blasphemous if He were not truly divine.

⚑ The Gospel of Mark

If the gospels were written down by eyewitnesses, then what do we do with the gospel of Mark as he was not one of the original 12 disciples? Well, there is good literary and historical evidence that inform us that Mark's gospel came from the teaching and preaching of the Apostle Peter (see Acts 12:12–17, 15:37; 1 Peter 5:13).[10] Interestingly, theologian David Garland notes, "Simon Peter is the first and last mentioned disciple in the gospel (1:16, where his name is mentioned twice in the Greek text; and 16:7). These 'two

---

9. See Andreas Köstenberger and Michael J. Kruger, *The Heresy of Orthodoxy* (Wheaton, IL: Crossway, 2010), p. 203–231.

10. It was understood that Papias, the early church bishop of Hierapolis in Phrygia, in the early 2nd century (101–108), wrote that Mark relied on the Apostle Peter for his information. For a defense of this view, see David E. Garland, *A Theology of Mark's Gospel: Biblical Theology of the New Testament* (Grand Rapids, MI: Zondervan, 2015), p. 53–67.

references form an inclusion around the whole story, suggesting that Peter is the witness whose testimony includes the whole.'"[11] Mark's gospel then is based upon a reliable historical witness. It was most likely written in Rome, to believers undergoing persecution (Mark 8:31–38; 10:30, 38–39), who were familiar with Scripture (Mark 1:2, 7:6, 9:12–13, 10:47–48, 12:26), who were non-Aramaic speakers (Mark 5:41; 7:11, 34; 14:36; 15:22, 34), sometime in the A.D. 60's, before the destruction of Jerusalem (Mark 13).[12]

It is important to realize that often in the synoptic gospels (Matthew, Mark, and Luke), early on in His ministry, Jesus chose to show who He is rather than proclaim who He is. A clear example of this comes after John the Baptist was put into prison and his disciples came to Jesus asking, "Are you the one who is to come, or shall we look for another?" (Matthew 11:3). The reason John's disciples ask this question is that they, like many of their contemporary Jews, were expecting a royal, conquering Messiah and not someone who, in their eyes, had come to preach and work miracles. How did Jesus answer John's disciples' question? Did He just come out and say who He was? No, Jesus didn't come out and give a simple answer to who He was, but He does it in an implicit way by telling John's disciples that they would know who He is by the things that He was doing:

> And Jesus answered them, "Go and tell John what you hear and see: the blind receive their sight and the lame walk, lepers are cleansed and the deaf hear, and the dead are raised up, and the poor have good news preached to them. And blessed is the one who is not offended by me" (Matthew 11:4–6).

The things that Jesus mentioned should have been evident to the disciples of John that the Messianic era was underway (see Isaiah 35:5–6; cf. 26:19, 61:1). Jesus answered this way to show who He was rather than explicitly state it. In other words, Jesus does the things that only God can do, which are implicit claims to His divinity. Jesus' implicit claims to divinity can be seen in the gospel of Mark on several different occasions when after the crowds or the disciples have been bewildered by His teaching or His miracles, questions regarding his identity come up:

> "What is this? A new teaching with authority! He commands even the unclean spirits, and they obey him" (Mark 1:27).

> "Why does this man speak like that? He is blaspheming! Who can forgive sins but God alone?" (Mark 2:7).

---

11. Ibid., p. 66.
12. Ibid., p. 67–82.

"Who then is this, that even the wind and the sea obey him?" (Mark 4:41).

"Where did this man get these things? What is the wisdom given to him?" ... "Is not this the carpenter, the son of Mary...?" (Mark 6:2–3).

Mark uses these questions to cause his readers to ask that same question — who is Jesus? Yet at the same time the audience of the gospel should know who Jesus is, as it has already been made clear at the beginning of the gospel, He is the Lord (YHWH) for whom the way is prepared (Mark 1:3; Isaiah 40:3) and the one who will baptize His people in the Holy Spirit (Mark 1:8; Isaiah 44:3). Although the gospel of Mark is seen by critical scholars as presenting Jesus as an "idealized human figure,"[13] the answer given to these questions show that Jesus is much more than a human figure, He is the divine Son of God who did not come from the world but came into the world (Mark 1:1, 11; 9:7; 14:61; 15:39).[14]

In Mark 2, Jesus is speaking at a home in Capernaum when a paralytic man is lowered down through the roof by his four friends so that Jesus can heal him.[15] Jesus seeing "their faith" (cf. Mark 5:34, 36; 10:52), rather than immediately heal the man He instead forgives his sins (Mark 2:5). This causes the scribes to question in their hearts, "Why does this man speak like that? He is blaspheming! Who can forgive sins but God alone?" (Mark 2:7; cf. 14:64). The scribes assume that Jesus has presumptuously forgiven the man's sins, which deserves death as it is blasphemous (Leviticus 24:15-16). If, as the Scribes recognize, only God can forgive sins, and Jesus forgives the man's sins, then what is Jesus saying of Himself?

On a previous occasion, the synagogue worshipers at Capernaum were also amazed at Jesus' authority when He exorcised an unclean spirit (Mark 1:26-27), because they recognized He was not like the scribes who were dependent on external authority (Mark 1:22). Nevertheless, Jesus, knowing the scribes' thoughts, something only God can do (1 Chronicles 28:9; Psalm 139:1-2), then provides evidence that the man's sins have been forgiven by healing him (Mark 2:11–12; cf. Psalm 103:3). Jesus' command to the man to get up and walk shows His authority on earth as the Son of Man,

---

13. J.R. Daniel Kirk, *A Man Attested by God: The Human Jesus of the Synoptic Gospels* (Grand Rapids, MI: W.B. Eerdmans Publishing Company, 2016), p. 580–581.

14. Mark's gospel also leaves no room for an Adoptionist Christology (the idea that Jesus, because of His perfect lifestyle, is adopted as God's Son at His baptism), as pre-existence is a necessary consequence of divinity.

15. The house would have had a flat roof, with a staircase at the side, making it possible for the friends to carry the man onto the roof and lower him down to Jesus.

an exalted human figure who has divine characteristics (Mark 2:10–11; cf. Daniel 7:13–14). After the man picks up his bed and walks away the crowd glorified God, as they had never seen anything like this (Mark 2:12).

As the Son of Man, Jesus not only shows His authority to forgive sins, but He will go on to identify Himself as the bridegroom, an image for God (Isaiah 54:5-8, 62:4–5), and to show that He is Lord of the Sabbath (Mark 2:28), and who is Lord of the Sabbath except the one who instituted it, God Himself (Genesis 2:1–3).

In Mark 4, after a long day of teaching in parables beside the sea (Mark 4:1–34), in the evening Jesus and His disciples get into a boat and go out onto the Sea of Galilee (c. 13 miles long and 8 miles wide) to cross to the other side (Mark 4:35). While they are on the sea a "great windstorm arose" (Mark 4:37), but whereas the skilled fishermen are terrified, Jesus, the carpenter[16] (cf. Mark 6:3), is asleep in the stern. Jesus being asleep is not only a sign of His trust in God but of His divine sovereignty (Isaiah 51:9–10; cf. Job 11:18–19; Psalm 3:5). The disciples woke Jesus and said, "Teacher, do you not care that we are perishing?" (Mark 4:38). The disciples question reflects a trust in Jesus to be able to save them (cf. Psalm 107:28–30). Jesus does not pray to God (the Father) for deliverance (cf. Jonah 1:6), but rather rebukes the wind and says to the sea, "Peace! Be still!" and the great windstorm ceases and turns into a great calm (Mark 4:39; cf. Jonah 1:15). Waves do not stop immediately after a storm, so the fact there is "perfect calm" afterward indicates this is a miracle. Jesus is more than a miracle worker or a prophet as He has the power to do what only the God who created the sea can do (Genesis 8:1; Psalm 65:7, 106:9). After calming the sea, Jesus offers a gentle rebuke to the disciples, "Why are you so afraid? Have you still no faith?" (Mark 4:40). Faith is to trust the divine power that is obvious in Jesus (cf. Mark 2:4–5, 5:34–36). The disciples have seen Jesus perform miracles before (Mark 2:11–12, 3:5), but after calming the storm the disciples' fear remains as they recognize they are in the presence of someone who can control creation: "Who then is this, that even the wind and the sea obey him?" (Mark 4:41).

Mark 6 contains another account of Jesus getting into a boat with the disciples and once again showing His authority over creation:

> Immediately he made his disciples get into the boat and go before him to the other side, to Bethsaida, while he dismissed the crowd. And after he had taken leave of them, he went up on the

---

16. In Mark 6:3 the Greek word for "carpenter" (*tektōn*) essentially means "craftsman" and so Jesus probably not only worked with wood but primarily with stone.

mountain to pray. And when evening came, the boat was out on the sea, and he was alone on the land. And he saw that they were making headway painfully, for the wind was against them. And about the fourth watch of the night he came to them, walking on the sea. He meant to pass by them, but when they saw him walking on the sea they thought it was a ghost, and cried out, for they all saw him and were terrified. But immediately he spoke to them and said, "Take heart; it is I. Do not be afraid." And he got into the boat with them, and the wind ceased. And they were utterly astounded, for they did not understand about the loaves, but their hearts were hardened (Mark 6:45–52).

Immediately, after the feeding of the five thousand (Mark 6:34–44), Jesus sends His disciples off into a boat to Bethsaida, dismisses the crowd, and then goes up on the mountain to pray. In the evening, Jesus sees that the disciples are "making headway painfully, for the wind was against them" (Mark 6:48). Jesus' omniscience is clear in the text as He can see beyond what can be seen by others. It was after evening, the wind was against the disciples, who were all the way out in the middle of the sea (c. about 3 miles from shore), yet despite these things Jesus can see the disciples struggling. Jesus comes to the disciples "about the fourth watch of the night" (between 3 a.m. and 6 a.m.) walking on the sea, something God alone can do (Job 9:8). Jesus not only walks on water, but He manages to catch up with the disciples — the impediment of the wind for the disciples was not an impediment for Jesus. When Jesus comes to the disciples, we are told that "He meant to pass by them" (Mark 6:48), which is Old Testament language connected to a theophany.[17] For example, in Exodus 33 Moses asks God to show him His glory, but God responds by passing before him and proclaiming His identity:

> And he said, "I will make all my goodness pass before you and will proclaim before you my name 'The LORD.' And I will be gracious to whom I will be gracious, and will show mercy on whom I will show mercy. But," he said, "you cannot see my face, for man shall not see me and live." And the LORD said, "Behold, there is a place by me where you shall stand on the rock, and while my glory passes by I will put you in a cleft of the rock, and I will cover you with my hand until I have passed by. Then I will take away my hand, and you shall see my back, but my face shall not be seen....The LORD descended in the cloud and stood with him there, and proclaimed the name of the LORD. The LORD passed

---

17. Garland, *A Theology of Mark's Gospel*, p. 295–297.

before him and proclaimed, "The LORD, the LORD, a God merciful and gracious, slow to anger, and abounding in steadfast love and faithfulness..." (Exodus 33:19–23; 34:5–6; cf. 1 Kings 19:11-12).

New Testament theologian David Garland notes, "This biblical background suggests that Mark portrays Jesus wanting to pass by his disciples to reveal his transcendent, divine majesty to them."[18] This interpretation is further supported by Jesus' response to the terrified disciples who think they have seen a ghost, "Take heart; it is I. Do not be afraid" (Mark 6:50). The reassurance "Take heart.... Do not be afraid" is language of a divine being in the Bible (see Genesis 15:1; Joshua 8:1; Luke 1:13). Jesus also greets the disciples with the use of the divine formula "it is I" (*egō eimi,* cf. John 8:58). The use of the divine formula is further supported by the Old Testament backdrop to this passage:

> Fear not, for I have redeemed you; I have called you by name, you are mine. When you pass through the waters, I will be with you.... For I am the LORD your God, the Holy One of Israel, your Savior (Isaiah 43:1–3).

In the same context God goes on to refer to himself as "I am" (*egō eimi* LXX):

> You are my witnesses," declares the LORD, "and my servant whom I have chosen, that you may know and believe me and understand that I am he. Before me no god was formed, nor shall there be any after me. I, I am the LORD, and besides me there is no savior (Isaiah 43:10–11).

The disciples who have been chosen by Jesus pass through the waters with Him and He is the one who only needs to say, "I am." This time, Jesus does not even need to rebuke the wind for the sea to be calm, but He simply gets into the boat and the wind ceases (Mark 6:51). Now is the perfect time for Jesus to reveal Himself to the disciples as it answers their previous question from the last time they were in a boat with Him: "Who then is this, that even the wind and the sea obey him?" (Mark 4:41). But after Jesus got into the boat the disciple's "were utterly astounded, for they did not understand about the loaves, but their hearts were hardened" (Mark 6:51–52; cf. 8:17). Just as the disciples had failed to see Jesus' divine power in feeding the 5,000 (cf. Mark 8:17–21), so they did not see the theophany of Jesus (cf. Job 9:11), and instead were afraid of a ghost. The disciples' failure to understand the identity of Jesus becomes an invitation for the readers of Mark's gospel to understand who Jesus is. Jesus is the transcendent Lord of

---

18. Ibid., p. 297.

creation who came to save sinners by giving His life as a ransom for many (Mark 10:45), through His death on the Cross and His Resurrection from the dead (Mark 8:31).

It is in the last week of Jesus' life where we see Him make what is probably the most explicit claim of His own divinity, using texts from the Old Testament to show this. Interestingly Mark's gospel begins and ends with a charge of blasphemy by the religious leaders against Jesus' own claim of divinity (cf. Mark 2:7). After Jesus' betrayal and arrest in the garden of Gethsemane, He is brought before the Jewish Sanhedrin for examination to face the high priest along with the chief priests, the elders, and the scribes.[19] The Jewish high priest asks Jesus the question, "Are you the Christ, the Son of the Blessed?" (Mark 14:61).[20] The title "The Blessed One" was a common paraphrase for God.[21] It is Jesus' reply to the high priest's question that causes controversy:

> "I am, and you will see the Son of Man seated at the right hand of Power, and coming with the clouds of heaven." And the high priest tore his garments and said, "What further witnesses do we need? You have heard his blasphemy. What is your decision?" And they all condemned him as deserving death (Mark 14:62–64).

Why did the high priest tear his garment and the Sanhedrin condemn Jesus to death over what He said? Jesus' reference to Himself as being "seated at the right hand of Power" is most likely a reference to Psalm 110:1 where king David speaks about the Messiah in an exalted fashion calling him "Lord":

> The LORD says to my Lord: "Sit at my right hand, until I make your enemies your footstool."

Jesus had argued previously, based on this Psalm, that the Messiah was greater than David (Mark 12:35–36). In order to appreciate the reaction of the Jewish leaders, we must keep in mind the court scene, as the Sanhedrin believed it was their right to judge the claims of Jesus. However, to be seated at the right hand of the LORD was to take a position above David and wait while God justifies the one who has been wronged by His accusers. In other words, those who are judging Jesus will one day be judged by Him. Other

---

19. This is not an official trial, as the Jewish authorities did not have the authority to put Jesus to death, and so they are trying to gather evidence that will convict Jesus to take to Pilate.
20. Interestingly, the title used by the high priest "Son of the Blessed" was used of Jesus by the Father at His baptism and at the transfiguration (Mark 1:9–11, 9:7). It was even used by Jesus of Himself in the parable of the tenants (Mark 12:6) and by the believing Roman centurion at the crucifixion (Mark 15:39).
21. Craig Keener, *The IVP Bible Background Commentary: New Testament* (Downers Grove, IL: InterVarsity Press, 1993), p. 178.

New Testament authors also take Psalm 110 to be speaking of Jesus who is not only greater than David but also than the angels (Acts 2:34; Hebrews 1:13). This shows that Jesus is not just a created being. Jesus' claim to be "seated at the right hand of Power" is also an allusion to His Resurrection from the dead. Jesus then quotes alongside Psalm 110 a text referring to "the Son of Man" who is "coming with the clouds of heaven." There is no evidence at the time of Jesus that "the Son of Man" was used as a Messianic title.[22] It seems Jesus "used the term publicly in reference to himself because it was sufficiently vague that he could fill it with his own meaning."[23] The title "the Son of Man" originates from Daniel's night vision where he appears before the Ancient of Days:

> I saw in the night visions, and behold, with the clouds of heaven there came one like a son of man, and he came to the Ancient of Days and was presented before him. And to him was given dominion and glory and a kingdom, that all peoples, nations, and languages should serve him; his dominion is an everlasting dominion, which shall not pass away, and his kingdom one that shall not be destroyed (Daniel 7:13–14).

It is clear here that "Son of Man" is an exalted human figure who has divine characteristics. The one like a Son of Man is seated on God's throne, comes in the clouds, a vehicle for God (Exodus 34:5; Isaiah 19:1), and boldly approaches the Ancient of Days (God the Father) but not in fear (see Isaiah 6:5). Importantly, the "Son of Man" is given a kingdom and all peoples, nations, and languages come and serve him. The Aramaic term for serve פְּלַח (pĕlaḥ) is used elsewhere in Daniel in the context of worship (Daniel 3:28, 7:27). What is interesting is that the Greek translation of the Old Testament, the Septuagint (LXX), translates the word pĕlaḥ in Daniel 7:14 as λατρεύουσα (from λατρεύω - latreuo), which refers to the highest form of religious worship (see Matthew 4:10; Luke 1:74; Acts 24:14; Revelation 7:15). Jesus is saying He is the glorious figure in Daniel's vision who is worthy of eternal worship. The religious leaders understand exactly what

---

22. Garland comments: "No evidence exists that there was a well-defined notion of the 'Son of Man' as a messianic figure or that the phrase was used as a messianic title. This assessment is supported by Mark's narrative. The phrase appears only on the lips of Jesus. Neither human characters nor the narrator calls Jesus 'the Son of Man.' When Jesus asks his disciples, 'Who do men say that I am?' the phrase 'the Son of Man' is not one of the conjectures (8:27–30). The high priest also does not charge Jesus with claiming to be 'the Son of Man' at his trial. While 'Son of Man' was not an established title, the figure was known from Dan 7:13–14, which I believe provides the backdrop for Jesus' usage and Mark's understanding of the phrase." Garland, *A Theology of Mark's Gospel*, p. 252.
23. Ibid., p. 252.

Jesus is saying in His use of Psalm 110:1 and Daniel 7:13–14, and that is why they cry "blasphemy" — because the claim to divinity brings with it the death penalty (see Leviticus 24:16). The irony of Jesus' examination before the Jewish Sanhedrin is that the person whose testimony is responsible for His crucifixion is Jesus Himself when He utters the words from Psalm 110 and Daniel 7. The Cross was not a surprise to Jesus, as the Son of Man willingly came to give His life as a ransom for sinners (Mark 10:45).

After the deadly decision of the Sanhedrin, "some began to spit on him and to cover his face and to strike him, saying to him, 'Prophesy!' And the guards received him with blows" (Mark 14:65). Prophesy was seen as a gift given to the Messiah (Isaiah 11:2–4). This is ironic because Jesus being mocked, spat upon, as well as Peter denying Him at that very moment were all evidence that His prophecies were already coming true (see Mark 10:33–34, cf. Mark 14:30, 66–72). The fact that Jesus' prophecies came true is evidence of the truth of the Son's coming again at a time no one knows, which is why we need to be ready and stay awake (Mark 13:32–36).

People may ask the question, "How would people know that Jesus said these things since there were no disciples around at this examination before the Sanhedrin?" Well, there would have been witnesses present at the Jewish Sanhedrin, such as Joseph of Arimathea and Nicodemus (Mark 15:43; John 19:38–39, cf. 3:1) who were members of this council and part of the early church. Therefore, these men would provide the valid eyewitness testimonies that were necessary. It is clear that in Mark 14:62 Jesus' own words are testimony that He claimed not only to be God but that He is worthy of worship.[24]

🕊 Gospel of John

The gospel of John is one of the most well-known and loved of all the gospels. The internal and external evidence show that the gospel of John was written by John the Son of Zebedee, the beloved disciple.[25] The evidence from the gospel indicates that it was written by a disciple who was at Jesus' side at the last supper (i.e., one of the 12), who was also at the scene of Jesus' arrest and trial, who witnessed Jesus' crucifixion and saw Him after His

---

24. In Mark 13:32, Jesus states, "But concerning that day or that hour, no one knows, not even the angels in heaven, nor the Son, but only the Father." Cults and other religions use this passage to argue that, since Jesus did not know all things, He cannot be God. Jesus' teaching, however, shows that His not "knowing" the day or the hour was a conscious self-limitation. As the God-man, Jesus possessed divine attributes, or He would have ceased to be God, but He chose not always to employ them. It is important to also note the ascending order in the verse, "no one," "the angels in heaven," "the Son," and "the Father." Jesus places Himself next to the Father in the divine hierarchy.

25. See Andreas Köstenberger, *A Theology of John's Gospel and Letters: Biblical Theology of the New Testament* (Grand Rapids, MI: Zondervan, 2009), 72-75.

Resurrection (see John 13:23, 18:15, 19:26, 20:2, 21:7, 21:24).[26] Scholars differ on the dating of John's gospel (60s, mid-80s or early 90s A.D.) (the earliest manuscript of John is dated to c. 125 A.D.).

The Apostle John begins his gospel by introducing us to a new era of salvation history:

> In the beginning was the Word, and the Word was with God, and the Word was God. He was in the beginning with God. All things were made through him, and without him was not anything made that was made. In him was life, and the life was the light of men. The light shines in the darkness, and the darkness has not overcome it (John 1:1–5).

The very first verse of the Bible tells us of the creation of the world: "In the beginning, God created the heavens and the earth" (Genesis 1:1). Interestingly, the opening words of Genesis 1:1 are echoed in John 1:1: "In the beginning" (*en archē*). John 1:1 follows the Greek translation (Septuagint, LXX) of Genesis 1:1. But it is not only the term "beginning" (*archē*) that Genesis 1 and John 1 have in common. Both Genesis 1 and John 1 also refer to: God (*theos*), light (*phōs*), darkness (*skotia*), and becoming (*ginomai*). These intertextual links show that there is no question that the Apostle John has the creation account in Genesis 1 in mind when he writes John 1.

Genesis 1:1–5	John 1:1–5
1 In the beginning [*en archē*] God [*theos*] created the heavens and the earth. 2 The earth was without form and void, and darkness was over the face of the deep. And the Spirit of God was hovering over the face of the waters. 3 And God said, "Let there be [*ginomai*] light," and there was light [*phōs*]. 4 And God saw that the light was good. And God separated the light from the darkness [*skotia*]. 5 God called the light Day, and the darkness he called Night. And there was evening and there was morning, the first day.	1 In the beginning [*en archē*] was the Word, and the Word was with God, and the Word was God [*theos*]. 2 He was in the beginning with God. 3 All things were made [*ginomai*] through him, and without him was not anything made that was made. 4 In him was life, and the life was the light [*phōs*] of men. 5 The light shines in the darkness [*skotia*], and the darkness has not overcome it.

Genesis 1 begins with the creation of the world; John 1 refers to a type of new creation that has come in Jesus (cf. 2 Corinthians 5:17; Galatians 6:15).

---

26. The witness of the early church was that the apostle John, the Son of Zebedee, wrote the gospel of John (see Irenaeus, *Haer.* 2.22.5, 3.3.4, 3.11; Eusebius, *Hist. eccl.* 3.23.3-4, 4.14.3-8, 5.8.4.).

John's gospel opens by informing us, "In the beginning was the Word, and the Word was with God, and the Word was God" (John 1:1). This one verse tells us three very important things about the Word (*logos*), who is identified as Jesus (John 1:17). First, the Word has eternally existed. The Greek word "was" (*ēn*),[27] which signifies existence, points to the Word (*logos*) already existing "in the beginning." The pre-existence of the Word is an incredible claim, but it is one that Jesus made Himself in His debate with the Pharisees (John 8:58) and when He prayed to the Father (John 17:5). Second, the Word has an eternal relationship with God (the Father, John 1:18). John describes the Word as being "with" (*pros*) God, which is a relational term showing that the person of the Word was with the person of God (the Father, cf. John 6:46; 1 John 1:2).[28] Third, the Word as to his nature is deity. The Word is not only distinct from God (the Word was with God), but the Word is God (*theos*).[29] An equally decisive statement about the deity of Jesus is made in John 1:18: "No one has ever seen God; the only God, who is at the Father's side, he has made him known." Once again, John not only speaks of Jesus as pre-existing and being relationally with God (the Only God, who is at the Father's side), but clearly states that He is God (the only God, *monogenēs theos*).[30] As the one who is at the Father's side, the Word makes the Father known to us (cf. John 14:9). Since the prologue of John (1:1–18)[31] clearly speaks of the deity of Jesus, it is not surprising that this finds an equally emphatic declaration throughout the gospel narrative (John 5:18, 8:58, 10:28–35) and at its end and climax when Thomas professed his faith in the resurrected Jesus: "My Lord and my God!" (*ho kyrios mou kai ho theos mou*) (John 20:28).

John 1:1 not only tells us who the Word was before creation, but John 1:3 tells us what He did in creation: "All things were made through him,

---

27. The Greek verb ἦν (*ēn*) is an imperfect form of the verb εἰμί (*eimi*, I am) and is used to show continuous action in the past.

28. The context of John 1:1–18 makes it clear that the Word is clearly a person and not an abstraction (i.e., as Unitarians believe), for example, people become children of God by believing in His name (John 1:12).

29. In John 1:1c "*kai theos ēn ho logos*" ("and the Word was God") the subject of the verse is highlighted by the article (*ho logos*, the Word), and God (*theos*) is a predicate nominative; *theos* does not take the article, it comes before the linking verb "was" (*ēn*), and therefore tells us that the Word is deity.

30. This reading of *monogenēs theos*, as opposed to the variant *ho monogenēs huios* found in many later *mss*, "is supported by the best mss (P66 א *BC*L), and the reading with *theos* is also supported by P75 אc, though both include the definite article before *theos*." See Grant Osborne, *The Gospel of John: Cornerstone Biblical Commentary* (Wheaton, IL: Tyndale House Publishers, 2007), p. 21.

31. John 1:1–18 is often referred to as a prologue because it forms an introduction to the gospel of John and is the interpretive lens by which to view the rest of the gospel.

and without him was not any thing made that was made." Greek Stoic philosophers used the term *logos* to refer to the rational principle by which everything exists. But this is not the primary point John is making here, as the Old Testament often speaks of God's Word as His self-expression in creation, revelation, and salvation (Jeremiah 1:4; Isaiah 55:11; Psalm 107:20).[32] By stating that "all things were made through him [*logos*]," John clearly is referring to the Jewish understanding of God's Word as the means by which creation came into being: "By the word [*logos*, LXX] of the LORD the heavens were made" (Psalm 33:6). This is seen in Genesis 1 when God creates, not by means of natural processes, but by supernaturally speaking things into existence in the space of six days (Genesis 1:3, 6, 9, 11, 14, 20, 24, 26; cf. Exodus 20:11). John applies the title of the Word to the person of Jesus who is the Creator of all things (cf. Colossians 1:16; Hebrews 1:2–3, 10–12). This is evident in His incarnation when Jesus performed other miracles — turning water into wine, feeding the five thousand (John 6:1–14), walking on water (6:16–21), and the miraculous catch of fish (John 21:4–8).

Most importantly, several verses later, John writes that the Word who was with God in the beginning "became flesh and dwelt among us" (John 1:14). Notice that John does not say that the Word stopped being God. The verb "became" (*egeneto*) does not mean there was a change in the deity of the Word; rather, He took on a human nature (cf. Philippians 2:5–8). In fact, John uses a very particular term here: *skenoo* "dwelt," which means he "pitched his tent" or "tabernacled" among us. This is a direct parallel to the Old Testament record of when God "dwelt" in the tabernacle that Moses told the Israelites to construct (Exodus 25:8–9, 33:7). John is telling us that in the person of Jesus, God "dwelt" or "pitched his tent" among us. The incarnate Word has appeared to us as a person (Jesus) and communicates to us by His Word (the Scriptures), and by believing His words we have eternal life (John 5:24).

Not only does the author (the Apostle John) identify Jesus as divine, but he accurately records Jesus identifying Himself as divine. At the Feast of Tabernacles/Booths (John 8:12), a harvest festival (15 to 21 Tishri, early October), Jesus claims, "I am the light of the world." (John 8:12). The Pharisees challenge Jesus to the validity of this claim (John 8:13). Jesus counters the challenge from the Pharisees by providing two witnesses that confirm his identity: Himself and the Father who sent Him (John 8:18). So the Pharisees respond by asking Jesus who His Father is (John 8:19). Jesus' response affirms His oneness with the Father, which is misunderstood by the Jewish

32. Carson, *The Gospel According to John*, p. 115–116.

leaders (John 8:22). Jesus told them, "I told you that you would die in your sins, for unless you believe that I am he (*egō eimi*) you will die in your sins" (John 8:24). The Jewish leaders reacted to Jesus' statement by asking Him, "Who are you?" (John 8:25). Jesus tells them that it will not be until they have "lifted up" (the Cross) the Son of Man that they will know His true identity (John 8:28). What follows is a discussion of what it means to believe in Jesus: "As he was saying these things, many believed in him. So, Jesus said to the Jews who had believed him, 'If you abide in my word, you are truly my disciples, and you will know the truth, and the truth will set you free'" (John 8:30–32; cf. 2:23–25).

The Pharisees take exception to Jesus teaching that the truth would set them free — they claim they have never been enslaved to anyone (John 8:33). However, these Jewish leaders were self-deceived. At that time, politically speaking, the Jewish people were currently enslaved to the Romans and in the past had been enslaved by the Babylonians. But Jesus was talking about their spiritual slavery to sin, and only Jesus could free them from it (John 8:34–36). The Pharisees dispute with Jesus grows more heated when they claim that their descent from Abraham is enough to save them (John 8:39). However, Jesus makes it plain to the Pharisees that it is not physical descent from Abraham that counts, but they must have the same faith as Abraham (John 8:39; cf. Galatians 3:7, 9). Jesus tells the Pharisees that unlike them, Abraham did not try and kill Jesus (John 8:40 cf. Genesis 18). Jesus gets straight to the point with the Pharisees and explains that the reason they want to kill Him is that they are off their father the devil (John 8:44). The reason that the Pharisees did not hear Jesus' words is that they were not of God (John 8:47; cf. 10:26). The Pharisees reply that Jesus is demon possessed, but Jesus responds that His followers will never see death (John 8:51). The Pharisees respond that is impossible because even Abraham died, and surely, Jesus is not greater than Abraham. Again, they ask Jesus who He makes Himself out to be (John 8:53). Jesus replies that Abraham rejoiced to see his day (John 8:56), but the Pharisees misunderstand, and ask how Jesus could have seen Abraham when he is not even 50 years old (John 8:57). Jesus responds to them: "Truly, truly, I say to you, before Abraham was [became], I am (*egō eimi*)" (John 8:58).[33] The Jewish leaders responded as they had done previously, and as they will do again, by picking up stones to throw at Him (John 8:59; cf. 5:18; 10:31). This is because they recognized that not only was Jesus claiming the divine title (YHWH) but was saying He pre-existed Abraham.

---

33. The verb "became" (cf. John 1:3) has to do with coming into existence whereas "I am" (*egō eimi*) has to do with pre-existence (cf. John 1:1).

Jesus "I am" (*ego eimi*) statement was His clearest example of His proclamation, "I am Yahweh," from its background in the Book of Isaiah (Isaiah 41:4; 43:10–13, 25; 46:4; 48:12; 52:6; cf. John 4:26; 13:19; 18:6).[34] The fact that there is one LORD (YHWH) who is not like the pagan gods of the nations is argued at length by the prophet Isaiah. In Isaiah 40–45, in what is often called the trial of false gods (see Isaiah 41:21), God repeatedly declares His identity to His people Israel who have strayed away from Him and calls them into judgment for their idolatry. The nation of Israel went into exile because it had mixed pagan idolatry with the worship of God (Isaiah 40:19, 41:7, 42:17, 45:16–20):

> "You are my witnesses," declares the LORD, "and my servant whom I have chosen, that you may know and believe me and understand that I am he. Before me no god was formed, nor shall there be any after me. I, I am the LORD, and besides me there is no savior. I declared and saved and proclaimed, when there was no strange god among you; and you are my witnesses," declares the LORD, "and I am God. Also henceforth I am he; there is none who can deliver from my hand; I work, and who can turn it back?" (Isaiah 43:10–13).

In Isaiah 43:10 (LXX) the LORD (YHWH) not only states that "I am he" (*ego eimi*), but "before me no god was formed [became]" (*emprosthen mou ouk egeneto allos theos*), which is the same contrast that Jesus makes with Himself and Abraham: "before Abraham became, I am" (*prin Abraam genesthai ego eimi*).[35] In John 10, just before the Feast of Dedication Jesus gives His "good shepherd" discourse (John 10:1–21), which speaks against the false shepherds (Pharisees) who were leading God's people astray (see Ezekiel 34). After Jesus' "good shepherd" discourse, at the Feast of Dedication (November/December), Jesus returns to the topic of sheep (assuming the same audience of 10:1–21), and says, "I give them eternal life, and they will never perish, and no one will snatch them out of my hand" (John 10:28). The words "and no one will snatch them out of my hand" (*kai ouch harpasei tis auta ek tēs cheiros mou*) is what the LORD (YHWH) says in Isaiah 43:13 "none who can deliver from my hand" (*kai ouk estin ho ek tōn cheirōn mou exairoumenos*). The only other time the phrase "none who can deliver from my hand" is found in the Bible is in the Song of Moses in Deuteronomy

---

34. John uses *ego eimi* in the absolute sense, without a predicate (see John 4:26; 6:20; 8:24; 13:19; 18:5-6, 8).

35. In the LXX of Isaiah 43:10, the word for "became," *egeneto*, is a form of the word *ginomai*, and the Greek of John 8:58 uses the word *genesthai* which is also a form of the word *ginomai*.

32:39. Deuteronomy 32 is "the interpretive lens through which to understand and interpret Isaiah through Malachi."[36]

Deuteronomy 31:10–11 tells us that the Torah was meant to be read to Israel every seven years at the Feast of Tabernacles (when Israel would celebrate the fact that God had tabernacled among them). Deuteronomy 32 then would have been part of the final portion of their reading during that festival. In Deuteronomy 32, in obedience to the LORD's command, Moses writes a song to teach to the Israelites, in the form of a covenant lawsuit, outlining Israel's history. The song would serve as a witness against Israel (Deuteronomy 31:19) when, after the death of Moses, they entered the land of Canaan and would "whore after the foreign gods" (Deuteronomy 31:16). When the Israelites committed apostasy against the LORD (YHWH) by going after other gods, God said He would "hide his face" from that wicked generation who had turned their backs against him (Deuteronomy 31:17–18). In contrast to the pagan gods of the nations, the Song of Moses emphasizes the LORD (YHWH) alone exists (cf. Deuteronomy 4:39; 6:4):

> See now that I, even I, am he, and there is no god beside me; I
> kill and I make alive; I wound and I heal; and there is none that can
> deliver out of my hand (Deuteronomy 32:39).

The LORD (YHWH) is not only the one who alone exists, but He is the ultimate cause of death and source of all life (divine prerogatives). The gods of the nations were powerless, whereas none could deliver out of the LORD's hand. Not only does Deuteronomy 32:39 (LXX) contain the first "I am" (*ego eimi*) statement in the Bible but it also contains the phrase "and there is none that can deliver out of my hand" (*kai ouk estin hos exeleitai ek tōn cheirōn mou*). The phrase "no one can deliver out of my hand" in Deuteronomy 32:39 and Isaiah 43:13 are both spoken by the LORD (YHWH) and are in conjunction with an "I am" (*ego eimi*) statement. Why is this significant? The context of Jesus' "I am" (*ego eimi*) statement in John 8:58 was at the last day of the Feast of Tabernacles (see John 7:2, 37; 8:12). When Jesus spoke these words on the last great day of the Feast of Tabernacles the Jewish leaders would have had the Song of Moses ringing in their ears. How does Jesus respond to the Jewish leaders who are in opposition to Him? The text tells us that: "Jesus hid himself and went out of the temple." (John 8:59; cf. Deuteronomy 31:17–18). This is what God said He would do when His covenant people (Israel) were in apostasy against Him (see John 10:1–21). The context of John 10:28 is that Jesus gives eternal life to His sheep, a

---

36. Miles Van Pelt, *A Biblical-Theological Introduction to the Old Testament* (Wheaton, IL: Crossway: 2016), p. 37.

divine prerogative, and no one can snatch them out of His hand (cf. Deuteronomy 32:39). Jesus employs terminology that His audience would be familiar with so that there could be no mistake about who He truly is, the LORD (YHWH).

Chapter 10
The Last Adam: His View of Scripture

When it comes to our view of Scripture, and what we should believe about it, whether it is inspired or not inspired, does it contain errors or not, who should we listen to? Should we listen to famous academics and theologians or even respected pastors who deny or re-interpret the inspiration of Scripture? After all, these are learned men who are trained in the Scriptures. Well, as Christians, who better to listen to when it comes to the authority and accuracy of Scripture than the Lord Jesus Christ? This may seem like the obvious answer, but when it comes to the authority of Scripture many Christians seem to want to listen to respected academics or theologians rather than to Jesus. As the incarnate Son of God, however, who is better to teach us about our doctrine of Scripture? Only Jesus has the authority to tell us what to think about the Bible. Think about it — if you wanted to know what to believe about the book series *The Lord of Rings,* would you ask someone who had done their PhD on them, or, if you had the opportunity, would you ask the author himself (J.R.R. Tolkien)? No matter what someone who had intensely studied *The Lord of the Rings* books had to say about them, it would not compare to the author's opinion. When it comes to the authority of Scripture, Jesus is *the* ultimate authority as there is no higher standard that we should listen to than Him. Although some people want to "unhitch" the Old Testament from Jesus, the truth of Jesus and the truth of Old Testament depend on one another as they are linked together:

> For if you believed Moses, you would believe me; for he wrote of me. But if you do not believe his writings, how will you believe my words? (John 5:46–47).

Jesus linked the truth He was teaching about Himself to Moses, the author of the Torah. Jesus believed the Old Testament was true, and that they were His own words as He is the eternal Word of God made flesh (cf. John 1:1–3; Psalm 12:6; 18:30). So, if you believe the Scriptures are wrong, then so is Jesus. Jesus and Scripture are linked together in such a way that we cannot unwind them, which means what Jesus says about the Scriptures matters because it reflects on His own testimony. This also means that Jesus is the primary lens by which we understand and interpret the Old Testament and Scripture as a whole. After His death and Resurrection, Jesus reminded the men on the road to Emmaus and His disciples that the purpose of the Old Testament is to point us to Himself (Luke 24:25–27, 44–46).

It is important to keep in mind that when Jesus came into the world there was no New Testament Scripture, there was only the Old Testament (Hebrew Scriptures). Since there was no New Testament in Jesus day, when we talk about Jesus' view of Scripture, we are talking about the Old Testament Scriptures. But did Jesus have anything to say about the New Testament Scriptures? If Jesus believed the Old Testament was inspired, then implicitly this means that He would believe the New Testament is inspired (see John 14:25–26).

🥢 Jesus Believed the Old Testament Was Historical

In the Old Testament, God revealed Himself to the people of Israel and not any other nation (Psalm 147:19–20). It was the Jewish people to whom the oracles of God were entrusted (Romans 3:2). The canon of the Old Testament, the Law (Torah), the Prophets (Nevi'im), and the Writings (Ketuvim), was well established by the time of Jesus (see Luke 24:44). According to the first century Jewish historian Josephus, the Old Testament consisted of "only twenty-two books" that were considered sacred (Josephus, *Against Apion*, 1.41).[1] Josephus rejected the Apocryphal books (i.e., Maccabees, Judith, etc) as sacred Scripture.[2] This is consistent with Jesus, and the Apostles view of the canon, as they never quote or reference the Apocryphal writings as being authoritative Scripture.

---

1. The reason Josephus says 22 books and not 39 (like today's O.T) is that Jews counted books differently (for example, Genesis, Exodus, Leviticus, Numbers and Deuteronomy were considered one book, The Torah, the book of Moses). Ruth is attached to Judges; other books are combined – 1 and 2 Samuel, 1 and 2 Kings, 1 and 2 Chronicles and Ezra and Nehemiah. Lamentations is joined to Jeremiah and the 12 minor prophets are one book.

2. Josephus states: "It is true, our history hath been written since Artaxerxes very particularly, but hath not been esteemed of the like authority with the former by our forefathers, because there hath not been an exact succession of prophets since that time." (Josephus, *Against Apion*, 1.41)

The Torah	The Nevi'im	The Ketuvim
Genesis	**The Former Prophets**	**Poetry**
Exodus	Joshua	Psalms
Leviticus	Judges	Proverbs
Numbers	Samuel	Job
Deuteronomy	Kings	**The Megilloth**
	The Latter Prophets	Song of Songs
	Isaiah	Ruth
	Jeremiah	Lamentations
	Ezekiel	Ecclesiastes
	The Twelve	Esther
		History
		Daniel
		Ezra-Nehemiah
		Chronicles

Although the Old Testament is sometimes a problem for people's trust in the Bible, Jesus loved the Old Testament and quoted from it extensively. Jesus did not see the events in the Old Testament (creation, the Flood, the exodus, etc.) as parable or myth, but as events that happened in history. Jesus interpreted the Old Testament as a historical narrative, straightforward history. This does not mean He denied there were figures of speech, metaphors, or symbols in it, as there are poetic portions, the Psalms, and apocalyptic portions which are highly symbolic, Ezekiel. Jesus also regarded the Old Testament's historicity as impeccable, accurate, and reliable. Jesus often chose for illustrations in His teaching the very persons and events that are the least acceptable today to critical scholars. This can be seen from his references to Adam, Abel, Noah, Abraham, Lot, Sodom and Gomorrah, Moses, and Jonah.

When it comes to the discussion over creation, a historical Adam, the Fall, the Flood, and the age of the earth, many people mistakenly think that the issues only involve the interpretation of Genesis 1–11. In the gospels, Jesus refers to the historicity in Genesis 1–11 to make several theological points. In His reference to Genesis 1–11, Jesus is obviously not addressing the modern-day debate over the age of the earth (this would be anachronistic), however, He is saying things that are fully consistent with a young-earth creation position, that are relevant to the creation/evolution debate, and that are impossible to align with an old-earth creation or theistic evolutionary position.

In Mark 10:6–8, Jesus, in a debate with the Pharisees, quotes from Genesis 1:27 and 2:24 in a straightforward, historical manner:

> But from the beginning of creation, 'God made them male and female.' 'Therefore a man shall leave his father and mother and hold fast to his wife, and the two shall become one flesh.' So they are no longer two but one flesh. What therefore God has joined together, let not man separate.

Jesus' use of Scripture here is authoritative in settling a dispute over the question of divorce, as it is grounded in the creation and purpose of the first marriage (cf. Matthew 19:4–6). Jesus points out that God's purpose for marriage is to be found in the creation account in Genesis 1–2. God created marriage to be between one man and one woman under a lifelong covenant, but it was because of people's "hardness of heart" that Moses allowed for a certificate of divorce (Mark 10:4–5). The "hardness of heart" was not the condition of man's heart before the Fall but is a result of it. Mark 10:6–8 is especially significant, as Jesus said in verse 6, "But from the beginning of creation, God made them male and female." When Jesus speaks of "creation" He is referring to the creation that God created, the whole created realm. In his gospel, Mark uses the term "beginning" (*archē*) in a chronological sense (Mark 1:1; 13:8, 19). The statement "from the beginning of creation" (*apo archēs ktiseōs* — cf. Mark 13:19–20; 1 John 3:8) is a reference to the beginning of creation and not simply to the beginning of humanity (cf. Genesis 1:1, *en archē*, LXX). In Mark 10:6, Jesus was saying that Adam and Eve were there at the beginning of creation, on day six (this was not billions of years after the beginning). It is estimated today, by naturalistic scientists, that the universe is around 13.8 billion years old. This means that if you try to argue for theistic evolution or an old earth creation position, then man was created after 99.99997 percent of those billions of years had passed. The evolutionary timeline makes no sense considering what Jesus says about creating man at the beginning of creation or with what the Bible teaches about God forming the earth to be inhabited (cf. Isaiah 45:18).

Jesus not only implicitly refers to Adam and Eve ("made them male and female" in Mark 10:6) but explicitly refers to their son Abel. Jesus believed that Abel, like Adam, existed at the "foundation of the world" and that Adam, Eve, and Abel were historical.

> [S]o that the blood of all the prophets, shed from the foundation of the world, may be charged against this generation, from the

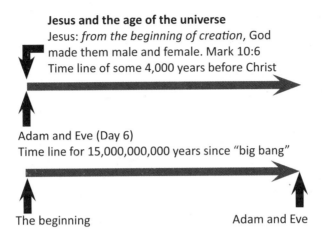

Jesus and the age of the universe
Jesus: *from the beginning of creation*, God made them male and female. Mark 10:6
Time line of some 4,000 years before Christ

Adam and Eve (Day 6)
Time line for 15,000,000,000 years since "big bang"

The beginning   Adam and Eve

blood of Abel to the blood of Zechariah, who perished between the altar and the sanctuary. Yes, I tell you, it will be required of this generation (Luke 11:50–51).

In this passage, Jesus talks about the blood of all the prophets shed from the foundation of the world. The foundation period begins with the initial creation week in Genesis 1 (see Hebrew 4:3–4). Jesus is paralleling the murder of the first martyr, Abel (Genesis 4:8), with the last martyr in the Old Testament, Zechariah (2 Chronicles 24:22). Theologian Jud Davis rightly asks the question of Jesus' words in Luke 11:50–51: "Would this be true if millions of years of human evolution preceded Adam and Eve? Were there really no murders before Adam's time?"[3] The first human murder recorded in the Bible is that of Abel (Genesis 4:8). There were no other murders before this. Jesus accepted the early history in the Book of Genesis as being reliable and accurate.

In His confrontation with the Pharisees, Jesus said to them that if God was their "Father" they would love Him (John 8:42). Since they did not, they must have another "Father," who Jesus identifies as the devil:

You are of your father the devil, and your will is to do your father's desires. He was a murderer from the beginning, and does not stand in the truth, because there is no truth in him. When he lies, he speaks out of his own character, for he is a liar and the father of lies (John 8:44).

Jesus says that lies and murder were on Satan's mind "from the beginning," a clear reference to the garden in Eden, where God had placed Adam and Eve, who were made in His image (Genesis 1:27, 2:8). Because Satan was in

3. Jud Davis, "Unresolved Major Questions: Evangelicals and Genesis 1–2," *Reading Genesis 1–2: An Evangelical Conversation* (Peabody, MA: Hendrickson, 2013), p. 211.

rebellion against God, he wanted to destroy man whom God had made. In his temptation, Satan deprived Adam and Eve of spiritual life, and physical death was brought into the world (cf. Romans 5:12). After seeing Adam and Eve fall from grace in Eden, Satan provoked the first human murder — of Abel by his brother Cain (1 John 3:12).

In speaking to His disciples, Jesus speaks of the historical judgment of the Flood in Noah's day:

> Just as it was in the days of Noah, so will it be in the days of the Son of Man. They were eating and drinking and marrying and being given in marriage, until the day when Noah entered the ark, and the flood came and destroyed them all (Luke 17:26–27).

Jesus did not consider the account of the Flood a myth or legend: the meaning of the passage would lose its force if it were. Jesus not only refers to the individuals as historical but cites parts of the narrative as real historical events, such as eating, drinking, marrying, and entering the ark. These terms obviously need to be considered with how Genesis describes the people in those days: "wicked," "corrupt," "violent," and "evil hearts," (Genesis 6:5, 11–13). The people of Noah's day seemed unconcerned with God and concerned only about life and celebration. The Flood is not just a story with a theological point, as Jesus uses it as analogy for a real judgment.[4] The Flood not only destroyed human life that inhabited the world at that time, but it also destroyed and reshaped the entire physical world (Genesis 6:13). In fact, the Flood was so severe that the earth was reversed to its original state on Day 2 of creation week (Genesis 1:6–8), before God created dry land — the whole earth was covered with water (2 Peter 3:5–6). The word Luke uses for "flood" also sheds light on the nature of the Flood. It comes from the Greek word *kataklysmos* from which we derive our English word cataclysm — a clear reference to a global catastrophe. If Luke had believed that the Flood in Genesis 6–8 was local, covering only the region of Mesopotamia, then why did he not use the Greek word for an ordinary local flood, *plemmura* (Luke 6:48)? Because Jesus believed the Flood was a real historical global catastrophe and not a local one.

Many Christian scholars today say they do not accept the Bible's account of origins in Genesis when it speaks of Adam and Eve, and God destroying the world in a global catastrophic Flood. This cannot be said, however, without overlooking the clear teaching of our Creator, the Lord Jesus, on the matter and the clear testimony of Scripture (Genesis 2:7, 22, 6–9; 1

---

4. Christians disagree as to whether Jesus is referring to judgment on Jerusalem in A.D. 70 or the final judgment at the end of the age.

Timothy 2:12–14; Peter 3:3–6), which He affirmed as truth (John 17:17). If we confess Jesus is our Lord, we must be willing to submit to Him as the teacher of the church. Theologian Robert Reymond states:

> To question the basic historical authenticity and integrity of Genesis 1–11 is to assault the integrity of Christ's own teaching.[5]

Moreover, if Jesus was wrong about Genesis, then He could be wrong about anything, and none of His teaching would have any authority. The importance of all this is summed up by Jesus in declaring that if someone did not believe in Moses and the prophets (the Old Testament) then they would not believe God based on a miraculous resurrection (Luke 16:31).

Jesus not only believed that the events described in Genesis 1–11 were true but so were the rest of the events in the Old Testament. The names Sodom and Gomorrah are infamous for God's judgment upon the wickedness of the people who lived in those cities (cf. Genesis 13:13). Just as Jesus pointed to the Flood as a guarantee of judgment, so He also pointed to God's judgment of Sodom by fire as a guarantee of judgment:

> Likewise, just as it was in the days of Lot — they were eating and drinking, buying and selling, planting and building, but on the day when Lot went out from Sodom, fire and sulfur rained from heaven and destroyed them all — so will it be on the day when the Son of Man is revealed. (Luke 17:28–30)

Just as with the days before the Flood, Jesus spoke of the days before the destruction of Sodom as a time when people were indifferent and solely concerned with the things of this life: eating and drinking, buying and selling, planting and building. In other words, people were caught up with material things of life, which caused them to have a lack of concern for the things of God. Then the destruction by fire and sulfur came quickly and unexpectedly, destroying them all. If Sodom and Gomorrah were fictional accounts, then how could they serve as a warning for future judgment?

The historical event of the exodus, when the LORD (YHWH), through Moses, led the people of Israel out of Egypt with a display of overwhelming power, is *the* major event of the Old Testament (Deuteronomy 7:18–19; Psalm 105:23–45, 106:7–32; Nehemiah 9:9–12). The exodus is of foremost importance because it marks God's redemption of His people, whom He took from slavery to freedom and made into a nation of His own possession (Exodus 19:5–6; cf. 1 Peter 2:9). Since the rise of higher criticism in the 18th century, many archaeologists and biblical scholars have questioned

5. Reymond, *A New Systematic Theology of the Christian Faith*, p. 118.

whether this event really happened and see it as a myth or a fable that is based more on tradition than history.[6] However, Jesus believed that Moses existed, and that God had given him the Law (Matthew 19:7–8; Mark 7:10; Luke 16:31; John 7:19). When Jesus met with Nicodemus, a ruler of the Jewish people and the teacher of Israel (John 3:1, 10), He spoke to him of what it means to be born again (John 3:3), and concluded with these words:

> And as Moses lifted up the serpent in the wilderness, so must the Son of Man be lifted up, that whoever believes in him may have eternal life (John 3:14–15).

To switch from His explanation of being born again (spiritual life, John 3:3) Jesus moves to the event of the bronze snake in the wilderness where God gave new (physical) life to the people of Israel (see Numbers 21:4-9). Because of the lack of food in the wilderness the people of Israel wanted to return to Egypt (Numbers 21:5–6). In response to their complaint, God sent them serpents (a symbol of lower Egypt) that bit the people and many of them died (Numbers 21:6). God in His mercy had Moses make a bronze serpent that was set on a pole that the people had to look at to be healed (Numbers 21:8–9). In the same way, Jesus would be physically "lifted up" on the Cross (John 8:28; 12;32, 34). Jesus became that symbol of death in order that eternal life may come to those who look to Him in faith (cf. 2 Corinthians 5:21). Jesus' use of the exodus account strongly supports the belief that this event occurred in history. In fact, according to Jude, it was "Jesus, who saved a people out of the land of Egypt" (Jude 5).[7] Moreover, as the Son of God, Jesus, came to affect a new exodus (Mark 1:1–3; Luke 9:31), which was accomplished through His redemptive work on the Cross (Mark 14:22–25). Jesus also made a strong connection between Moses' teaching and His own (John 5:45–47), and Moses made some very astounding claims about six-day creation in the Ten Commandments, which he says were penned by God's own hand (Exodus 20:8–11, 31:17–18).

Many people struggle with the account of Jonah because of his being swallowed by a great fish, and therefore suggest it is an allegory or parable. However, the Old Testament presents Jonah as a historical person (2 Kings

---

6. For evidence of the historicity of the exodus see Scott Stripling, "The Fifteenth-Century (Early Date) Exodus View," in *Five Views on the Exodus* (Grand Rapids, MI: Zondervan: 2021), p. 25–52.

7. This verse is a debated textual variant, however, the textual evidence strongly supports the view that the original reading was "Jesus." See note 24 in "Jude" https://netbible.org/bible/Jude+1.

14:25), who prophesied under the reign of Jeroboam II (793–753 B.C.). Jonah was a Hebrew who feared the LORD, the God of Heaven, who created the sea and the dry land (Jonah 1:9). In the account of Jonah, God not only appoints a huge fish to swallow Jonah (Jonah 1:17), but He also appoints a plant, a worm, and a scorching east wind to teach Jonah a lesson (Jonah 4:6–8). Moreover, Jesus appealed to Jonah as the very reason he would be in the grave for three days and three nights:

> Then some of the scribes and Pharisees answered him, saying, "Teacher, we wish to see a sign from you." But he answered them, "An evil and adulterous generation seeks for a sign, but no sign will be given to it except the sign of the prophet Jonah. For just as Jonah was three days and three nights in the belly of the great fish, so will the Son of Man be three days and three nights in the heart of the earth. The men of Nineveh will rise up at the judgment with this generation and condemn it, for they repented at the preaching of Jonah, and behold, something greater than Jonah is here (Matthew 12:38–41).

The people of Nineveh repented without ever recognizing the sign, whereas the Jewish leaders were too hard-hearted to repent even though Jesus had shown them many signs (Matthew 11:20–24). The people of Nineveh simply needed to hear Jonah's preaching (Jonah 3:4–5), and yet Jesus was greater than Jonah. Jesus did not see Jonah as a myth or legend; the meaning of the passage would lose its force if it was. How could Jesus' death and Resurrection serve as a sign, if the events of Jonah did not take place? Furthermore, Jesus says that the men of Nineveh will stand at the last judgment because they repented at the preaching of Jonah, but if the account of Jonah is a myth or symbolic, then how can the men of Nineveh stand at the last judgment?

☙ Jesus and the Inspiration of the Old Testament

Because of the influence of evolution, which gave rise to higher criticism, there are those who want to redefine the authority of Scripture as being relevant to only spiritual issues. The theistic evolutionary organization BioLogos makes it clear that they tolerate the view that the Bible has errors:

> Some in BioLogos would not be comfortable with the word "inerrancy." They don't see it as a useful concept; it's not how they would characterize their view of Scripture. But others would be

comfortable with the Bible being inerrant in terms of what God has to teach in matters of faith and practice.[8]

But if Scripture is incorrect in its history (i.e., Genesis 1–11), then why should we trust it in what it teaches in matters of faith (theology) and practice (morality) that is grounded in that history (e.g., marriage, sexuality etc.)? The Bible's morality and theology cannot be separated from its history (see Exodus 20:1–17; 1 Corinthians 15; Matthew 22:23–33). Because God does not change and neither does His truth, what was true in Jesus' day is so today and will be in the future. The passage of time does not change the truth of God's Word, as the truth of God's Word is not an ever-changing matter based on evolutionary considerations. Theistic evolution must be tested by Scripture, and when it is, it fails. It fails to do justice to the goodness of God in creation (Genesis 1:31), it fails to do justice to the impact of sin on creation (Genesis 3:17; Romans 5:12, 8:20), it fails to do justice to the redemptive work of Christ (Romans 8:21; Colossians 1:20), and it fails to do justice to the truth of God's Word (2 Timothy 3:16). Theistic evolution is not derived from Scripture but is an extra biblical (philosophical) system that is imposed upon it. As such, theistic evolution needs to be abandoned as it weakens the Christians ability to trust in the authority of Scripture.

In Matthew 4, Jesus' response to being tempted by Satan in the wilderness was to quote sections of Scripture from Deuteronomy (8:3; 6:13, 16) demonstrating His belief in the final authority of the Old Testament. Jesus overcame Satan's temptations by quoting Scripture to him "It is written …" which has the force of or is equivalent to "that settles it"; and Jesus understood that the Word of God was sufficient for this. Jesus' own view of Scripture was that of verbal inspiration, which can be seen from His statement in Matthew 5:17–18:

> Do not think that I have come to abolish the Law or the Prophets; I have not come to abolish them but to fulfill them. For truly, I say to you, until heaven and earth pass away, not an iota, not a dot, will pass from the Law until all is accomplished.

For Jesus, Scripture is not merely inspired in its general ideas or its broad claims or in its general meaning, but is inspired down to its very words (*iota* and *dot* are the smallest marks in the Greek and Hebrew languages) because those words come "from the mouth of God" (Matthew 4:4). Every word of

---

8. Deborah Haarsma "Discussing Origins: Biologos, Reasons to Believe, and Southern Baptists, Part 2," BioLogos, January 27, 2015, http://biologos.org/blogs/archive/discussing-origins-biologos-reasons-to-believe-and-southern-baptists-part-2.

the Old Testament (Law and the Prophets) stands in God's purposes and will not pass away. There is an eternality to the Word of God (cf. Luke 16:17). Whereas Scripture provides us with the very voice of God, human tradition not founded upon Scripture, as Jesus reminded the Pharisees, makes "void the word of God" (Matthew 15:6).

When Jesus was confronted by the Sadducees (who denied the Resurrection, Acts 23:8) they asked Him a trick question regarding the future Resurrection, He reminded them:

> But Jesus answered them, "You are wrong, because you know neither the Scriptures nor the power of God. For in the resurrection they neither marry nor are given in marriage, but are like angels in heaven. And as for the resurrection of the dead, have you not read what was said to you by God: 'I am the God of Abraham, and the God of Isaac, and the God of Jacob'? He is not God of the dead, but of the living" (Matthew 22:29–32).

This text is important for a couple of reasons. First, those who make the charge that the Scriptures contain error find themselves in the same position as the Sadducees who were rebuked by Jesus ("you are wrong"). The implication by Jesus here is that the Scriptures themselves do not err, as they speak accurately concerning history and theology (in context, the Patriarchs and the Resurrection). Second, Jesus points to Scripture "have you not read" as the focus of His argument. Jesus points to the words from the Book of Exodus (3:6) concerning Abraham, Isaac, and Jacob not only as being the very words of God but also as being applicable even to correct the Sadducees' misunderstanding of the Resurrection in the first century. Jesus held the Sadducees accountable to the scriptural revelation that God had spoken 1,400 years earlier. The concept of Scripture being "God-breathed" was not invented by Paul (2 Timothy 3:16), it was something Jesus believed. Scripture is not bound by time and culture but is living and active (cf. Hebrews 4:12).

Although Jesus disagreed with the Pharisees over many issues (i.e., Sabbath, purity laws), the one thing He did not disagree with was the authority and inspiration of the Old Testament. In John 10, when Jesus is debating the Pharisees, He appeals to Scripture to settle a dispute: "If he called them gods to whom the word of God came — and Scripture cannot be broken" (John 10:35). The word "broken" means that Scripture cannot be falsified or proven wrong, it is a foundation that will hold strong. Jesus was telling the Jewish leaders that the authority of Scripture could not be denied. Jesus clearly believed that Scripture was God's Word and therefore truth (John 17:17). In John 17:17, notice that in Jesus' prayer to the Father, He says

"Sanctify them in the truth; your word is truth." Jesus did not say that "your word is true" (adjective), rather He says, "your word is truth" (noun). The implication is that Scripture does not just happen to be true; rather the very nature of Scripture is truth, and it is the very standard of truth to which everything else must be tested and compared. It is Scripture, not philosophy or science, that is the standard of truth.

Jesus regularly refers to the words of the Old Testament as the words of God. Jesus does not just cite the Old Testament but often indicates that God is speaking or that the author is speaking by the Holy Spirit. In Mark 12:36, Jesus quotes Psalm 110:1 and says that when David spoke, he spoke by the Holy Spirit. In Matthew 19:4–5, when Jesus said "Have you not read that *he who created them* from the beginning made them male and female, and *said*, 'Therefore a man shall leave his father and his mother and hold fast to his wife, and the two shall become one flesh" [italics mine] he quotes from Genesis 2:24 and attributes those words to God. Although Genesis 2:24 was written by Moses, it is not him speaking, as Jesus sees it as God speaking. This means that for Jesus, when the Old Testament speaks, God speaks.

Jesus' use of Scripture was authoritative and infallible as He spoke with the authority of God the Father (John 5:30, 8:28). Jesus taught that the Scriptures testify about Him (John 5:39), and He showed their fulfillment in the sight of the people of Israel (Luke 4:17–21). Jesus even declared to His disciples that what is written in the prophets about the Son of Man will be fulfilled (Luke 18:31). Furthermore, He placed the importance of the fulfillment of the prophetic Scriptures over escaping His own death (Matthew 26:53–56). After His death and Resurrection, He told His disciples that everything that was written about Him in Moses, the Prophets, and the Psalms must be fulfilled (Luke 24:44–47), and rebuked them for not believing all that the prophets have spoken concerning Him (Luke 24:25–27). The question then is how could Jesus fulfill all that the Old Testament spoke about Him if it is filled with error?

As Christians, if we do not have Jesus' view of Scripture then we have the wrong view of Scripture.

❧ Jesus Believed the Old Testament Was Authoritative

The Old Testament was the source Jesus went to in order to settle any debate, whether it was with Satan (Matthew 4:4, 6, 7, 10), the Sadducees (Matthew 22:31), or the Pharisees (Matthew 22:41–43). In some of those debates Jesus even asks a prominent counter question by stating "have you not read" (Matthew 19:4, 21:16). Jesus also counters questions from His opponents with a prominent counter question based on the authority of the Old Testament (Matthew 12:10–12, 15:2–3). Jesus not only answers a question with a question to make His opponent think, but to point His opponents to the Scriptures for the answer. The Old Testament was also Jesus' final court of appeal in all ethical debates, as He regularly appealed to the Law of God:

> But when the Pharisees heard that he had silenced the Sadducees, they gathered together. And one of them, a lawyer, asked him a question to test him. "Teacher, which is the great commandment in the Law?" And he said to him, "You shall love the Lord your God with all your heart and with all your soul and with all your mind. This is the great and first commandment. And a second is like it: You shall love your neighbor as yourself. On these two commandments depend all the Law and the Prophets" (Matthew 22:34–40).

Jesus even saw His own words as authoritative, "Heaven and earth will pass away, but my words will not pass away" (Matthew 24:35). If we are ashamed of Jesus' and His words, He will be ashamed of us (Mark 8:38). It is because Jesus' words are authoritative that we are to teach them to the nations: "And Jesus came and said to them, 'All authority in heaven and on earth has been given to me. Go therefore and make disciples of all nations, baptizing them in the name of the Father and of the Son and of the Holy Spirit, teaching them to observe all that I have commanded you. And behold, I am with you always, to the end of the age'" (Matthew 28:18–20).

In the four canonical Gospels, when Jesus speaks to people He often calls them to hear what He is saying (Matthew 7:24; Mark 7:14–15; Luke 11:28; John 10:27). In the parable of the Sower, Jesus begins and ends by telling His audience to listen to what He is saying (Mark 4:3, 9). Jesus not only calls people to listen, but He often asks questions of people to get them to give an account for their motives for doing something (Matthew 15:3, 19:17, 22:18, 26:10). It is not only important that we listen to Jesus' words but that we listen and obey, or we deceive ourselves (cf. James 1:22).

It is not just Jesus' words that are authoritative, but the Apostles are as well. This is because Jesus sent the Apostles into the world (John 20:21) and it was not them speaking but the Spirit and the Father speaking through them (Matthew 10:20). Hearing and rejecting the words of the Apostles will lead to greater condemnation (Matthew 10:14). The Holy Spirit not only spoke through the Apostles, but He also taught them the words of Scripture (John 14:26, 16:12–15). The four canonical Gospels are inspired by the Holy Spirit, who is the Spirit of truth (John 14:17). This sets the stage for a New Testament containing Gospels (words of Jesus) and letters (words of Apostles). The Apostles were God's eschatological "ministers of a new covenant" (2 Corinthians 3:6). But to recognize the authority and the divine origin of Scripture, the Holy Spirit must open our eyes. The Holy Spirit helps us see the divine quality of Scripture that is objectively there. For example, Jesus makes a similar point "My sheep hear my voice, and I know them, and they follow me" (John 10:27). Jesus' sheep will not listen to the voice of a stranger (John 10:5). The authority of Scripture is recognized by those who have the Holy Spirit dwelling in them (John 14:17).

Did Jesus' Assume the "Erroneous" Ideas of His Day?

It is important to understand that in Jesus' incarnation (John 1:14), He not only retained His divine nature, but He also took on a human nature. With respect to His divine nature, Jesus was omniscient (John 1:47–51; 4:16–19, 29), having all the attributes of God, yet in His human nature He had all the limitations of being human, which included limitations in knowing. For example, in Mark 13:32, when Jesus is talking about His return, he says, "But concerning that day or that hour, no one knows, not even the angels in heaven, nor the Son, but only the Father." Does this mean that Jesus was somehow limited? How should we handle this statement by Jesus? The text seems straightforward in saying there was something Jesus did not know. Jesus' teaching shows that what He knew or did not know was a conscious self-limitation. The God-man possessed divine attributes — otherwise He would have ceased to be God — but He chose not always to employ them. The fact that Jesus told His disciples that He did not know something is an indication that He did not teach untruths, and this is confirmed by His statement "If it were not so, I would have told you" (John 14:2). Furthermore, not knowing the future is not the same as making an erroneous statement. If Jesus had predicted something that did not take place, that would have been error.

Was Jesus in His humanity capable of error or ignorance in the things He taught? Does our human capacity to err apply to the teaching of Jesus? Because of His human nature, questions are raised about Jesus' beliefs concerning certain events in Scripture. Yet the Chicago Statement on Biblical Hermeneutics (1982) says: "We deny that the humble, human form of Scripture entails errancy any more than the humanity of Christ, even in his humiliation, entails sin."[9] Because of the impact evolutionary ideology has had on the scientific realm as well as on theology, it is reasoned that Jesus' teaching on things such as creation and the Mosaic authorship of the Torah was simply

---

9. https://www.leaderu.com/theology/chicago.html.

wrong. It is argued that Jesus would have been unaware that the Torah was written by multiple authors (Documentary Hypothesis) rather than a singular author (Moses). It is reasoned that in His humanity Jesus was limited by the opinions of His time. Therefore, He cannot be held accountable for holding to a view of Scripture that was prevalent in His culture. It is argued that Jesus erred in what He taught because He was accommodating the erroneous Jewish traditions of His time. For example, Old Testament theologian Peter Enns objects to the idea that Jesus' belief in the Mosaic authorship of the Torah (Pentateuch) is valid, arguing that Jesus simply accepted the cultural tradition of His day:

> Jesus seems to attribute authorship of the Pentateuch to Moses (e.g., John 5:46–47). I do not think, however, that this presents a clear counterpoint, mainly because even the most ardent defenders of Mosaic authorship today acknowledge that some of the Pentateuch reflects updating, but taken at face value this is not a position that Jesus seems to leave room for. But more important, I do not think that Jesus's status as the incarnate Son of God requires that statements such as John 5:46–47 be understood as binding historical judgments of authorship. Rather, Jesus here reflects the tradition that he himself inherited as a first-century Jew and that his hearers assumed to be the case.[10]

Enns uses the accommodation theory to argue for human errors in Scripture. He believes that the Christological argument (i.e., Christ's divine nature) cannot serve as an objection to the implications of accommodation. In his objection to the validity of Jesus' belief in the Mosaic authorship of the Torah, Enns is too quick to downplay the divine status of Jesus in relation to His knowledge of the authorship of the Torah. This overlooks whether the divinity of Christ meant anything in terms of an epistemological relevance to His humanity, and raises the question of how the divine nature relates to the human nature in the one person. We are told on several occasions, for example, that Jesus knew what people were thinking (Matthew 9:4, 12:25), which is a clear reference to a divine attribute. A.H. Strong gives a good explanation as to how Jesus' human nature existed in union with His divine nature:

> [T]he Logos did not take into union with himself an already developed human person, such as James, Peter, or John, but human nature before it had become personal or was capable of receiving a

---

10. Enns, *The Evolution of Adam*, 153.

name. It reached its personality only in union with his own divine nature. Therefore we see in Christ not two persons — a human person and a divine person — but one person, and that person possessed of a human nature as well as a divine.[11]

There is a personal union between the divine and the human nature, with each nature entirely preserved in its distinctness, yet in and as one person. Although some appeal to Jesus' divinity in order to affirm Mosaic authorship of the Torah, it is not necessary to do so, since:

> There is no mention in the Gospels of Jesus' divinity overwhelming his humanity. Nor do the Gospels refer his miracles to his divinity and refer his temptation or sorrow to his humanity, as if he switched back and forth from operating according to one nature to operating according to another. Rather, the Gospels routinely refer Christ's miracles to the Father and the Spirit.... [Jesus] spoke what he heard from the Father and as he was empowered by the Spirit.[12]

The context of John 5:45–47 is important in understanding the conclusions we draw concerning the truthfulness of what Jesus taught. In John 5:19 we are told that Jesus can do nothing of Himself. In other words, He does not act independently of the Father, but He only does what He sees the Father doing. Jesus has been sent into the world by God to reveal truth (John 5:30, 36) and it is this revelation from the Father that enabled Him to do "greater works." Elsewhere in John we are told that the Father teaches the Son (John 3:32–33; 7:15–17; 8:28, 37–38; 12:49–50). Jesus is not only one with the Father but is also dependent upon Him. Since the Father cannot be in error or lie (Numbers 23:19; Titus 1:2), and because Jesus and the Father are one (John 10:30), to accuse Jesus of error or falsehood in what He knew or taught is to accuse God (the Father) of the same thing. Jesus went on to acknowledge that the Old Testament required a minimum of two or three witnesses to establish the truthfulness of a person's claim (Deuteronomy 17:6, 19:15). Jesus produced several witnesses corroborating His claim of equality with God:

- John the Baptist (John 5:33–35)
- His works (John 5:36)
- God the Father (John 5:37)
- The Scriptures (John 5:39)
- Moses (John 5:46)

---

11. A.H. Strong, *Systematic Theology: The Doctrine of Man*, Vol. 2. (Valley Forge, PA: Judson Press, 1907), p. 679.
12. Horton, *The Christian Faith*, p. 469.

Jesus tells the Jewish leaders that it is Moses, one of the witnesses, who will hold them accountable for their unbelief in what he wrote concerning Him, and that it is he who will be their accuser before God. New Testament scholar Craig Keener comments, "In Palestinian Judaism, 'accusers' were witnesses against the defendant rather than official prosecutors (cf. 18:29), an image which would be consistent with other images used in the gospel tradition (Matt. 12:41–42; Luke 11:31–32). The irony of being accused by a person or document in which one trusted for vindication would not be lost on an ancient audience."[13]

In order for the accusation to hold up, however, the document or witnesses need to be reliable (Deuteronomy 19:16–19), and if Moses did not write the Torah, how could the Jews be held accountable by him and his writings? It was Moses who brought the people of Israel out of Egypt (Acts 7:40), gave them the Law (John 7:19) and brought them to the Promised Land (Acts 7:45). It was Moses who wrote about the coming prophet that God would send Israel and to whom they should listen (Deuteronomy 18:15; Acts 7:37). What is more, it was God who would put words into the mouth of this prophet (Deuteronomy. 18:18). Moreover, Jesus "opposed the pseudo-authority of untrue Jewish traditions … [and] disagrees with a pseudo-oral source, the false attribution of Jewish oral tradition to Moses [Mark 7:1–13]."[14] Thus, the basis for the truthfulness and inerrancy of what Jesus taught does not have to be resolved by appealing to His divine knowledge (although it can be); it can be understood from His humanity through His unity with the Father. Jesus' teaching is therefore true. The simple fact is that scholars who reject the Mosaic authorship of the Torah and embrace an accommodation approach to the evidence of the New Testament are as unwilling as the Jewish leaders (John 5:40) to listen to the words of Jesus on this subject.

The accommodation approach also leaves us with a Christological problem. Since Jesus clearly understood that Moses wrote about Him, this creates a serious moral problem for Christians, as we are told to follow the example set by Christ (John 13:15; 1 Peter 2:21) and have His attitude (Philippians 2:5). Yet, if Christ is shown to be approving falsehood in some areas of His teaching, it opens a door for us to affirm falsehood in some areas as well. The belief that Jesus accommodated His teaching to the beliefs of His first century hearers does not square with the facts.

13. Craig Keener, *The Gospel of John: A Commentary*, Vol. 1. (Peabody, MA: Hendrickson Publishers, 2003), p. 661–662.

14. G.K Beale, *The Erosion of Inerrancy in Evangelicalism: Responding to New Challenges to Biblical Authority* (Wheaton, IL: Crossway, 2008), p. 145.

For those who hold to an accommodation position, this overlooks the fact that Jesus never hesitated to correct erroneous views common in the culture (Matthew 7:6–13, 29). Jesus was never constrained by the culture of His day if it went against God's Word. He opposed those who claimed to be experts on the Law of God, if they were teaching error. His numerous disputes with the Pharisees are testament to this (Matthew 15:1–9, 23:13–36). The truth of Christ's teaching is not culturally bound, but transcends all cultures and remains unaltered by cultural beliefs (Matthew 24:35; 1 Peter 1:24–25). Those who claim that Jesus in His humanity was susceptible to error and therefore merely repeated the ignorant beliefs of His culture are claiming to have more authority, and to be wiser and more truthful than Jesus.

The Apostle Paul issued a warning to the Corinthian Church: "But I am afraid that as the serpent deceived Eve by his cunning, your thoughts will be led astray from a sincere and pure devotion to Christ." (2 Corinthians 11:3). The serpent's (Satan) method of deception with Eve was to get her to question God's Word (Genesis 3:1). Unfortunately, many scholars and Christian lay people today are falling for this deception and are questioning the authority of God's Word. We must remember, however, that Paul exhorts us that we are to have "the mind" of Christ (1 Corinthians 2:16, Philippians 2:5). Therefore, as Christians, whatever Jesus' belief was concerning the truthfulness of Scripture should be what we believe; and He clearly believed that Scripture was the perfect Word of God and, therefore, truth.

Chapter 11

The Last Adam: His Life-Giving

Resurrection

Today we are seeing the decline in the impact of the church all over the Western world.[1] While different influences have played their part in this, we cannot overlook the fact that this decline has come about largely because of the church's acceptance of the day's philosophy: evolution and millions of years. The appeal to the church to accept the philosophy of the day, however, is not new to modern times. The Apostle Paul often found himself in a cultural context in which he had to deal with many objections to the Christian faith. In 1 Corinthians 15, for example, the Corinthian congregation was questioning the future resurrection of believers: "How can some of you say that there is no resurrection of the dead?" (1 Corinthians 15:12). Paul saw this as a threat to the gospel (1 Corinthians 15:1–11) and treated it with the utmost seriousness (1 Corinthians 15:33–34).

Corinth was one of the major city centers of the ancient Mediterranean and one of the most diverse cities in the Roman empire. Although it was a Greek city by location, it had become a Roman colony (44 b.c.) about a century before Paul wrote his letter (c. a.d. 52–55). The Corinthian church was established on Paul's second missionary journey (Acts 18:1–18). Paul spent 18 months there on this visit around a.d. 51–52 (Acts 18:11–12).[2]

In his letter to the Corinthians, Paul treats the wisdom of the world in a negative sense (1 Corinthians 1:18–2:5) and will correct it with the wisdom of the cross and the spirit (1 Corinthians 2:6–3:4). In their worldly wisdom,

---

1. This does not mean that the church is defeated (see Matthew 16:18).
2. During Paul's second missionary journey Gallio was the Roman proconsul in Corinth, whose time there is dated from midsummer of a.d. 51 to midsummer of a.d. 52 (see Acts 18:12).

the Corinthians struggled with the idea of a bodily resurrection because it did not fit into their cultural worldview. The city of Corinth was permeated with Greek philosophy. The Greeks loved speculative philosophy and were proud of their intellect as they sought after and trusted in the "wisdom of men" (1 Corinthians 1:22, 2:5). This wisdom is "folly with God" (1 Corinthians 3:19). In their own wisdom, some of the Corinthians rejected the physical resurrection from the dead because of the Greek idea of the immortality of the soul apart from the body. In their dualistic worldview (a division between matter and spirit) many Greeks saw the body (matter) as corrupt, a prison for the spirit and not worthy of any form of immortality. For the Greeks, the spirit's escape from the body was a good thing, and it made no sense to them for God to want to raise a physical body from the dead. If there is no resurrection from the dead, then the Epicureans denial of the afterlife follows (1 Corinthians 15:32). Based on their worldview, a future physical resurrection from the dead was foolishness to them. Therefore, they mocked the idea that the body would be physically resurrected from the dead (Acts 17:32).

Two thousand years later, not much has changed. Just as the culture in Paul's day was permeated with Greek philosophy, so it is today. The worldview that undergirds Darwinian evolutionary thought is essentially Greek at its core. Many Christians are still integrating Greek philosophy into Christianity; however, we have just given it the name *science* rather than *philosophy*.[3] In his Epistle to the Colossians, Paul wrote to them so that no one would "delude you with plausible arguments," (Colossians 2:4) and to warn them not to be taken captive by "philosophy...according to human tradition" (Colossians 2:8). In the midst of the false teaching that took place in Colossae, Paul wanted his readers to recognize who Jesus is and what He has done. He is the creator of all things (Colossians 1:16), and therefore has something to say when it comes to science, history, and philosophy. The reason Paul emphasizes the centrality of Jesus in the life of the church is that he wants them to know it is in Him that "are hidden all the treasures of wisdom and knowledge" (Colossians 2:3). For Christians, this is a statement relevant to all other philosophical statements regarding origins. Paul is saying that all knowledge, not just spiritual knowledge, is to be found in Jesus. Therefore, Jesus triumphs over all other claims of wisdom and knowledge because of the fact that He is the Creator of all things and therefore knows all things. Acknowledging this is the only way that we will not be deceived by persuasive arguments based on the philosophy of the

3. By this I mean a worldview by which data is interpreted. Most scientists today view the world according to the philosophy of naturalism.

world. The only philosophy we are to be taken captive by is the philosophy that is "according to Christ" (Colossians 2:8).

Whereas Paul specifically asked how the Corinthians could say there is no resurrection, today's Christians must ask, "How do some among you say there is no first man Adam?" Because Greek thinking has been synthesized with biblical thinking, it is becoming increasingly popular among many evangelicals to either reject a historical Adam or reinterpret Adam as something other than the first man who existed. For example, theistic evolutionist Denis Lamoureux believes not only that Adam never existed, but also that this fact has no impact whatsoever on the foundational beliefs of Christianity. Commenting on 1 Corinthians 15:1–7 he states:

> This is the Gospel as stated in the Bible, and there is no mention whatsoever of Adam and whether or not he existed. Christian faith is founded on Jesus, not Adam.... We must also separate, and not conflate, the historical reality of Jesus and His death and bodily resurrection from the fact that Adam never existed.[4]

Lamoureux acknowledges that the Apostle Paul understood Adam to be a real person. However, he rejects this as a reason for us to believe in a historical Adam since, he believes, Paul's view of Adam was based upon an ancient view of science.[5] Just as the Resurrection is central to the gospel, the idea of there being a first man, Adam, is foundational to the gospel and to the doctrines that are built upon it. While Paul's background for the physical bodily resurrection of the dead is the Old Testament (Isaiah 26:19; Daniel 12:1–3), his "argument seems to be especially dependent upon the creation material (Genesis 1–2; Psalm 8) for its way of telegraphing what God's original intentions were for humanity and, therefore, where the story of creation must be headed."[6] Those references to Genesis provide some of the foundational points in Paul's argument for the restoration of creation and mankind.

🌿 1 Corinthians 15:1–8

The uniqueness of Christianity is that it is grounded in history. The gospel is based upon the historicity of the life, death, and Resurrection of Jesus Christ. This is why whenever the history of the Christian faith is under attack from false teaching, then eyewitness testimony is appealed to (see 2

4. Denis Lamoureux, "Was Adam a Real Person? Part 3," BioLogos, September 17, 2010, http://biologos.org/blog/was-adam-a-real-person-part-iii/P60.
5. Denis Lamoureux, "Evolutionary Creation View," in *Four Views on the Historical Adam* (Grand Rapids, MI: Zondervan, 2013), p. 61–62.
6. Ciampa and Rosner, *The First Letter to The Corinthians,* p. 740–741.

Peter 1:16–18; 1 John 1:1–3). It is to the eyewitness testimony of history that Paul appeals in order to defend the Resurrection of Jesus Christ:

> Now I would remind you, brothers, of the gospel I preached to you, which you received, in which you stand, and by which you are being saved, if you hold fast to the word I preached to you — unless you believed in vain. For I delivered to you as of first importance what I also received: that Christ died for our sins in accordance with the Scriptures, that he was buried, that he was raised on the third day in accordance with the Scriptures, and that he appeared to Cephas, then to the twelve. Then he appeared to more than five hundred brothers at one time, most of whom are still alive, though some have fallen asleep. Then he appeared to James, then to all the apostles. Last of all, as to one untimely born, he appeared also to me (1 Corinthians 15:1–8).

In verses 1–2 Paul makes four initial remarks about the gospel. First, the gospel was the message that Paul preached to the Corinthians when he first came to them (c. A.D. 51, Acts 18:12–17). This was the message of Jesus Christ crucified (1 Corinthians 2:1–2). The gospel is what defined the ministry of the Apostle Paul, as it was a divinely commissioned activity (1 Corinthians 1:17; cf. Romans 10:15). Paul will go on to remind the Corinthians that this gospel was the basis of their faith (1 Corinthians 15:11). Second, the gospel is the message of salvation, how God saves sinners (cf. Romans 10:14–17). This is the gospel by which, Paul says, the Corinthians "are being saved" (present continuous, cf. 2 Corinthians 2:15).[7] Paul is referring to God's ongoing work in the life of a believer, which He will bring to completion at the end (cf. Philippians 1:6). Third, the Corinthians received the gospel message just as Paul himself received it from the early church (cf. Galatians 1:12, 2:1–9). The gospel is a message that must be received by those who hear it (1 Thessalonians 1:6, 2:13). Fourth, the gospel message entails "holding fast to the word" preached (cf. Philippians 2:16). The gospel must be believed and be active in the life of believers or it has been believed "in vain" (1 Corinthians 15:58).

In 1 Corinthians 15:3–7, Paul develops the content of the gospel he preached to the Corinthians which he had received in the form of a tradition (cf. 1 Corinthians 11:2, 23). This early credal tradition came from the eyewitnesses of the risen Jesus and pre-dates the writing of the letter to the Corinthians by several years, with some scholars placing its formulation to

---

7. Paul also speaks of believers as "having been saved" (past, Romans 8:24; Ephesians 2:8) and that they "will be saved (future, Romans 5:9-10; 1 Corinthians 3:15).

within almost months (some scholars say 2–3 years) of the actual event of the crucifixion. New Testament scholar James D.G. Dunn says of the credal statement in 1 Corinthians 15:3–7: "This tradition, we can be entirely confident, was formulated as tradition within months of Jesus' death."[8] In these verses Paul uses four verbs to summarize the gospel message: Christ *died*, was *buried*, was *raised*, and *appeared* to different people. The death and Resurrection of Jesus Christ are the central events and message of the gospel.

The first point of the tradition is that Christ died for our sins. That Christ's' death was for our sins may be an allusion to Isaiah 53:5–6, 11-12. But why did Christ have to die for our sin? In his letter to the Romans, Paul argued that it was through one man that sin entered the world, and death through sin (Romans 5:12–16). Christ had to die for sin on the Cross because Adam had brought sin and death into the world. Therefore, just as God provided an atonement for Adam's sin (cf. Genesis 3:21), so Christ has provided atonement for our sins because we are "in Adam" (1 Corinthians 15:22). Christ's death was an atoning sacrifice for sin (cf. Romans 3:24–25). It is important to keep in mind that atonement involves a blood sacrifice (1 Corinthians 5:7; cf. Hebrews 9:22), which implies violence and death. However, this surely makes no sense in a theistic-evolutionary worldview where violence and death have been a part of God's process of creation over millions of years. Accepting millions of years of human and animal death before the Creation and Fall of man undermines the teaching of the atoning work of Christ. Theistic evolution does not just undermine Genesis and the supernatural creation of Adam, but it also undermines the doctrine of the atonement.[9] Furthermore, although Paul does not make specific mention of Adam in 1 Corinthians 15:1–7, he understands that Adam is foundational for sharing the gospel. For example, in a pagan culture he begins with a biblical understanding of creation (Acts 14:15–17, 17:24–28), specifically with reference to all people coming from one man (Acts 17:26), which leads him to speak of Jesus and the Resurrection, calling all men to repent in light of God's judgment of sin (Acts 17:30–31).

The next two verbs tell us that Jesus was buried and raised from the dead. Paul will go on to tell the Corinthians that if Christ was not raised

---

8. James D.G. Dunn, *Jesus Remembered* (Grand Rapids, MI: W.B. Eerdmans Publishing Company, 2003), 825.

9. The Biologos website had many different authors present various ways to understand the atonement in light of evolution. See Joseph Bankard, "Substitutionary Atonement and Evolution, Part 1," BioLogos, June 9, 2015, http://biologos.org/blogs/archive/substitutionary-atonement-and-evolution-part-1 See AiG's response, Tim Chaffey, "Evolution and the Atonement of Jesus Christ," Answers in Genesis, August 28, 2015, https://answersingenesis.org/jesus-christ/evolution-and-atonement-of-jesus-christ/.

from the dead then his preaching and their faith is in vain, and even futile, but most importantly they would still be in their sins (1 Corinthians 15:14, 17). Paul, however, is certain that Christ was raised, which is consistent with his preaching. In Acts 13, Paul preaches at the synagogue in Antioch in Pisidia on the Sabbath day about Jesus' Resurrection from the dead:

> this he has fulfilled to us their children by raising Jesus, as also it is written in the second Psalm, "You are my Son, today I have begotten you." And as for the fact that he raised him from the dead, no more to return to corruption, he has spoken in this way, "I will give you the holy and sure blessings of David." Therefore he says also in another psalm, "You will not let your Holy One see corruption." For David, after he had served the purpose of God in his own generation, fell asleep and was laid with his fathers and saw corruption, but he whom God raised up did not see corruption (Acts 13:33–37).

Paul argued that God had raised Jesus from the dead in fulfillment of Psalm 2:7 and Psalm 16:10. Psalm 16:10 cannot refer to David, as he died, was buried, and his body underwent corruption. The fact that Jesus' body did not see corruption demonstrates that He is the Jewish Messiah (cf. Acts 2:29–32). Paul's application of Jesus' Resurrection is that forgiveness and justification come through faith in Him (Acts 13:38–39; cf. Romans 4:25). This is the same method Paul used in the synagogue in Thessalonica when, "he reasoned with them from the Scriptures, explaining and proving that it was necessary for the Christ to suffer and to rise from the dead, and saying, 'This Jesus, whom I proclaim to you, is the Christ'" (Acts 17:2–3; cf. Acts 26:22–23).

Paul states that Jesus' death, burial, and His Resurrection from the dead on the third day was according to the Scriptures (Old Testament). This is what Jesus told His disciples before and after His death and Resurrection (see Luke 18:31–33; 24:44–47). But does the Old Testament say that the Messiah (Jesus) would rise from the dead on the third day?[10] Some scholars say there is little evidence for this. Interestingly, in the Old Testament reference to the "third day" can often refer to something that is fulfilled or completed (see Genesis 22:4; Exodus 19:10–11; Jonah 1:17; cf. Matthew 12:40). Moreover, the Old Testament describes the nation of Israel's exile and restoration in terms of the nation's death and resurrection (Ezekiel 37; Hosea 6:1–2). In their commentary on 1 Corinthians, New Testament scholars Ciampa

---

10. The phrase "according to the Scriptures" may modify "was raised" rather than "on the third day."

and Rosner explain, "A crucial part of the Old Testament background for understanding Christ's death and resurrection appears to be found in the ubiquitous prophetic tradition of Israel's own prophesied and then historical exile and (promised) restoration and the early Christian understanding (originating with Christ himself) that the Messiah's destiny was bound up with that which God had appointed for Israel, the nation he led and represented."[11] If this is the case, Paul is saying, just as it happened to the nation of Israel, so it would happen with the Messiah (see Matthew 2:15).

In 1 Corinthians 15:5–7 the final verb (appeared) is the only one that is repeated (four times) as Paul gives a list of resurrection appearances, beginning with Peter (Cephas) and to the 12, then to 500 brothers (of whom most were alive, but some were dead), then to James, and then to the Apostles. Last of all, Jesus appeared to Paul (1 Corinthians 15:8). Peter was one of the early leaders of 12 disciples and a leader of the Jerusalem church (Acts 15:7; Galatians 2:9). The 12 is probably a reference to the name that represented Jesus' closest followers (Judas was dead by this time and had been replaced by Matthias, see Acts 1:21–26). The 500 brothers are probably listed as a group, other than those close to Jesus (disciples), who were still living and could testify to the Resurrection. The James who is mentioned is the brother of Jesus who was an important leader in the early church (James, the son of Zebedee was killed by Herod; Acts 12:2). All the Apostles may refer to Christ's appearance at the time of His ascension (Acts 1:6–11). Lastly, Jesus appeared to Paul who was "least of the apostles" (1 Corinthians 15:8–9; cf. Galatians 2:7–9). That the risen Christ "appeared" (*ōphthē*) to Paul is not expressly stated in his conversion narrative in Acts 9:3–9 (even though Jesus identifies Himself as a person; "I am Jesus, whom you are persecuting"). It is, however, confirmed by Ananias (Acts 9:17) and Barnabas (Acts 9:27). Paul's own testimony to his conversion also tells us that he not only heard the voice of Christ but saw Him (1 Corinthians 9:1; Galatians 1:16; cf. Acts 22:14, 26:16) Just as the risen Jesus had appeared to Peter, James, and the Apostles, so he also appeared to the Apostle Paul.

Despite the naturalistic and materialistic worldview that rejects the Resurrection of Jesus, the evidence for it is verifiable. Jesus' death by crucifixion is one of the best-established facts of ancient history, something even atheist scholars admit. Atheist professor of the history and literature of early Christianity Gerd Lüdemann admits: "Jesus' death as a consequence of crucifixion is indisputable."[12] We know Jesus was alive after His death because His

11. Ciampa and Rosner, *The First Letter to The Corinthians*, p. 747.
12. Gerd Lüdemann, *The Resurrection of Christ: A Historical Inquiry* (Amherst, NY: Prometheus Books, 2004), p. 41.

many post-Resurrection appearances proved He had risen from the dead. It did not happen in secret. There were numerous eyewitnesses to it and trustworthy pieces of evidence to support it, such as the conversion of skeptical witnesses, the empty tomb, etc. What is more, even Lüdemann recognizes that Jesus' disciples were convinced that they had seen Jesus alive after His death: "It may be taken as historically certain that Peter and the disciples had experiences after Jesus' death in which Jesus appeared to them as the risen Christ."[13] Lüdemann, however, believes these events were the product of hallucinatory experiences probably brought about by guilt-complexes. However, after His Resurrection Jesus not only appeared to numerous individuals, but He also appeared at least three times to groups of people (Matthew 28:16; Luke 24:13–15, 36–39; John 20:11–23, 21:1–14). Generally, groups of people do not hallucinate at the same time as it is not contagious but is a personal experience. Moreover, hallucination does not account for the empty tomb or the conversion of Paul (Saul), as he was not grieving but trying to destroy the church (Acts 9:1–5; Galatians 1:13). Given the historical evidence for the Resurrection of Jesus, it would seem the reasons to reject it would either be a prior commitment to naturalism or the implication that we need to listen to what He says when it comes to sin, judgment, and salvation (see Mark 8:34–38).

Paul will go on to argue that to deny the believers' bodily resurrection from the dead is to deny Christ's bodily Resurrection from the dead (1 Corinthians 15:12–19). To deny the future bodily resurrection of believers or to treat it as a spiritual experience that has already taken place, is the mark of false teaching (2 Timothy 2:18). It is based on a dualistic worldview which sees the physical as evil and the spiritual as good (cf. 1 Timothy 4:3). The hope of the Christian faith is the future physical resurrection of the dead, which is mocked at by unbelievers because of their false worldview (Acts 17:31–32).

✖ 1 Corinthians 15:20–22

In these verses, Paul connects Christ's death and Resurrection to the foundational historical events of Genesis 1–3. The Christian faith is dependent upon the historicity of these events.

> But in fact Christ has been raised from the dead, the firstfruits of those who have fallen asleep. For as by a man came death, by a man has come also the resurrection of the dead. For as in Adam all die, so also in Christ shall all be made alive (1 Corinthians 15:20–22).

13. Gerd Lüdemann, *What Really Happened to Jesus: A Historical Approach to the Resurrection* (Louisville, KY: John Knox Press, 1995), p. 80.

Paul has already established the fact that Jesus has been raised from the dead (1 Corinthians 15:4–8). Now considering that, Paul states Christ is the "first fruits" of those who have died (fallen asleep). The phrase "first fruits" (*aparchē*) is a metaphor for the first portion of a crop offered in thanksgiving to God, which signifies the assurance of the rest of the harvest (Leviticus 23:9–14). Jesus was not the first to rise from the dead, as He had already raised the dead (John 11:38–44; cf. Mark 5:41; Luke 7:14–15). But He was the first to be raised from the dead, and never die again like those He had raised before, with a glorified body which guarantees that those who believe in Him even when they die will be resurrected one day with a glorified body (cf. John 11:25). Christ's Resurrection from the dead is the guarantee that there is more of the same to come. But as Paul will show, resurrection is more than the restoration of the soul to the body as there is transformative aspect of the body to come.

Paul then moves on to show the similarity and differences between Adam and Christ who are representative heads of mankind. The expressions "in Adam" and "in Christ" emphasize the idea of corporate solidarity that is in the first fruits metaphor. The first contrasting realities are that both death and resurrection came about "by man" or "through a man" (*di' anthrōpou*). This is what Adam and Christ both have in common. They are both individuals whose respective actions affect those who belong to them. Death was brought about by a man, Adam, and resurrection was brought about by a man, Christ. Paul uses the Adam-Christ typology to explain the reason for the resurrection to life. Those who have not trusted in Christ remain in Adam and receive what Adam brought into the world, namely death. On the other hand, those who have trusted in Christ receive new life, and will be "made alive." Just as Adam's sin had far-reaching negative consequences, so Christ's Resurrection from the dead has far-reaching positive consequences. As the last Adam, Christ, in His humanity, rescues humanity, and becomes the head of a new humanity who guarantees the resurrection of those who belong to Him. Even though we do not yet see it completely, Christ's Resurrection reversed the effects of Adam's sin.

The claim that Adam was not historical overlooks the fact that the parallel between Adam and Christ is too close for one to be historical and not the other. Moreover, how could a mythological figure affect mankind in such a negative way? What about those who accept Adam as some sort of historical figure but argue that Adam's fall only brought spiritual death into creation? Not only does this miss the meaning of Genesis 2:17 and Genesis 3:19 (see chapters 3 and 4) but it overlooks the parallel Paul draws between Adam and Christ. The focus throughout 1 Corinthians 15 is on Christ's Resurrection from the dead — a physical Resurrection with spiritual implications. Those who argue that the death (*thanatos*) Adam brought into the world was only spiritual must answer the question as to why Christ had to die physically. If we reject the biblical revelation that God created Adam supernaturally, and he instead developed from a lower form of a pre-existing hominids, then we must reject that physical death came about because of his disobedience. Then there really is no need for the Cross, atonement, or a new heavens and earth. Biblically, all of these are needed because death and suffering entered creation through Adam's disobedience toward God in Genesis 3 (Romans 5:12–21, 8:19–22; Revelation 21:4, 22:3).

❧ 1 Corinthians 15:25–26

After Paul explains that it was through Adam that death entered the world, he then moves to explaining that it is through Christ that death will be ultimately defeated:

> For he must reign until he has put all his enemies under his feet.
> The last enemy to be destroyed is death (1 Corinthians 15:25–26).

Paul states that Christ's present "reign" (*basileuein*, present infinitive) will last until He has put all His enemies under His feet. Then death will be destroyed as the last enemy, i.e., "[The] death is last enemy."[14] Christ's reign will not be complete until death is destroyed.[15] At the end of the age, death will be destroyed and be stripped of its power. It will no longer be victorious as it will have lost its sting (1 Corinthians 15:54–55). Therefore, to say that Paul is only talking about spiritual death undermines the power of Christ's victorious Resurrection from the dead. It is because of His defeat of death on the Cross and His physical Resurrection from the dead that those who trust in Him will no longer die physically. From a theistic evolutionary viewpoint, however, death is not an enemy — it's a God-ordained part of the process of the creation of life on earth. But Jesus did not die on the Cross to defeat an enemy He made at the beginning of creation. The fact that death is called an "enemy" implies that it is not natural, and therefore cannot have been part of the original state of creation in which God created mankind. In Romans 5:14, Paul says death reigned from the time of Adam, while Romans 5:21 suggests that the dominion of death is tied to that of sin since "sin reigned in death." It was Adam's disobedience (Genesis 2:17, 3:17–19) that brought

---

14. ἔσχατος ἐχθρὸς καταργεῖται ὁ θάνατος. In verse 26 "death" is the subject (it has the article) and "last enemy" is the predicate nominative (it lacks the article).
15. Jesus is currently reigning over all things in heaven (Ephesians 1:20–22).

death into the world, which is why Paul believes death to be an enemy that will be destroyed.

Jesus' Resurrection was ultimately a victory over death, which is why we even see our Lord outraged over the physical death of His friend Lazarus (John 11:35). John 11:33 tells us that Jesus was "deeply moved" and the verb in Greek *embrimaomai* "always speaks of deep-seated anger and does not connote mere emotional upheaval."[16] Why was Jesus angry? Because of the power of sin and death that was reigning in the world. Christ came to overcome death, and we need to live in the light of that fact.

✄ 1 Corinthians 15:35–49

In 1 Corinthians 15:35-49, Paul goes on to speak about the nature of the resurrection body. New Testament scholar N.T. Wright argues "the key to understanding [verses 35–49] is to realize that they, like verses 20–28, are built on the foundation of Genesis 1 and 2."[17] Paul's argument then is based on ideas drawn from the creation account. Paul begins his argument by stating: "How are the dead raised? With what kind of body do they come?" (1 Corinthians 15:35). Paul answers this question by using an agricultural metaphor of a seed (1 Corinthians 15:36–37). The seed must die before it can really live (cf. Genesis 1:11–12). The life of the seed parallels the resurrection from the dead (cf. 1 Corinthians 15:42, 43, 44). In 1 Corinthians 15:39–41 Paul mentions various bodies (humans, animals, birds, fish, sun, moon, stars) that correspond to three days of creation in reverse order (6th day, 5th day and 4th day). Paul's "point is that there are various kinds of bodies and different levels of splendour for each (so it would be a mistake to think a human body would always have to be the same kind of human body, with the same level of splendour)."[18] Just as there are many kinds of bodies in existence, so there is another kind of body for resurrection existence.

In verses 42–44, Paul points out that our new bodies will have a glory that our present ones do not have. The reason we need new bodies is the result of the corruption (*phthora*) brought about through Adam's disobedience (cf. Genesis 3:19).[19] However, unlike the Greek view of the afterlife, Paul does not teach that our future bodies will be made from spirit (cf. Luke 24:39). Just as there is a temporal sequence between the firstfruits

---

16. Osborne, *The Gospel of John*, p. 171.

17. N.T Wright, *The Resurrection of the Son of God* (Minneapolis, MN: Fortress Press, 2003), p. 340.

18. Ciampa and Rosner, *The First Letter to The Corinthians*, p. 804.

19. The Greek word for corruption, *phthora*, (1 Corinthians 15:42) is the same word used in Romans 8:21 where Paul refers to the creation's bondage to decay.

and the rest of the harvest, so there is between the "natural" (*psychikos*) body and the "spiritual" (*pneumatikos*) body (1 Corinthians 15:44; cf. 2:14). The "natural" body we have now is suited for this life, but that body will need to be changed for the next life. The resurrected body will be a "spiritual" body (not made from spirit) that is directed and empowered by the Spirit of God (cf. 1 Corinthians 12:1). Elsewhere, Paul tells us that we have been sealed by the Spirit (Ephesians 1:13) and that the Holy Spirit is the "guarantee" (Ephesians 1:14) of our redemption, which suggests that our resurrection experience could not exist without the Holy Spirit. In Adam, people receive one kind of body, and in Christ, believers receive a different type of body.

Paul already showed the similarity between Adam and Christ, their common humanity, but in verses 45–49 he shows the difference between the two heads of humanity to explain how there can be a resurrection body:

> And so it is written, "The first man Adam became a living being." The last Adam became a life-giving spirit. However, the spiritual is not first, but the natural, and afterward the spiritual. The first man was of the earth, made of dust; the second Man is the Lord from heaven. As was the man of dust, so also are those who are made of dust; and as is the heavenly Man, so also are those who are heavenly. And as we have borne the image of the man of dust, we shall also bear the image of the heavenly Man (1 Corinthians 15:45–49; NKJV).

In order to make his point about the nature of the body, Paul typically makes his appeal to Scripture. In verse 45, Paul quotes from Genesis 2:7 where God made the first Adam from the dust of the ground and gave him a soul, a living being. The first Adam was simply a living being, who passed on his nature to those who come after him. Paul knows Adam is a life-giving spirit from Genesis 2:7, but how does he know the last Adam, Christ, became a life-giving spirit? The reference to Christ being "a life-giving spirit" may be an allusion to Genesis 5:3 whereby he functions typologically as an Adamic figure by passing his image to believers (cf. 1 Corinthians 15:49).[20] Or it could be that Paul is reading Genesis 2:7 in light of Ezekiel 37. Ciampa and Rosner comment: "In Genesis 2:7 it is when God breathed into the man that he came to life. In Ezekiel 37:6, 9, 10, 14 God repeatedly says, echoing Genesis 2, that it is by putting His breath or Spirit

---

20. See Benjamin L. Gladd, "The Last Adam as the 'Life-Giving Spirit' Revisited: A Possible Old Testament Background of One of Paul's Most Perplexing Phrases." *WTJ* 71 (2009): p. 297–309.

(the same word in both Hebrew and Greek) in His people that they would be brought to life. Ezekiel 37 describes 'a life-giving spirit' in the context of the resurrection of the dead, or the restoration of Israel described as a resurrection of the dead."[21] Christ, as the life-giving spirit, is not only the guarantee of the resurrection to come but He is the source of the body's transformation, as He gives it life. The title Paul uses of Christ as "the last Adam" is also significant, as New Testament scholar Leon Morris notes: "In modern times we often read of 'the second Adam,' but Paul never uses this term.... There is a finality about the 'the last Adam': There will be no other Head of the human race."[22]

Paul had also just spoken of the first and last Adam but now he speaks of them in terms of the first and second man. Paul uses the word "first" before "man" to draw the contrast between Adam and Christ. He also uses Adam as a proper name to identify the man in Genesis 2:7. In doing this, Paul clearly establishes Adam as the first man in relationship of order to mankind. Furthermore, the fact that Paul states that Adam was *the* first man should alone refute the idea that he was anything other than the first creature God created, as all theistic evolutionary and Old-earth creation views allow for pre-Adamite "humans."

In verse 46, Paul talks about the chronological order of creation and new creation. His argument has been that there is a difference between our present bodies and our resurrection bodies that is parallel to Adam's bodily existence and Christ's resurrection body (1 Corinthians 15:44–45). The natural body (Adam) comes first and then the spiritual (Christ). Believers have only yet experienced the first bodily existence; therefore, we can look forward to the bodily existence that comes after the first one.

In verse 47, the first man, Paul says, was from the earth and the second man is from heaven. Paul previously contrasted the "natural" and "spiritual" but now he expands the contrast to "earth" and "heaven" to explain what he meant by the first by stressing the origins of the two men. Some scholars believe the "earthly" vs "heavenly" categories come from the Jewish diaspora philosopher Philo. In his *Allegorical Interpretation,* Philo exegetes Genesis 2:7 and contrasts the "heavenly man" of Genesis 1:26–28 with the earthly man of Genesis 2:7. The heavenly man is made in God's image and has dominion over all creation, and the earthly man, who is formed from the dust, shares a corruptible and earthly substance. However, Philo allegorizes the text in order to speak of two different kinds of people in the world,

---

21. Ciampa and Rosner, *The First Letter to The Corinthians*, p. 820.
22. Leon Morris, *1 Corinthians: Tyndale New Testament Commentaries* (Nottingham: Inter-Varsity Press, 1985), p. 218.

whereas Paul sees the earthly man as Adam and the heavenly man as Christ. Furthermore, Paul's terminology differs significantly from that of Philo.[23]

That Adam is of the "dust" in verse 47 is a reference to Genesis 2:7. Paul is reminding the Corinthians that man is made from the dust and will return to the dust and lives only because of the spirit of God that is within him (Ecclesiastes 3:20, 12:7; Psalm 104:29). It emphasizes mankind's perishability given their earthly origin. In verse 49, Paul notes that every person has borne the image of Adam, but those who trust in Christ now bear His image (Colossians 3:10). Just as the first man was of the earth and therefore the originator of humanity, so Jesus Christ, the second man, is from heaven, and is the originator of a new humanity. Christ's people will one day be like Him (1 John 3:2). Although our earthly lives are spent in perishable bodies that we have inherited from Adam (post-Fall), in the age to come our bodies will be like Christ's after His Resurrection from the dead (Luke 24:36–43; John 21:9-14). The resurrection body of the Lord Jesus is a glimpse of what it will be like for believers in the age to come. The Apostle Paul does not separate Christ's work of redemption of humanity and creation from Adam's disobedience (Romans 8:19–22).

Some have argued that Paul changed his position on life after death because of the supposed change in language between 1 Corinthians 15 and 2 Corinthians 5. The argument being that in 2 Corinthians 5 Paul's language reflects a platonic division between the body and soul. But this is certainly not the case. In 2 Corinthians 5:1, Paul states, "For we know that if the tent that is our earthly home is destroyed, we have a building from God, a house not made with hands, eternal in the heavens." Paul knows about the resurrected body because he has encountered the risen Jesus (Acts 9:1–9), heard the eyewitness accounts (1 Corinthians 15:3–8) and has a biblical understanding of the Resurrection. So what Paul knows helps us understand what will happen to our bodies after death. Paul speaks of the body as a "tent" (or residence) that can be "destroyed," an image for death (see Isaiah 38:12 LXX). Paul states that if death comes to a believer before Christ returns "we have a building from God." The word for "building" (*oikodomēn*) speaks of a structure that stands because of a building process.[24] Paul states that this heavenly building originates with God (John 14:2). This building is "not made with hands" because it "refers to an immortal body, which only God can provide to the believer at the resurrection of the

---

23. See Ciampa and Rosner, *The First Letter to The Corinthians*, p. 819.
24. See George H. Guthrie, *2 Corinthians: Baker Exegetical Commentary on the New Testament* (Grand Rapids, MI: Baker Academic, 2015), p. 278

dead."[25] It is a resurrected body (see John 2:21–22). This "building" is characterized as being "eternal" and "in the heavens." The eternal "building" is in contrast with the "earthly home" (mortal body) which is made of "clay" (2 Corinthians 4:7), a temporary body that is subject to death. The place of this "body" will be "in the heavens," which indicates that it will be suitable for that state of existence (see 1 Corinthians 15:47–50). This is not referring to the believer going "to heaven" after death, rather that this body will be fit for the future, the new heavens and earth (see 1 Corinthians 15:50). Paul sees continuity between this life now and life after death, as when we die, we will be "home with the Lord" (2 Corinthians 5:8), but "there will also be a 'life after life after death' … when the mortal puts on immortality through the resurrection."[26]

Paul brings the chapter to a magnificent conclusion by noting that flesh and blood (mortals) cannot inherit the kingdom of God (1 Corinthians 15:50). Paul tells us a "mystery,"[27] that in a moment, at the last trumpet, the dead will be raised, and our bodies will be changed (1 Corinthians 15:51–52). This marks the end of the things we now know, and when this happens, we will not return to the sort of life we are now living in perishable bodies, but they will be imperishable (1 Corinthians 15:53). This will also signal the end for death (1 Corinthians 15:55). Knowing this future, we can serve God in the present steadfastly, immovably, and abundantly (1 Corinthians 15:58).

In 1 Corinthians 15, Paul grounds the bodily death and Resurrection of our Lord Jesus in the reality of the history of Genesis. It was a real man, Adam, who brought about physical death and corruption into God's very good world (Genesis 1:31). This is the reason Paul says Jesus came to earth as a real man in order to undo the work of the first man. If we reject the supernatural creation of Adam, then why should we accept the future supernatural resurrection from the dead? Many theistic evolutionists inconsistently reject the supernatural creation of Adam yet accept the reality of the Resurrection of Christ and the future bodily resurrection of the dead. This is equally at odds with the truth claims of the secular scientific majority who deny any form of supernatural resurrection. This inconsistency is the sign of a failed argument.

---

25. Ibid., p. 278.
26. Ibid., p. 279.
27. The Greek word "mystery" (*mystērion*) does not refer to something that is hard to figure out, but to something that was once hidden that has now been revealed (1 Corinthians 2:7).

Those who reject a historical Adam or reinterpret him as something other than the first man God created, do so because they have elevated the wisdom of men over the revelation of God. However, Paul reminded the Corinthian church that human wisdom cannot benefit us before God, as He rejects all that rests on human wisdom (1 Corinthians 1:20–25, 3:19). Instead, Paul reminded them that Christ, who is the wisdom of God (1 Corinthians 1:24; cf. Colossians 2:3), is far superior to that of any philosophy. The wisdom of the Greeks could not recognize the most profound wisdom of all when they were challenged with it. The truth of the creation of the first man, Adam, embodies true wisdom — the wisdom of God, not the wisdom of the age.

Chapter 12

The Last Adam: The Gospel Begins in Creation

The greatest message of all is the gospel of the Lord Jesus Christ (cf. Acts 10:36). The word gospel (*euangelion*) means "good news," and it is so-called because it addresses the serious problem of the bad news (that we are guilty sinners "in Adam"). The message of the gospel is not "you can have a relationship with God," although there may some truth to it. The fact of the matter is that every person has a relationship to God. People are either related to God in Christ, by grace, or related to God in Adam, according to wrath (Romans 5:12–19; 1 Corinthians 15:22). The message of the gospel is that our sins can be forgiven, and we can pass from wrath to grace by trusting in what Jesus accomplished in His life, death, and Resurrection from the dead (John 3:36, 5:24; Romans 2:8, 5:2). The gospel is a message about our reconciliation to God (the Father), through the atoning work of the Lord Jesus, by which we become "new creations" (2 Corinthians 5:17–21). Nevertheless, in our own day when the gospel is preached it is often not understood by people in our post-secular Western pagan culture. This is because Western culture now has a substantially different worldview to that of Christians. It is essential therefore that we understand the content and the context of the gospel message.

The gospel does not start with the Cross and Resurrection (these are its climax), it begins with creation and the Fall (cf. Genesis 3:15). If we are going to share the gospel with people from other religions (other systems of belief that is a person's ultimate standard for reality,—,their worldview) then we need to start to plot the course of the gospel from creation so that they begin to comprehend its full scope and its significance for their lives. The good news of the gospel cannot be understood without its broader context. For example, if I told you, "There's good news, the war is over!" Unless you knew that there had been a war going on you would be thinking, "What war, how and when did it start, and who was involved?" Those details provide the context for the headline good news. If you explain to somebody today that they are a sinner and they need to repent, one of the first questions people normally ask is "What is sin?" and "Which God?" or they may even respond "I don't believe in God." It is important that we know how to respond to those questions.

The world we live in today has lost the context of the wider narrative of the Bible and rejects the existence of a self-existent, eternal, and transcendent God. The western world today is essentially neo-pagan, or monistic (attributing oneness or singleness to existence). In a monistic worldview, which presupposes materialistic worldview, everything is made up of the same stuff, all distinctions are removed, and essentially everything has the same worth. The goal of neo-paganism is to relativize everything that seems different, to join the opposites and get rid of the distinctions God has made in His creation because of their belief that all is "one" (i.e., pantheism). For example, heterosexuality celebrates otherness (Greek, *héteros* = other) whereas homosexuality (Greek, *homo* = same) celebrates the sameness of everything, which is the definition of the neo-pagan worldview. The one solution to this problem of the neo-pagan worldview is the biblical worldview, as it rightly sees distinctions in the world, the main one being that God is our Creator and mankind is His creation. The first bit of good news the Bible presents to us is that everything originally was "very good" (Genesis 1:31). But when we look at the world today it is obviously not "very good." Something has happened (see Genesis 3). Therefore, we must go back to the beginning. Since Jesus is the Last Adam, we must trace the gospel back to the first Adam.

It is also important to understand that the gospel is not just for unbelievers. In Romans 1:15 Paul said, "So I am eager to preach the gospel to you also who are in Rome." Evangelism for Paul was about much more than initial salvation. He wanted believers to be discipled as well as to fully know and be obedient to the gospel message (Romans 1:5, 16:26). For those Christians in Rome who came from a Greco-Roman background, it was important that they not only understood that the God of creation had clearly revealed Himself from the beginning in Genesis 1, but also that people sinfully suppress that truth and create idols for themselves instead of worshiping the one true God (Romans 1:18–23). Paul wanted them to understand the foundational history in Genesis so they could fully grasp the gospel message. They needed to remember that the only way for a person to be liberated from the reign of sin, brought into the world by the first man Adam, is through the righteousness bought by the obedience of Jesus (Romans 5:12–21). The idea that we need to go back to the beginning, creation, is not adding to the gospel; rather, it grounds the gospel message in its overall biblical context by adhering to its biblical foundation for the gospel. In Colossians 1:15, Paul's reference to "image" harks back to Genesis 1:26–28 when God made the first man and woman in His own image. This image, however, has been distorted by the Fall. Yet, through the proclamation of the gospel, the image in the life of the Christian is "being renewed in knowledge after the image of its creator" (Colossians 3:10).

In our own day, the churches' role in spreading the gospel in the west has been hindered by the influence of the Enlightenment, the so called "age of reason" (1685–1815), that basically said religion is part of the private sphere and not something that should be brought into the public square. However, this differs with the meaning of the Greek word *ekklēsia* ("church" or rather congregation or assembly, Acts 7:38, 19:32), which refers to "a gathering of citizens called out from their homes into some public place; an assembly."[1] The message of the gospel is not meant to be left at home and kept to ourselves, but it should rightly be proclaimed in the public sphere to all people in order to transform lives and culture (Acts 1–28).

Paul's speech to the Greek philosophers at the Areopagus in Athens (Acts 17:16–34) is the classic text for sharing the gospel with those from different religious backgrounds. To engage with his audience in Acts 17, Paul uses the biblical meta-narrative of the Creation, Fall, redemption, and consummation. Before we look at Acts 17, since Paul deals with other religious beliefs there, it is important to see what the Bible says about religion and where it comes from.

❧ What Is Religion and Where Does it Come From?

In the ESV translation of the Bible, the term religion (religious) is translated six times from two different Greek words (*deisidaimonia*: religion, superstition, and *threskeia*: religion, worshiping). By itself it is a neutral term. It can refer to Jewish-Christian faith (*deisidaimonia*, Acts 25:19), Judaism (*threskeia*, Acts 26:5), self-made religion (*ethelothrēskia*,[2] Colossians 2:23), or failure to tame the tongue (*threskeia*, James 1:26). But religion that is acceptable to God is "to visit orphans and widows in their affliction, and to keep oneself

---

1. J.H. Thayer, *Thayer's Greek–English Lexicon of the New Testament*, 8th ed (Peabody, MA: Hendrickson, 2007),p. 195–196.

2. In Colossians 2:23, the Greek word *ethelothrēskia* is made up of two words: *ethelo* (will) *thrēskia* ("worship," "religion," "service"). It is probably best understood as worship freely chosen.

unstained from the world" (*threskeia*, James 1:27). In Acts 17:22, Paul calls the Greek philosophers very "religious" (*deisidaimonesteros*, see below).

It is particularly difficult to define religion since there is no one universally accepted definition. The Oxford English dictionary defines religion as "the belief in and worship of a superhuman controlling power, especially a personal God or gods."[3] Under this definition, belief systems such as Atheism and Buddhism would not be viewed as religions. Nevertheless, the dictionary also defines religion as "a particular system of faith and worship" and "a pursuit or interest followed with great devotion." Under this definition of religion, however, atheism is religious. Many atheists spend much of their time railing against the Creator that they believe doesn't exist, and hold their cause with great devotion and faith. Furthermore, atheists themselves have a worldview based upon certain beliefs, such as the belief that the universe, including life, came about by natural processes. This is a belief based upon faith — blind faith!

While there may be several ways to define religion, I believe a more biblical view of the definition is "a system of belief that is a person's ultimate standard for reality — their worldview." A worldview is basically a perspective by which someone sees and interprets the world around them. One is revealed in God's Word and the other is based upon man's opinion in its many variations. For example, in His own lifetime, Jesus contrasted those who lived their lives based upon the traditions of men over the Word of God (Mark 7:1–13). Because God has clearly revealed Himself in creation, religion is first of all a response to God's revelation — either in faith or rebellion. It is either based on God's Word or man's word. God's image bearers have suppressed His revelation in creation; therefore, other religions are an idolatrous response to God's revelation, which are subversively fulfilled in the gospel.

In today's Western culture it is common to hear people say: "God didn't invent man, man invented God." Evolutionists often argue that religion is part of an evolutionary accident. Richard Dawkins states this in his book *The God Delusion*:

> … religious behaviour may be a misfiring, an unfortunate by-product of an underlying psychological propensity which in other circumstances is, or once was, useful.[4]

For the evolutionist, religion evolved in the mind of man early on in human history. It went through a developmental process, beginning in its most

3. Oxford English Living Dictionaries, "Religion," https://en.oxforddictionaries.com/definition/religion.
4. Richard Dawkins, *The God Delusion* (Great Britain: Bantam Press, 2006), p. 202.

simple form before becoming more developed: animism, polytheism, heno-
theism, and then monotheism emerged. The obvious problem with this suggestion is its basis in an evolutionary view of history. It is also contradicted
by cultures all around the world that were originally monotheistic.[5] The
Bible, however, reverses this idea and gives us the true explanation of how
religion originated.

If we want to know the meaning of anything, we must understand its
origin. Genesis is often known as the book of beginnings. It is in Genesis
1–11 that we learn the origin of time, space, matter, mankind, marriage, sin,
civilization, and much more. But it also speaks about the origin of religion
and its diversity. The origin of religion began in the garden when God clearly
revealed Himself to Adam. However, Adam and Eve rejected that revelation
and instead chose to believe a falsehood about Him. Their sin was that they
wanted to be gods themselves (Genesis 3:4–5). In this act of disobedience,
Eve believed Satan and adopted his own worldview over God's worldview.
Adam's disobedience had consequences for the rest of his descendants since
it not only brought death into the world (Genesis 2:17; Romans 5:12, 19),
but also it affected how they viewed God and creation (Romans 1:21, 28).

The event of the Tower of Babel in Genesis 11 was a triggering point
to explain the explosive diversity of religion, not through developmental
stages but through an act of rebellion and separation. While the account
of the Tower of Babel has to do with the origin of different people groups,
it also gives us a historical and theological account of the modern origin
of false religion. The events at Babel occur several hundred years after the
global Flood in Genesis 6–8. At the beginning of the Babel account, the
whole earth had one language and one speech, which meant that mankind
was united in both its language and habitation (Genesis 11:1). After the
people journeyed from the east, they settled on a plain in the land of Shinar
(Genesis 11:2). It is here that they decide to build "a city and a tower whose
top is in the heavens" (Genesis 11:4). But why did the people choose to
build a tower, and what was the tower and its purpose? The text gives two
reasons for the people's desire to build the tower: to make a name for themselves and to avoid being scattered (Genesis 11:4). The builders' desire to
make a "name" for themselves also reveals mankind's common ideological
purpose: usurping God. This was a foolish notion, as it is God who makes
man's name great (Genesis 12:2). The building of the city and tower was
also rebellion against God, as the people were resisting His command to
"increase" and "fill the earth" (Genesis 9:1, cf.1:28). There is an interesting

---

5. See Winfried Corduan, *In the Beginning God: A Fresh Look at the Case for Original
Monotheism* (Nashville, TN: B&H Publishing Group, 2013).

text in Deuteronomy 32:8–9 that helps us understand some of the details of Babel, as it has its background in the Table of Nations of Genesis 10 (cf. Acts 17:26).

> When the Most High gave to the nations their inheritance, when he divided mankind, he fixed the borders of the peoples according to the number of the sons of God. But the LORD's portion is his people, Jacob his allotted heritage.[6]

The question is, when did God (Most High; cf. Genesis 14:19) divide mankind (i.e., the nations)? This is obviously a clear reference to the event of the Tower of Babel. The verb translated "divided" (*pārad*) is used in the division of the nations in Genesis 10:5, 32, and here it refers to the dividing out of mankind (*běnê 'ādām*, "the sons of Adam"; NKJV) over the earth. With the close connection between Genesis 10 and 11, this then gives us a behind-the-scenes look at what happened at the Tower of Babel. The text speaks of God having divided "mankind" (or "the sons of Adam"), among "the sons of God" (*běnê hā 'ĕlōhîm*), heavenly beings (cf. Job 1:6, 2:1, 38:7). Because the people at Babel had disobeyed God by staying in one place and desired to make a name for themselves, it resulted in Him judging them by dispersing them over the earth and by giving them over to idolatry by allocating these fallen heavenly beings to the nations, who became their objects of worship (Deuteronomy 4:19, 29:24–26; cf. Daniel 10:20). Mankind's disobedience by staying in one place rather than spreading out across the earth led to their devolution into demonically influenced idolatry (see Deuteronomy 32:16–17, 21; c.f. Psalm 106:37; 1 Corinthians 10:19–20).

Three times Genesis 10 tells us that each nation that spread across the earth had their own local language (Genesis 10:5, 20, 31). This did not happen until God confused the one united language at Babel into many languages (Genesis 11:1–9). At Babel, mankind was united in its habitation and language as the "whole world" (*kāl-hā 'āreṣ*) had "one language" (*śāpâ 'eḥāt*) and the "same words" (*děbārîm 'ăḥādîm*); literally "one lip and one [set of] words." The repetition of the adjective "one" stresses the unity of the language and indicates that the whole world had a specific language in common.[7] The one language came to an end when God "confused their language" so that the people could no longer "understand one another's speech" (Genesis 11:7). God destroyed the unity of the people's "language"

---

6. Deuteronomy 32:8 in the Masoretic text reads "sons of Israel" (*běnê yiśrā 'ēl*), but the nation of Israel did not exist at Babel, so this reading makes no sense in context. However, the LXX and Qumran fragment 4Q read "sons of God" (*běnê hā' ĕlōhîm*).
7. Mathews, *Genesis 1–11:26*, p. 477.

by confusing their "lips" which resulted in their dispersion across the "face of all the earth." (Genesis 11:9; cf. 1:28).

The dispersion of mankind at the Tower of Babel took place in Peleg's day as it was in his day that "the earth was divided" (Genesis 10:25). This "division of the earth" is speaking of the confusion of languages and the dispersion of mankind at the Tower of Babel. Peleg (פֶּלֶג)[8] comes from the verb פָּלַג "to cleave or divide" and is a wordplay on his name because it was in his days that "the earth was divided." A related word play occurs later with Babel (בָּבֶל, *Bābel*), where God confused (בָּלַל, *bālal*) mankind's language (Genesis 11:9). This helps explain how the earth was divided. The earth (*'ereṣ*) refers to the people of the world (Genesis 11:1, 9; cf. 9:19). Although the word "dispersed" (*pûṣ*) (Genesis 11:8, 9; cf. 10:18) is not the same as the word "divided" (פָּלַג, *pālag*) (Genesis 10:25), the word for "divided" is used in the context of confusing language (Psalm 55:9). The overall context of Genesis 10 points to a spreading out or dividing (פָּרַד, *pārad̠*) of the nations across the earth (Genesis 10:5, 32; cf. Deuteronomy 32:8). The genealogy in Genesis 10 lists a total of 70 nations to show the totality of all peoples on the earth: 14 from Japheth, 30 from Ham, and 26 from Shem. This may be intended to foreshadow the 70 descendants of Jacob that went into Egypt with him (Genesis 46:27; Exodus 1:5).[9] The Jewish notion was at Babel the nations of the world were divided into 70 nations (שׁוּבְעִין עַמְמַיָּא, *Targum. Jer.* on Genesis 11:8; cf. *Sanhedrin* 17a).

At the Tower of Babel, the concept of the unity and absoluteness of God had begun to be lost. When the people were dispersed at Babel, they would have taken with them a hybrid truth of the living God mixed with the twisted and distorted truth of that revelation about Him. The loss of a unified language led to the loss of unified religion; every people and nation now deviated to worship its own national or regional god.[10] At Babel, monotheism degenerated into animism, sorcery, magic, and polytheism — though some still retained it (e.g., Melchizedek, Genesis 14, Noah — who lived for another 350 years or so after the Flood). The pure revelation of God had been generally lost, corrupted, and perverted by sin, leading to religious idolatry,

---

8. As a common noun פֶּלֶג refers to a "stream, channel" (Psalm 1:3).

9. In both Genesis 46:27 and Exodus 1:5 the LXX reads "seventy-five" as does Stephen's sermon in Acts 7:14.

10. The Bible identifies several of the "gods" of the nations: Marduk the god of the Babylonians (Jeremiah 50:2); Egyptians had multiple gods (Exodus 12:12); Ba'al the supreme god of the Canaanites (1 Kings 18); Dagon god of the Philistines (1 Samuel 5); Milcom god of the Ammonites (1 Kings 11:5); Chemosh national god of the Moabites (1 Kings 11:7); Molech Canaanite god associated with child sacrifice (Leviticus 18:21). Ashtoreth goddess of the Sidonians (Canaanites) (1 Kings 11:5).

and giving rise to religious pluralism (Joshua 24:2). In Akkadian, the word for the city of Babylon means "gateway of the gods" (*bāb-ili, bāb-ilāni*),[11] whereas in Hebrew the word Babel sounds like the word "confusion." The pagans saw Babel as a way to access the divine, whereas the Bible states that God judged the people at Babel because of their disobedience by confusing their languages and spread them across the whole earth.

In the New Testament, after His death and Resurrection, Jesus commissioned His disciples to be His witnesses in all the world (Acts 1:8). This began on the day of Pentecost when the Holy Spirit fell upon the gathered devout Jews and devout men from "every nation under heaven" (Acts 2:5), and "divided tongues as of fire" rested on them and "they were bewildered, because each one was hearing them speak in his own language" (Acts 2:3, 6; cf. Zephaniah 3:9). The connection between Genesis 10–11 and Pentecost can be seen in the use of two terms. In Acts 2:3, the word "divided" (*diamerizō*) is the same word used in Deuteronomy 32:8 (LXX), and in Acts 2:6 the Greek word "bewildered" (*sugcheo*) is the same word in Genesis 11:7, 9 (LXX). Those men who were gathered from the nations at Pentecost would now take the gospel back with them to the nations that had been separated in Genesis 10. Although the names of the nations in Acts 2:9–11 are different from those in Genesis 10 there is a correlation with those nations that spread out over all the earth; Medes (Madai, Genesis 10:2), Elamites (Elam, Genesis 10:22), Egypt (Mizraim, Genesis 10:6), Libya (Put, Genesis 10:6), Cyrene (Lehabim, Genesis 10:13), and Cretans (Caphtorim, Genesis 10:14). Later in Acts we see other nations that are mentioned in Genesis 10 reached with the gospel: Ethiopia (Cush, Genesis 10:6; Acts 8:25–27), Cyprus (Elishah, Genesis 10:4; Acts 11:19–20, 13:4, 15:39), and Greece (Javan, Genesis 10:2; Acts 17:16–34). Even though he did not get there before his death, the Apostle Paul desired to reach the nation that was farthest west, Spain (Tarshish, Genesis 10:4), with the gospel (Romans 15:22–28). Pentecost was the beginning of the reversal of Babel, as through the preaching of the gospel people from all tribes, languages, and nations have access to the one true and living God (Revelation 5:9; 22:1–3).

❧ How Does the Bible View Other Religions?

This is an important question, since our answer will determine how we engage other religions with the gospel. We need to keep in mind the theological reality that God is our Creator, and man is in rebellion against Him. The Apostle Paul tells us:

---

11. Mathews, *Genesis 1–11:26*, p. 469.

For the wrath of God is revealed from heaven against all ungod-liness and unrighteousness of men, who suppress the truth in unrighteousness, because what may be known of God is manifest in them, for God has shown it to them. For since the creation of the world His invisible attributes are clearly seen, being understood by the things that are made, even His eternal power and Godhead, so that they are without excuse (Romans 1:18–20; NKJV).

From Paul's teaching in Romans 1:18–20, we can understand that religious consciousness is a product of two things: God's revelation and suppression of that revelation. Because God has clearly revealed Himself in creation, there is no one excused from believing in His existence. However, because of mankind's fallen nature, the truth of God's revelation is suppressed. The suppression of that revelation ultimately expresses itself in idolatry. Idolatry is not just the carving of something out of wood or stone, but it is also the pursuit of anything in this world other than the glory of the one true and living God (see Philippians 3:19; Colossians 3:5). The Bible views the pagan worship of idols as a grave error and foolish vanity (Acts 14:15; 1 Thessalonians 1:9–10; 1 John 5:21). The false "gods" of the nations (Exodus 15:11; cf. 9:14) are not in in the same category as the LORD (YHWH), as He defines the category of God: self-existent and uncreated (Exodus 3:14; Isaiah 43:10). The gods of the nations are not actually gods but demons (Galatians 4:8; cf. Deuteronomy 32:17; 1 Corinthians 10:19–20). The message of the Bible is that the LORD is the Creator, and the gods of the nations are idols (Psalm 96:5), so it is foolish to trust in other deities (Isaiah 43:11, 44:6, 45:5), as the attribute that separates the LORD from all other deities is that of creating (Isaiah 40:28, 42:5). Idols are counterfeit gods that are parasitic on the truth.

To capture the essence of human fallenness, the reformer John Calvin said that man, in his mind, is a "maker of idols."[12] Idolatry is exchanging the glory of God for worship of the creature. As theologian D.A. Carson says, "[It is] the de-godding of God."[13] In exchanging the truth of God's revelation for a lie, that revelation is transformed into idolatry; religion, therefore, is a subjective response to objective divine revelation which only has negative consequences: sin → suppression of the truth → exchange for idolatry → darkness → guilt = God's wrath (Romans 1:18–32). The origin of idolatry then begins in the human mind. We must remember that even

12. Calvin, *Institutes of the Christian Religion*, p. 55.

13. D.A. Carson, *Christianity and Culture Revisited* (Grand Rapids, MI: W.B. Eerdmans, 2008), p. 46.

as Christians, we still have the capacity to commit idolatry if we do not allow Scripture to renew our minds (Romans 12:2). Because the gods of the nations are idols (Jeremiah 10:1–11; Acts 19:26) only God's special revelation in the gospel can turn people from their idolatry to trust in the living and true God (1 Thessalonians 1:5, 9).

⚓ Acts 10 — Peter in Caesarea

Before we look at how Paul communicates the gospel to the philosophers in Athens, it is instructive to look at how the Apostle Peter communicated the gospel to those who feared God. Both accounts help us deal with the challenge of pluralism and inclusivism, the belief that there is access to salvation outside of Jesus.

The Apostle Peter, Simon Bar-Jonah (Matthew 16:17), the fisherman who grew up in Bethsaida (John 1:44) along the coast of the Sea of Galilee, Peter was called into ministry by Jesus (Mark 1:16–18) and was one of His original 12 disciples (Mark 3:13–16). A man of great boldness, courage, and self-confidence, Peter would not only physically defend Jesus (John 18:10) but also deny that he knew Him (Mark 14:66–72), though he was later restored to fellowship by Jesus after His Resurrection (John 21:15–19). Peter was a key leader in the Early Church and preached the very first sermon, at Pentecost, when 3,000 people were saved on that day (Acts 2:14–41). He not only continually defended the faith by boldly preaching the gospel, but he also suffered greatly for it (Acts 4:8–12, 5:17–18, 40–41, 12:1–5). As one of the leaders in the Early Church, he was, according to the Apostle Paul, called to minister to his fellow Jewish people (Galatians 2:8). Nevertheless, God also used him to minister to people from the nations (*ethnos*, Acts 15:7; cf. 1 Peter 1:1).

In Acts 10 we meet a centurion of the Italian Cohort known as Cornelius, a devout man who fears the God of Israel (Acts 10:1-2; cf. 13:16, 26). In the afternoon, at his regular hour of prayer, an angel of God tells Cornelius to send men to Joppa to bring Peter to him (Acts 10:5). The next day as the men sent from Cornelius are on their way to Joppa, the Apostle Peter sees a vision about food with all kinds of animals, reptiles, and birds that he is told to kill and eat (Acts 10:9–13). This was unthinkable for the Jewish apostle — as such, Peter had never eaten anything unclean (Acts 10:14) or had associated with anyone from another nation (Acts 10:28). Peter, whose full name is Simon Bar Jonah, was in Joppa, the same place where the prophet Jonah was reluctant to preach to those from the nations (see Jonah 1:1–3, 4:1–3). The purpose of the vision (Acts 10:17), however, was to show that a new-covenant era has arrived, and that God now accepts those from the nations (Acts 10:34–35; cf. Acts 15:1–21).

The Roman centurion Cornelius is often used as an example of someone from the nations whose faith in God was accepted without him knowing about Jesus. It is true that Cornelius is described as a "devout man who feared God" (Acts 10:2), and as Peter himself said, "Truly I understand that God shows no partiality, but in every nation anyone who fears him and does what is right is acceptable to him" (Acts 10:34–35). But does this mean that Cornelius did not need to hear about Jesus to be saved? We need to keep in mind the context, which is that those from the nations, as well as the Jewish people, need to hear the gospel. Peter explains this as "preaching good news of peace through Jesus Christ" (Acts 10:36). He also ends his message by stating that "everyone who believes in him receives forgiveness of sins through his name" (Acts 10:43). Cornelius's salvation occurred during Peter's presentation of the gospel, since Peter himself says, "He will declare to you a message by which you will be saved, you and all your household" (Acts 11:14). This is consistent with the message Peter proclaimed to the religious rulers and elders in Jerusalem: "And there is salvation in no one else, for there is no other name under heaven given among men by which we must be saved" (Acts 4:12).

❧ Acts 17 Paul in Athens

Now while Paul was waiting for them at Athens, his spirit was provoked within him as he saw that the city was full of idols. So he reasoned in the synagogue with the Jews and the devout persons, and in the marketplace every day with those who happened to be there. Some of the Epicurean and Stoic philosophers also conversed with him. And some said, "What does this babbler wish to say?" Others said, "He seems to be a preacher of foreign divinities" — because he was preaching Jesus and the resurrection. And they took him and brought him to the Areopagus, saying, "May we know what this new teaching is that you are presenting? For you bring some strange things to our ears. We wish to know therefore what these things mean." Now all the Athenians and the foreigners who lived there would spend their time in nothing except telling or hearing something new (Acts 17:16–21).

The Apostle Paul was Jewish, held Roman citizenship from birth, and was born in Tarsus in Cilicia (Acts 21:39; 22:3, 25–28). Paul was educated by Gamaliel (Acts 22:3), the leading Pharisaic teacher of his day (Acts 5:34) and excelled as a student (Galatians 1:14). The city Paul grew up in, Tarsus, was noted for its schools dedicated to rhetoric and philosophy. The Stoic philosopher Zeno was from there (Paul was probably exposed to Greek thinking at an early age). At his conversion on the road to Damascus, Paul (Saul) was called by Jesus to preach to the nations (Acts 9:15; cf. Galatians 1:15–16). Given his biblical training in the Scriptures and his knowledge of Greek culture, Paul was the ideal person to take the gospel to the nations.

Athens was the capital of ancient Attica, in the Roman province of Achaia, and was considered the philosophical center of the ancient world. At his arrival in Athens, Paul sees that the city is full of idols, which to him are not gods at all (1 Corinthians 8:4; Galatians 4:8 cf. Acts 19:26). In fact, he believes that demonic influence lies behind them (1 Corinthians 10:20; 1 Timothy 4:1). Paul would have understood the idolatry in Athens as evidence of suppressing the truth of God's revelation in creation (Romans 1:18–20). The Greeks had suppressed God's revelation in creation and had become fools (Romans 1:21–22). When we realize that misdirected religion is a human idolatrous response to God's revelation, behind which are demonic influences, it will help us think about communicating the gospel to those of other religions. Nevertheless, Paul was so "provoked"[14] at seeing the idolatry in the city that he was moved to preach the gospel in the marketplace. Paul's provocation regarding the idolatry in Athens was because he knew what was written in the Law of God (Exodus 20:1–6). In Paul's day, the marketplace was the place where the different philosophical ideas of the day were shared and discussed.

Paul's interaction with the Greek philosophers is a valuable lesson for Christians, as many Christians believe that the way to impact the culture is to become like it. The idea is that when we go out into the world, we should not be overtly Christian so as not to offend. Apart from overlooking the fact that the gospel is already foolishness and a stumbling block to unbelievers (1 Corinthians 1:18, 23), this belief is antithetical to the apostolic example of preaching to a pagan culture. Wherever the Apostle Paul went in his missionary journeys there was either a revival (Acts 13:48–49, 16:5, 19–34, 17:4) or a riot (Acts 13:50, 14:19, 16:19–24, 17:5). Those early Christians were not persecuted because the message of Christianity was different to that of the Greeks and Romans (i.e., monotheism vs polytheism) but because of its unique and authoritative claim that Jesus is Lord of all, and we must submit to Him (Acts 10:36; 17:6–7; cf.1 Thessalonians 1:9–10). When it came to the biggest stage of his ministry, the Areopagus on Mars Hill in front of the leading intellectuals of his day, the Apostle Paul did not compromise by

---

14. The Greek verb παροξύνω (*paroxuno*) means "provoke" and is used of God's anger at idolatry in the Old Testament (Deuteronomy 31:20 LXX; Psalm 73:10 LXX [74:10 Eng].

trying to become like the people in order to win them over. Paul was not invited to speak because he looked or thought like the world, but because he was preaching Jesus and the Resurrection (Acts 17:18), something the Greeks were philosophically opposed to (Acts 17:32). As Christians we do not need to intentionally hide the message of the Bible to get an opportunity to speak with people about it. God gave Paul the biggest platform of his day, and Paul did not shrink back from declaring the truth of the gospel.

It was because Paul was openly preaching about Jesus and the Resurrection (Acts 17:18–19) that some Epicurean and Stoic philosophers wanted to converse with him. Some thought Paul was a "babbler" (*ho spermologos*) or literally a "scavenger" (a bird who picks up seed) as though he had picked up bits of information and passed them off as if he knew what he was talking about. Others saw Paul as a "proclaimer" (*katangeleus*) of "foreign divinities." The Epicurean and Stoic philosophers wanted to know what these "strange things" were, so they invited Paul to the Areopagus to know more of what he was teaching (Acts 17:19–20). But what was the Areopagus? The Areopagus could refer to either a location or a council. The contextual clues point to a council: (1) the reference to Paul standing in the midst (Acts17:22) is referring to a council who is hearing Paul out; (2) more decisive is the reference to Dionysius the Areopagite (Acts 17:34), the latter term clearly refers to a member of the council.[15] The Greek philosophers invited Paul to speak at the Areopagus as they loved nothing more than to hear new ideas (Acts 17:21).

Paul would have been well aware that the philosophies of the Epicureans and Stoics were completely different from his own worldview. For example, the Epicureans were indifferent to the gods because they believed the gods were too removed to be objects of concern; the Epicureans were basically like today's atheistic materialists. They argued that the chief human good was "pleasure" and that the gods did not interfere in human affairs. The Epicureans did not believe in an afterlife but rather believed that at death the body merely returned to its various elements. The Stoics, on the other hand, were pantheists who argued for the unity of humanity and relationship with the divine. Both the Epicureans and Stoics were essentially materialists who, unlike Paul, did not believe in one God who created the world and was sovereign over it (Acts 17:24–26; cf. 14:16). Paul did not look for some supposed neutral ground between himself and his Greek audience by speaking about God in generic terms to win the people over; this is important to keep in mind. This is because the Bible clearly tells us that there is no neutral

---

15. Witherington III, *The Acts of the Apostles*, p. 515.

ground between the believer and unbeliever when it comes to worldview issues (Romans 1:18, 21, 8:6–8; 1 Corinthians 1:20–25, 2:14).

One of the primary problems in Christian apologetics today is that, rather than defending the faith, many Christians end up defending a generic theism. Paul was not defending the "probability" for the existence of a god in his encounter with the Greek philosophers. We must realize that theism does not equal Christianity. As Christians, we are not meant to make theists out of people; we are called to defend the Christian faith and preach the gospel of Jesus Christ. This means sharing what the triune God of creation has done for us in the gospel and standing on the authority of Scripture.

So Paul, standing in the midst of the Areopagus, said: "Men of Athens, I perceive that in every way you are very religious. For as I passed along and observed the objects of your worship, I found also an altar with this inscription: 'To the unknown god.' What therefore you worship as unknown, this I proclaim to you. The God who made the world and everything in it, being Lord of heaven and earth, does not live in temples made by man, nor is he served by human hands, as though he needed anything, since he himself gives to all mankind life and breath and everything. And he made from one man every nation of mankind to live on all the face of the earth, having determined allotted periods and the boundaries of their dwelling place, that they should seek God, and perhaps feel their way toward him and find him. Yet he is actually not far from each one of us, for 'In him we live and move and have our being'; as even some of your own poets have said, 'For we are indeed his offspring.' Being then God's offspring, we ought not to think that the divine being is like gold or silver or stone, an image formed by the art and imagination of man. The times of ignorance God overlooked, but now he commands all people everywhere to repent, because he has fixed a day on which he will judge the world in righteousness by a man whom he has appointed; and of this he has given assurance to all by raising him from the dead" (Acts 17:22–31).

Paul begins his speech by noting that the Athenians are "very religious" (Acts 17:22, *deisidaimonesteros*), a term which itself is ambiguous since it can be used either in a positive (religious) or negative (superstitious) sense. Paul knows these sophisticated Greek philosophers are basically materialists, yet he calls them "very religious" or rather superstitious (see Acts 17:16; 25:19). For a rhetorical device, Paul deliberately chooses a word which would draw his audience into the context of his explanation of God, creation, mankind, redemption, resurrection, and judgment. Paul preached to the Athenians in this unique way because he recognized that his worldview was different from theirs; they were basically evolutionary in their thinking. Paul was able to do this because he was not ignorant of the culture, nor was he consumed by it; but he observed the culture with the intent of proclaiming the gospel to it (Acts 17:16, 23). If we are to be better communicators of the gospel to people from other religions, it is important that we know something about what they believe. Just as Paul and Barnabas did when they visited Lystra and spoke to pagan farmers who worshiped other gods, they gave a basic appeal to God's revelation in creation and called them to turn from their idolatry (Acts 14:15–18). Those men did not have the same philosophical background as the Athenians, so Paul and Barnabas only had to make a general appeal to God's revelation in creation (cf. Psalm 19:1).

🌿 Encountering and Exposing the Unbelieving Worldview: Creation and Fall

Since Paul understood the people he was preaching to and their religious background, he knew the topics he needed to address. For instance, after seeing the idol to an "Unknown God," Paul used it as a springboard for explaining who God really is — he is "The God who made the world and everything in it...." Paul was pointing out that God is distinct from His creation, He is not a part of it (the Stoics were pantheists). Pantheism is the belief that creation is made up of God's own being (the world is God and God is the world) so that creation itself is divine. Pantheism is a failure to distinguish between the Creator and His creation. God is not what He created, but rather what He has created reflects who He is. When you observe the heavens, you do not observe God, you observe what God has created (Psalm 19:1). The Creator and the creation are two ontologically distinct things. Pantheism tends toward foolishness, as it worships that which is unworthy of worship: creation (Romans 1:22, 25). This is because Pantheism is the result of a natural theology that rejects divine revelation. By explaining who God is, Paul deliberately went against the philosophies of the people in his preaching by proclaiming God as Creator of everything (Isaiah 42:5; Exodus 20:11; Nehemiah 9:6).[16] Paul also proclaimed that the God of creation does not live in a temple made by humans. The God of creation cannot be reflected by an idol! Paul's statements in his speech about the God of creation are rooted in the Old Testament Scriptures and not the god of philosophy.

---

16. The reference to God as the creator of everything in Isaiah 42:5 is in the context of an anti-idol polemic.

Paul goes onto explain that God "made from one man every nation of mankind to live on all the face of the earth." The question is, who is the "one man" that Paul was referring to? John Walton, in his book *The Lost World of Adam and Eve*, argues that it is a reference to Noah.[17] The reference to creation in Acts 17:24, however, makes the Adam connection much more likely, and this is recognized by most biblical commentators (cf. 1 Clement 29:2).[18] It also agrees with Paul's anthropology in his epistles (Romans 5:12; 1 Corinthians 15:45). This idea, that mankind came from one man, contradicted the Athenians belief that they originated from the soil of the ground.[19] Schnabel explains:

> The reference to one ancestor in Acts 17:26…is an unambiguous reference to the biblical tradition of the beginning of all human existence in the creation of Adam, the first man whom God brought into being (Gen 1:26–27, 2:7). There is no clear parallel in Greek thought or mythology to this conviction that the human race can be traced back to one man who was created by God.[20]

Paul deliberately refers to Adam to show that all people have their roots in the one man God originally created. The background of Acts 17:26–27 is Deuteronomy 32:8, which asserts monotheism in the face of polytheism, with the division of the nations mentioned in Genesis 10 and 11 as the remote background.[21] This serves to highlight how God has providentially arranged the movements of the nations of mankind so that they may seek Him. The Creator who Paul is communicating to the Greeks is the God of history, which is not random but is providentially arranged. However, Paul tells the Athenians that their fallen attempt to seek after and find God is ultimately a failed one. In Acts 17:27, the term "grope" (*pselapheseian*) is used "in both classical and biblical texts…refers to the groping of a blind person or the fumbling of a person in the darkness of night."[22] New Testament scholar Ben Witherington notes,

17. Walton, *The Lost World of Adam and Eve*, p. 186–187. For a refutation of this see Simon Turpin, "Adam or Noah: Who Is the 'One Man' in Acts 17?" May 30, 2020, https://answersingenesis.org/bible-history/adam-or-noah-who-is-one-man-in-acts17/.

18. See F.F. Bruce, *The Book of Acts: New International Commentary on the Old Testament* (Grand Rapids, MI: W.B. Eerdmans, 1988), p. 337; Marshall, *Acts*, p. 287; Witherington, *The Acts of the Apostles*, p. 526; Bock, *Acts*, p. 566.

19. See Bruce, *The Book of Acts*, p. 337.

20. E.J. Schnabel, "Other Religions: Saving or Secular?" in *Faith Comes by Hearing: A Response to Inclusivism*, C.W. Morgan and R.A. Peterson, eds. (Nottingham, England: Apollos, 2008), p. 115.

21. See Witherington, *The Acts of the Apostles*, p. 527.

22. Witherington, *The Acts of the Apostles*, p. 528. The biblical texts are Isaiah 59:10; Judges 16:26; Deuteronomy 28:29; Job 5:13–14, 12:25.

The image is not an encouraging one, even when coupled with what follows it — "and yet God is not far from each one of us." The overall effect of this verse is to highlight the dilemma and irony of the human situation. Though God is omnipresent, and so not far from any person, ironically human beings are stumbling around in the dark trying to find God. When one is blind, even an object right in front of one's face can be missed. The sentence does not encourage us to think the speaker believes that the finding of the true God is actually going on, apart from divine revelation. To the contrary, the true God remains unknown apart from such revelation.[23]

This is why Paul will go on to present the revelation of the light of the gospel so that it can shine through the darkness of idolatry in Athens (cf. 2 Corinthians 4:6). Paul was once blinded by his sin and needed his eyes opening to the truth of who Jesus is (Acts 9:3–18). After his conversion, the Lord Jesus called Paul to preach to the nations, so that his witness of Christ would "open their eyes, so that they may turn from darkness to light and from the power of Satan to God, that they may receive forgiveness of sins and a place among those who are sanctified by faith in me [Jesus]" (Acts 26:18).

Exploring and Evangelizing the Unbelieving Worldview: Redemption and Consummation

For the Athenians to relate to what he was saying, Paul connected the truth of who the Creator God is with the truth that God has already given to them by way of natural revelation. Paul did this by quoting two Greek poets to these Athenian philosophers (Acts 17:28). The quotation "In him we live and move and have our being" is probably from Epimenides of Crete, while the quotation "For we are indeed his offspring" is from Aratus' poem "Phaenomena." Paul used these Greek poets as a part of his defense and persuasion of the gospel. By taking what they already knew and bringing it to his defense, Paul used God's revelation in nature to persuade them of what they already knew to be true. Paul connected that inner knowledge to who God is, adding explicitly Christian content to it. This connection with the knowledge of God that the Athenians already have leads to a bridge for Paul to share the gospel. Paul then tells the Athenians that God has overlooked the ignorance of the nations who find themselves in need of repentance and being reconciled to God through Christ (Acts 17:30). The term *ignorant* is used of Jews and people from the nations since they both need to repent and be reconciled to God through Christ (Acts 3:17). God in His mercy

---

23. Ibid., p. 528–529.

has not judged the idolatry of the nations as severely as He might have (see Romans 3:25).

In this way, the gospel can be seen as subversively fulfilling world religions. The gospel is subversive because it stands as the contradiction and confrontation to all manifestations of world religions. It makes a call for repentance from idolatry to the true and living God (Acts 17:30, 14:15; cf. 1 Thessalonians 1:9). But it is also the fulfillment of what these false religions seek. Since idols are counterfeits of the one true God, the metaphysical, ethical, and epistemological questions that other religions ask (but ultimately cannot answer) are answered by the triune God alone.[24] The subversive fulfillment approach can be practically applied in evangelistic conversations by following three steps: exploring the truth that has been distorted; exposing that distortion; and then evangelizing by showing how the gospel alone offers the true answer.

	Explore	Expose	Evangelize
Atheism	Morality	Atheism has no foundation for absolute morality	Absolute morality needs an absolute moral lawgiver
Islam	Monotheism	The Islamic view of God is Unitarian Monotheism	The biblical view of God is Trinitarian monotheism (Father, Son, and Holy Spirit)
Jehovah's Witnesses	Belief in Jesus	The Jehovah's Witnesses believe that Jesus is a created being and should (the archangel Michael) not be worshiped.	The Bible teaches that Jesus is the Creator of all things and therefore is worthy of our worship
Neo-paganism	Belief in the divine	God is not part of his creation	God is the Creator who transcends and exists before creation

Unlike the Stoics, who had a cyclical view of the world, Paul concludes that there will be a definitive judgment on the world by Christ, so it is incumbent of all men to repent of their sin and turn to Him. The Resurrection of Jesus is the proof that there will be a final judgment.

---

24. See Daniel Strange, *For Their Rock is Not As Our Rock: an evangelical theology of religions* (England: Apollos, 2014), p. 268–271.

> Now when they heard of the resurrection of the dead, some mocked. But others said, "We will hear you again about this." So Paul went out from their midst. But some men joined him and believed, among whom also were Dionysius the Areopagite and a woman named Damaris and others with them (Acts 17:32–34).

There was a threefold reaction to Paul's mention of the resurrection and future judgment. First, it is mocked (Acts 17:32) by the Athenians. The reason the Greek philosophers in Athens rejected Paul's message (which included the resurrection of the dead) was not because of the evidence but because it did not fit their worldview. The Stoics who had a pantheistic concept of God believed reason was "the principle which was inherent in the structuring of the universe and by which men ought to live."[25] The Epicureans, however, had a similar worldview to today's atheists in that they were materialists, believing in the atomic theory, and so "for them either the gods did not exist, or they were so far removed from the world as to exercise no influence on its affairs."[26] The idea of "rising" (*anistēmi*) from the dead was literally "to raise up by bringing back to life."[27] This view was incompatible with the Athenian view of life, as they believed that "once a man dies and the earth drinks up his blood, there is no resurrection."[28] This is why many of them scoffed at the resurrection; by the cultural standard of wisdom, it was foolishness to them (cf. 1 Corinthians 1:23).

Paul did not present the Resurrection of Jesus as a neutral fact, open to the interpretation of the Athenian philosophers, but as the focal point of the history of redemption. As part of the history of redemption, Paul proclaimed the fact of creation (Acts 17:24), the fact of the human race being in Adam (Acts 17:26), and the fact of the Resurrection, which leads to the fact of the final judgment (Acts 17:31). Any apologetic perspective that leaves you appealing to the person as an autonomous authority to judge the evidence as to what is acceptable is not biblical. This does not fit with the authoritative proclamation that we see in Acts 17, where Paul speaks of the future judgment of the world; there is no opting out of it if you do not agree with the evidence.

The second reaction is that some wanted to hear Paul again about this. Third, there was a positive response as some believe that Jesus is the Christ (Acts 17:34). Contrary to what some have wanted to suggest, Paul's apologetic methodology was not wasted in Athens, as Witherington comments,

---

25. Marshall, *Acts*, p. 284.
26. Ibid., p. 284.
27. BDAG, p. 83.
28. Bruce, *Acts*, p. 343.

While some have suggested that 1 Cor. 2:1–4 indicates that Paul renounced his approach in Athens when he arrived in Corinth, and instead resolved to stick with the heart of the kerygma, this is probably reading too much in this text.... It is hard to doubt that Luke sees this speech in Acts 17 as something of a model for how to approach educated pagan Greeks, and means it to reflect positively on his hero Paul, especially since he records only three major speech summaries from Paul's travels, and this is the only major one specifically directed at Gentiles. It is surely not seen as merely a record of a unique occasion, or of something tried, which failed and was later discarded. Athens is one of the few places on this journey where Paul is not in fact run out of town.[29]

Paul message to the Greek philosophers was successful, in that it gave the Athenians the foundation for understanding the gospel message and should be seen as a model of how to approach those who are "Greek" (evolutionary) in their thinking. In contrast, Peter's message to the Jewish proselytes in Acts 2 is seen by some as being more "successful" because 3,000 were converted in one day (Acts 2:41). But this is to forget that they already believed in the one true God who created the heavens and earth, and believed in the authority of the Old Testament Scriptures. All Peter had to do was show them that Jesus was the fulfillment of that which the prophets had spoken about (Acts 2:16–41). Paul was able to reach some of those who were in the Areopagus with the gospel because he painted to them a total picture of the Christian philosophy of life (creation, Fall, redemption, and consummation). In his evangelistic efforts Paul (and Peter) was not involved in inter-faith dialogue but sought to bring people to faith in Christ.

World religions are a rebellious, idolatrous response to God's revelation of Himself in creation. Because God has made Himself known to every person, we need to communicate the truth of the gospel in such a way that it connects with the truth that God has already communicated by way of natural revelation. The good news is that God is now redeeming people from false religions throughout the earth and uniting them into one people of God through the gospel of Jesus Christ.

---

29. Witherington, *Acts of the Apostles*, p. 533.

A NEW TESTAMENT DEFENSE FOR THE BIBLICAL ACCOUNT OF CREATION

SCOFFERS

Responding to Those Who Deliberately
Overlook Creation and the Flood

SIMON TURPIN

978-1-68344-267-7

FOR at least the last 200 years, the Western world has openly scoffed at Christians and their beliefs about the Bible. Atheistic evolutionists or skeptics often ridicule Christians who accept the belief in the supernatural creation of the world and a global Flood by calling them "fundamentalists," "anti-intellectuals," "extremists," and "literalists." We must prepare to face the scoffers.